VOICING
RELATIONSHIPS

VOICING RELATIONSHIPS
A Dialogic Perspective

Leslie A. Baxter
University of Iowa

Los Angeles | London | New Delhi
Singapore | Washington DC

For information:

 SAGE Publications, Inc.
2455 Teller Road
Thousand Oaks,
    California 91320
E-mail: order@sagepub.com

SAGE Publications Ltd.
1 Oliver's Yard
55 City Road
London EC1Y 1SP
United Kingdom

SAGE Publications India Pvt. Ltd.
B 1/I 1 Mohan Cooperative
    Industrial Area
Mathura Road, New Delhi 110 044
India

SAGE Publications
    Asia-Pacific Pte. Ltd.
33 Pekin Street #02-01
Far East Square
Singapore 048763

Printed in the United States of America

Library of Congress Cataloging-in-Publication Data

Voicing relationships: a dialogic perspective/edited by Leslie A. Baxter.
    p. cm.
Includes bibliographical references and index.
ISBN 978-1-4129-2784-0 (cloth)
ISBN 978-1-4129-2785-7 (pbk.)
    1. Interpersonal relations. 2. Dialogue analysis. 3. Bakhtin, M. M. (Mikhail Mikhailovich), 1895-1975. I. Baxter, Leslie A.

HM1111.V65 2009
302.3'4601—dc22   2009031777

This book is printed on acid-free paper.

10   11   12   13   14   10   9   8   7   6   5   4   3   2   1

Acquisitions Editor:	Todd R. Armstrong
Assistant Editor:	Aja Baker
Editorial Assistant:	Nathan Davidson
Production Editor:	Brittany Bauhaus
Copy Editor:	Heidi Unkrich
Typesetter:	C&M Digitals (P) Ltd.
Proofreader:	Eleni-Maria Georgiou
Indexer:	Diggs Publication Services, Inc.
Cover Designer:	Bryan Fishman
Marketing Manager:	Helen Salmon

Contents

Preface

Writing this book was an experience in dialogic expansiveness: although the words written on the page are under my authorship, they are infiltrated with the words of many others who have engaged my thinking and improved the quality of my efforts. I thank first the many co-authors and students over the past decade and a half who have engaged me in dialogue about Bakhtin's notions of dialogue. I have benefitted especially from co-authorships with Dawn Braithwaite and exchanges with members of my 2007 and 2009 graduate seminars on dialogism. I value the long conversation I had with Barbara Montgomery in which I talked through the outline of the book and benefitted from her insights and support. I thank, as well, the following Sage reviewers of the initial draft of this book:

Tamara D. Afifi, *University of California, Santa Barbara*

Melissa Wood Alemán, *James Madison University*

Dawn O. Braithwaite, *University of Nebraska-Lincoln*

Kenneth N. Cissna, *University of South Florida*

Daena Goldsmith, *Lewis and Clark College*

Glen H. Stamp, *Ball State University*

Julia T. Wood, *The University of North Carolina at Chapel Hill*

You gave me detailed and thoughtful comments, and the volume is better for taking seriously both the comments with which I agreed and those with which I initially disagreed. Thanks are due, as well, to my longstanding Sage editor, Todd R. Armstrong. Todd proved once again that he is a wise thinker on a multitude of levels. I thank, as well, the members of the editorial staff at Sage who continue to bring me back to Sage whenever I have an idea for a book—working with them is a joy.

I also want to express my thanks to Purdue University Press for granting permission to reprint in Chapter 2 most of an essay I authored for Pat Arneson's 2007 edited volume, *Perspectives on Philosophy of Communication* ("Mikhail Bakhtin and the Philosophy of Dialogism," pp. 247–268).

Finally, I thank my daughter, Emma, who helps me realize, on most days, the joys of being her mother. Emma, more than anyone, has taught me the value of celebrating diverse discourses. She will have to read this book someday when she's older to understand what that means!

—Leslie A. Baxter
Iowa City, IA

1

Introduction

Theories, I have come to appreciate, are like living organisms. Growing a theory is a process akin to raising a child. A theory gestates quietly in a scholar's mind before it is birthed; it is presented to the world in the birth announcement of its formal articulation; it requires nurturance as it takes its initial steps into the scholarly conversation; and it ultimately establishes independence from the original scholar(s) who birthed it. Relational dialectics theory (RDT) was formally articulated in 1996 (Baxter & Montgomery, 1996), and I have been blessed to witness the use of the theory by many researchers of interpersonal and family communication (Baxter & Braithwaite, 2006b; Braithwaite & Baxter, 2008; Stamp, 2004). This book engages the RDT-informed research that has been published over the past decade and a half, embedding discussion of this work in an articulation of the next generation of RDT. A useful theory, after all, doesn't live off of its past. Theories are not static things; to stay alive, a theory must continue to develop and evolve. This latest articulation of RDT (which we might call RDT 2.0, but which I shall refer to hereafter simply as RDT) draws upon a richer palette of concepts than the 1996 statement of the theory. Like upgrades in computer operating systems, you don't need to be familiar with the 1996 statement of RDT to understand the current articulation; however, the endnote to this chapter highlights the main differences between RDT 2.0 and RDT 1.0 for the interested reader.[1]

RDT is a theory of relational meaning making—that is, how the meanings surrounding individual and relationship identities are constructed through language use. It is inspired by the scholarly work of the Russian theorist Mikhail Bakhtin, who wrote about culture, language, and literature from the 1920s into the 1970s and whose corpus of work has been labeled *dialogism* (Holquist, 2002). The core premise of dialogically grounded RDT is that meanings are wrought from the struggle of competing, often contradictory, discourses.

What's a discourse? Stated simply, a discourse is a system of meaning—a set of propositions that cohere around a given object of meaning. Let me illustrate the concept of a discourse with a simple example outside the realm of relating, drawn from Baxter and Babbie (2004). Suppose you are interested in what an apple means. Part of its meaning is captured by describing its attributes—its color (red, yellow, green), its size and shape (round with a diameter of about 3–4 inches), its taste (sweet or tart), and so forth. But the meaning of an apple doesn't stop here. Part of the meaning of an apple is its inclusion in the food group known as fruit. Part of the meaning of *apple* comes from understanding places where apples are grown, and in what seasons, and how they are grown and harvested. Part of the meaning of *apple* comes from understanding the various ways apples can be eaten—raw, cooked in an apple pie, and so forth. Part of what an apple means invokes beliefs about healthy eating ("An apple a day keeps the doctor away"). In short, the meaning of *apple* is pretty complex, consisting of many different propositions that collectively form a coherent web of meaning—a discourse—of appleness. All meaning making is similarly complex; the meaning of any concept is embedded in a larger web of meaning—a system of integrated bits of meaning.

RDT's core theoretical principle is that meaning in the moment is not simply the result of isolated, unitary discourses but instead is the result of the interplay of competing discourses. How do you know two or more discourses are in competition? Discourses are in competition when the meanings they advance negate one another in some way, more or less in a zero-sum manner. Thus, what an apple means in the moment when I walk into my kitchen and see one in the fruit bowl on my countertop is wrought from other discourses that might be circulating. For example, I might have just watched a TV program about the health dangers of pesticides used on apples, in which I was exposed to a discourse of healthy eating that excludes apples. I might have a memory flash of a recent conversation with a friend in which I was exposed to a discourse on the latest fad diet in which apples are believed bad for you. I might be attending to a discourse of gratification in which I talk myself into having earned a piece of cake instead of a less desirable apple as a snack for completing some task. According to RDT, what something means in the moment depends on the interplay of competing discourses that are circulating in that moment.

But let's move to an example a bit closer to the domain of meanings of relevance to this volume—how relationships come to have meaning. Consider this excerpt from an exchange between two young adult males who told me that they had been the best of friends for the past five years. This excerpt comes from a much longer conversation in which they were asked to reflect jointly on their relationship while being tape-recorded:

B: Of course you know your habits are different than mine. They don't, they're not a problem in our relationship, at all. I mean, I don't know if a lot of people can say that about someone that they're good, you know, that they've hung tight with for five years, you know, and I guess that's the only reason why we have hung tight for five years is cuz we're not hung up on the trivial. It's not a problem for me.

A: The one thing I guess we do is argue.

B: Yes!

A: About trivial things. But in a comedic way.

B: Yeah.

A: You know, in a nonthreatening [way].

B: That's a good way to put it.

A: We get on each other's case about, like you know, anything.

B: That shirt you're wearing. You look like a fruit!

A: And then the voices start to raise and we're a little louder, things start to, you know, rage. But that's just, I think, a rare, rare, rare, thing among friends is that we argue for fun.

B: With no repercussions. Yeah, with no repercussions.

A: You can tell by the tone of the voice.

B: And people see us doin' that and have said, you know, humorous things to me like, "Oh my God! What happened last night, you and him were in a huge fight." "I don't know what you're talking about."

A: Right.

B: We were playing off each other. It's a game. It's like who can push each other farther, you know, without crossing that line.

A: And the line is never even crossed. (Baxter, Foley, & Thatcher, 2008, IV#5)

This excerpt, like any conversational slice we could choose, is rich in dialogic overtones—competing discourses. The pair is involved in constructing their relationship communicatively. In this particular segment, the opening utterance says that the two are different in their habits. The friend concurs in this judgment, noting a bit later that they argue over their differences. The rest of the excerpt can be read as an attempt by these two friends to regulate and contain their differences—to minimize them, to trivialize them, to make light of them by attributing them to part of a humorous game. But why do the friends spend so much interactional effort in positioning their differences as nonproblematic? Why don't they simply take note of their differences in habits and move on in the conversation to the next topic? A RDT-informed analysis might note that the discourse of friendship in mainstream American culture is built on a premise of similarity, not difference. The fact that these two friends have different habits and argue is an anomaly to themselves, and to others, as well, based on one of B's later utterances. The only way for the friends to make sense of this discursive struggle—a cultural conception of friendship based on similarity against the discourse of their best friendship in which the proposition that they have differences features prominently—is to minimize those differences. Ironically, the two reconstruct their differences of habit into a similarity—a similarity of style in the ability they share to read each other's intentions and to play the game. The two friends not only talk about their ability to take difference and argument lightly, but they perform it for themselves and perhaps for the benefit of me, the researcher-addressee who would be listening to the tape of their conversation. B appears to insult his friend's taste in shirts, and his friend ignores the insult, thereby demonstrating their ability to trivialize their differences.

The conversation also deploys another element in the cultural discourse of friendship—the proposition that each relationship is somehow unique and private only to its two members. The friends appear to relish the fact that outsiders often misunderstand their arguments and incorrectly infer that something is wrong between them. This apparent satisfaction in outsiders' misunderstanding adds to their construction of their friendship as "tight," further offsetting the fact that they have different habits. Ironically, it is their realization of their differences—and how those are managed—that serves as the basis of uniqueness.

This short excerpt manifests two discourses, at a minimum, that are at play: (1) the cultural discourse of friendship in which similarity is expected and a given friendship is expected to demonstrate its unique and private nature and (2) the discourse of this particular A-B friendship in which difference is centered. The meaning that is made from the interanimation of these discourses is one that preserves the friendship's meaning as tight. By the end of the conversation, this pair celebrates their differences, but in a manner that simultaneously constructs an overarching similarity in the two friends in their mutual joy at the way they position their differences as a game to be played. Later in the book, we will encounter the concept of a transformational hybrid—a way in which seemingly competing discourses are somehow merged through their interplay in a way that achieves a both/and hybrid meaning. These two friends have arguably enacted a hybrid in the way these discourses interanimate in this conversation.

Notice that my brief analysis of this conversational excerpt focused on the interplay of competing discourses. I analyzed these utterances not as representations of the speakers' inner thoughts, motivations, and needs. Instead, I interrogated the utterances for the underlying systems of meaning—the discourses—that were animating the meaning that was constructed of the friends' relationship. Bakhtin (1981d) used the term *voice* to refer to any discourse (i.e., perspective, ideology, standpoint, or system of meaning) that was circulating in language use. The title of the book centers this concept and casts it in verb form to suggest that relationships achieve meaning through the active interplay of multiple, competing discourses, or voices. These discourses are given voice by speakers' utterances, but the focus is not on the individuals, per se, who speak them but on the discourses themselves and how they interanimate in talk. Thus, the book offers a theoretical understanding of how relationships (and individual identities in relationships) are constituted in communicative messages.

❖ EVALUATING RDT AS A THEORY

One of my foremost goals in writing this book is to better position scholars with guidelines for evaluating RDT as a theory, as well as evaluating RDT-based research. In particular, I have concerns with three important misunderstandings about RDT, which I hope to address over the course of the book. First, a number of scholars appear to ignore differences among various dialectical theories, collapsing them together as if they were a unitary dialectical perspective (e.g., Sabourin, 2006; Segrin & Flora, 2005). As addressed elsewhere (Baxter & Braithwaite, 2006c; Baxter & Montgomery, 1996; Montgomery & Baxter, 1998), RDT is but one of several theories that holds membership in a broader dialectical family, and differences are substantial from one dialectical theory to another. RDT is unique in its explicit grounding in Bakhtin's theory of dialogism. I will not elaborate on other dialectical theories in this book, because that has already been done elsewhere (e.g., Baxter & Braithwaite).

Second, a number of scholars have chosen to describe RDT as a model (e.g., Honeycutt & Cantrill, 2001) or perspective (e.g., Berger, 2005) rather than referring to it as a theory. The implication in these alternative labels is that RDT somehow falls short of theory status. Baxter & Montgomery (1996) readily admitted that RDT is not a postpositivist theory; that is, it is not a formal axiomatic theory of propositions and theorems designed to predict and causally explain an objective world. But they argued, it is still a theory. Turner (1986) wrote that "theory is a mental activity. . . . It is a process of developing ideas that can allow us to explain how and why events occur" (p. 4). Regardless of variations in types of theory, Turner further argued that theories have in common several basic building blocks: concepts, statements, and formats (p. 5). Concepts refer to abstract definitions of phenomena—features about the communicative world for communication theories—that are deemed important in the theory. The next chapter details the important root concepts in Bakhtin's theory of dialogism, and in RDT as well, given its status as an appropriation of dialogism to interpersonal and family communication. Theoretical statements, and their grouping together into a theoretical format, provide a theory's claims about how concepts work. Taken together, a communication theory's web of theoretical statements—its format—helps us explain the communicative social world, or that subset of it targeted for theoretical understanding. Turner presented several different kinds of theoretical statements and formats, of which his articulation of the descriptive/sensitizing analytic scheme probably comes closest to capturing Bakhtin's theory of dialogism and, in turn, RDT. Descriptive/sensitizing schemes can be understood as

> loosely assembled congeries of concepts intended only to sensitize and orient researchers to certain critical processes. . . . [They] are typically more skeptical about the timeless quality of social affairs [than are positivistic schemes]. Instead, they argue that concepts and their linkages must always be provisional and sensitizing because the nature of human activity is to change those very arrangements denoted by the

organization of concepts into theoretical statements. Hence, except for certain very general conceptual categories, the scheme must be flexible and capable of being revised as circumstances in the empirical world change. At best, then, explanation is simply rendering an interpretation of events by seeing them as an instance or example of the provisional and sensitizing concepts in the scheme. (p. 11)

RDT, and Bakhtin's theory of dialogism more generally, is a descriptive/sensitizing theory. Its format consists of a set of basic concepts and theoretical principles that can be brought to bear in analyzing communicative life.

Third, RDT is often critiqued because it is regarded as too descriptive with an inability to predict and causally explain communicative phenomena (e.g., Miller, 2005). This criticism reflects a basic misunderstanding about theory. Theories come in different stripes and are designed to perform different work. The goal of RDT, and Bakhtin's dialogism more generally, is not prediction and causal explanation, as is the case with positivistic theory. Rather, its goal is to function as a heuristic device to render the communicative social world intelligible. The criterion to ask of such a theory is whether it helps the user understand some phenomenon beyond what common sense, and other theories, would tell us. Rather than the falsifiability criterion applied to positivistic theory—the belief that a theory holds merit to the extent that it is not challenged, or falsified, by empirical facts—a descriptive/sensitizing theory is evaluated by its capacity for heurism—its ability to be useful in assisting us in seeing things in ways different from what otherwise would be the case.

One of the ways a descriptive/sensitizing theory is heuristic is by providing a different framing of the phenomena of interest than what can be found in alternative theories or through common sense. Its theoretic framework directs our attention to different aspects or features of the phenomena, providing us with an alternative lens with which to see the phenomena. By way of previewing the remainder of the book, the next section summarizes the theoretical framework of RDT by discussing five different "seeings" afforded by the theory. This framework asks us to productively rework five important assumptions that characterize the dominant theoretical lenses to be found in the scholarly research on interpersonal and family communication. These reworkings are not intellectual "business as usual" ; instead, they challenge taken-for-granted assumptions with respect to five basic issues that characterize mainstream interpersonal and family communication scholarship: the false binary of public/private, the bias against uncertainty, the illusion of the monadic individual actor, the inattention to power, and the illusion of relationships as containers.

❖ REWORKINGS: ALTERNATIVE FRAMINGS OF INTERPERSONAL COMMUNICATION

Reworking 1: The False Binary of Public/Private

Interpersonal and family communication scholars often presume a popular binary of public life and private life, which Gal (2005) argued has been foundational to Western political and economic theory since at least the eighteenth century. *Public* anchors places, realms and spheres in which "individuals and groups congregate to discuss matters of mutual interest and, where possible, to reach a common judgment" (Hauser, 1998, p. 86). It is the discursive place where society and culture are presumably located and where individuals assume a variety of social roles (e.g., worker, neighbor, citizen, and so forth). By contrast, *private* anchors the study of communication by interpersonal and family communication scholars: the privatized havens of individuality (over community), home (as opposed to work), sentiment (as opposed to rationality), and love (as opposed to money) (Gal, p. 25).

The public-private binary undergirds our very conception of interpersonal communication. In a highly influential conceptualization, Miller and Steinberg (1975) argued that communication is interpersonal when parties make predictions about one another based on individuated, psychologically oriented information as opposed to information about their social roles (e.g., bank clerk) or cultural roles (e.g., Asian American). On definitional grounds, in other words, interpersonal communication escapes from the public sphere into the private sphere. This scholarly tradition helps us to understand why psychologized approaches and perspectives have long dominated the interpersonal and family communication research (Baxter, 1998; Cronen, 1998).

Certainly, this tradition has produced a voluminous body of work over the past forty years. However, this accumulation has not been without cost. In particular, as Hawes (1998) has argued, the public/private binary has contributed to the trivialization of everyday relational communication relative to the presumed significance of public discourse. Public life, in other words, often has trumped private life among communication scholars in general. However, the position of RDT theory, and other social constructionist positions, is that sociocultural phenomena are constituted in the interactions of so-called private life as much as in the public discussions of the so-called public sphere. Sociocultural life is deeply relational. Although I choose to emphasize individual and relationship identities throughout the book, the theoretical implications of RDT extend to all types of meanings that emerge from the interplay of competing discourses. For example, when parties talk about the federal government, they are discursively constructing this social institution, giving it life as "real" through their talk.

Just as sociocultural life is deeply relational, so relating is a deeply sociocultural process. Traces of sociocultural discourses lurk in every utterance voiced by relationship parties—whether in joint conversations with their relational partner, in conversations with third parties (including fellow social network members or even strangers, including interviewers), or in the inner dialogues of intrapersonal communication in a speaker's mind. The utterance chain of talk is riddled with the potential for multiple discourses, many of which circulate in the broader public domain we refer to as *society* and *culture*. Taken as a whole, the argument of the book is that the binary of public/private is a false one. Instead, I argue the dialogic position that public and private interpenetrate in the utterance chain. For too long, scholars have perpetuated the tidy compartmentalization of knowledge in which culture, society, and relationships (both familial and nonfamilial) have occupied discrete domains. Taken seriously, dialogically based RDT obligates us to think outside these categorical boxes to understand their interpenetration in the utterance chain.

Reworking 2: The Bias Against Uncertainty

Relationships are constructed through time, and parties must address issues of continuity and change in the meanings of the relationship-of-the-past versus the relationship-of-the-present. At a given point in time, the interplay of competing discourses runs the risk of what shall later be labeled *dialogic contraction*—a discursive playing field so unequal that all but one monologic, authoritative discourse is silenced. If a discourse assumes an authoritative voice, meaning can become calcified because no alternative meanings are allowed. At stake in dialogically contractive talk is certainty in the centering of dominant discourses, perhaps to the extreme point of totalizing monologue. By contrast, at stake in dialogically expansive talk is uncertainty as silenced or marginalized discourses gain symbolic footholds in the negotiation of meaning, or as all competing discourses are supplanted by transformative meanings such as the hybrid meaning illustrated above with respect to the similar-yet-different friendship of the two young men. But I don't like the term *uncertainty* because of its negative connotations in existing research and theory in interpersonal/family communication. I prefer the term *dialogic creativity*.

As noted elsewhere (Baxter & Braithwaite, 2009; Baxter & Montgomery, 1996), existing work is biased in that certainty is viewed as positive, whereas uncertainty is regarded as negative and something people seek to reduce (Berger & Calabrese, 1975). Later scholarship on (un)certainty has embraced a more complex view in its recognition that uncertainty can be positive to individuals under certain circumstances (e.g., Afifi & Weiner, 2004; Babrow, 2001; Brashers, 2001). However, this later body of work—roughly glossed as the uncertainty management tradition (in contrast to the Uncertainty Reduction Theory of Berger and Calabrese)—still privileges certainty. As Baxter and Braithwaite (2009) have argued,

> Language use is not without tendency, thus it is significant to note that PIT [Problematic Integration Theory], UMT [Uncertainty Management Theory], and TMIM (the Theory of Motivated Information Management] are theories of uncertainty management, not theories of certainty management. Thus, the presumption is that it is uncertainty that requires management—sometimes managed toward reduction and sometimes not. The prospect that certainty requires management—including the possibility of reducing it—goes unconsidered. In this sense, extant theory and research still privileges certainty, while recognizing exceptions under which parties are not motivated to reduce it. (pp. 28–29)

By contrast, the position taken in this book is that dialogic interplay is, under conditions of dialogic expansiveness, indeterminate. That is, meaning making is an unfinalizable process—it is pregnant with potential for emergent meanings that have not been uttered before. This quality of surprisingness (Morson & Emerson, 1990, p. 37), dialogic creativity, is not possible except under conditions of uncertainty. Absolute certainty is a monologue.

Creativity has received scant attention by scholars of interpersonal/ family communication. Those few who attend to creativeness tend to view it as an individual accomplishment of message production (e.g., Greene, 2008). The kind of creativity envisioned by RDT (and dialogism more generally) is not something achieved by the individual; rather, it is a consequence of intertextuality. It is an emergent meaning in which old discursive positions are somehow shaken up—either by altering the playing field with respect to which discourse is centered and which is relegated secondary status, or by transforming meaning more fundamentally through semantic synergy of some kind.

The critique of the bias against uncertainty is more profound than legitimating uncertainty. Existing work on uncertainty reduction/ management operates with a presumption of a preformed self— that is, the view that an individual's identity is formed prior to the interaction and becomes knowable to another through the individual's self-disclosive revelations as well as a variety of information acquisition strategies deployed by the knower (Berger & Bradac, 1982; Berger & Calabrese, 1975). By contrast, the dialogic self conceived in this book is always under construction through interaction with others who are different from oneself. The parties' various horizons of discursive seeing are brought into play with and against one another, and selves are shaped out of this discursive interpenetration. Thus, communication is conceived not as an information carrier through which already-formed selves can be known—the view represented by the uncertainty reduction/management tradition. Communication is a dialogic struggle, and out of this struggle identities are shaped. Of necessity, these identities are always indeterminate, fluid and fleeting in the interactional moment.

Reworking 3: The Illusion of the Monadic Individual Actor

Interpersonal/family communication scholars have generally presumed that a monadic individual is the analytic linchpin in studying communication. In a classic articulation of the place of the individual in communication science, Hewes and Planalp (1987) explicitly stated that there are two fundamental properties of communication—impact and intersubjectivity— that support the centrality of the monadic individual. With reference to impact, Hewes and Planalp asserted, "Perhaps no other property of communication is so commonly linked to its definition than impact. If person A's behavior affects person B's subsequent behavior or cognitive/emotive state, then communication has taken place; if not, then it has not" (p. 147). Thus, by their criterion, an adequate account of human communication must identify the mechanism(s) that generates the degree of impact that a person's behavior has on another. With respect to intersubjectivity, Hewes and Planalp argued that shared knowledge between interactants is necessary for communication. Impact and intersubjectivity are so foundational, argued Hewes and Planalp, that they "are properties against which any explanation of human communication can be judged adequate" (p. 149).

Of course, impact and intersubjectivity are not neutral criteria by which to evaluate any theoretical approach to communication, because they presuppose the centrality of the individual as the key to meaning production. These may be perfectly legitimate criteria by which to judge individually centered theories of communication, but they are biased against more socially oriented approaches, such as RDT. The very language of these properties reveals their bias. Impact is calibrated by the extent to which one individual affects another individual's actions or inner states. Intersubjectivity presupposes preformed, intact subjects who can understand one another in varying degrees.

Both impact and intersubjectivity are subsumed in Deetz's (1992) property of effectiveness, which he argued has long been the dominant motif in mainstream communication research in general. With effectiveness as the dominant intellectual backdrop, it is hardly surprising to find that cognitively oriented work holds a place of prominence in current interpersonal/family communication research (Baxter & Braithwaite, 2008a). Researchers focus on how autonomous individuals plan and then implement communication messages; the metric of effectiveness is the extent to which a speaker's goals are accomplished.

RDT eschews the individual as the centerpiece of relational communication, arguing instead for a move to the social, in which meaning is located in the "between"—that is, in the interplay between competing discourses. After a decade of engaging students and fellow scholars on this point, I am convinced that this decentering of the individual is the single most challenging aspect of RDT for people to understand. Let me summarize in the following core premises the argument elaborated throughout the book:

- A speaker's utterance is not a mere representational expression of his or her inner state but is instead an intertextual utterance chain.
- An utterance chain is a profoundly social phenomenon in which the words of the moment respond to prior utterances and address anticipated responses not yet spoken.
- A speaker's utterance, understood as an utterance chain, is always part of a larger dialogue; there is nothing autonomous about a speaker's utterance because it is always already embedded in a larger utterance chain.
- The utterance chain is the site where discourses—systems of meaning constituted in language use—are at play in constructing meanings of the moment.
- Identities (of individuals and relationships) are meanings wrought from the interplay of competing discourses.
- Because individual and relational identities are constructed in the play of competing discourses, they cannot be finalized prior to communication.

Thus, from a dialogic perspective, the selves in communication are not preformed, autonomous entities but instead are constituted in communication. Speaker identities are subject to the discourses animating language use. As Deetz (1992) so eloquently put it, "The self is not independent of texts but always finds itself in them. Western linguistic conventions, however, name a subject, making the 'I' a possible object of concern" (p. 139). As Baxter and Montgomery (1996) observed, self as an autonomous monadic entity is a narrative that feels comfortable in mainstream U.S. society, but it is a narrative nonetheless. The monadic actor is a social construct that is produced from within a discourse of individualism, and it is reified as natural in mainstream U.S. communicative practices.

The focus of RDT is not on individual subjective experience. Certainly, discourses are voiced (in both said and unsaid ways) when individuals talk. However, the focus is not on the individual but on the discourses that are circulating in that talk. The goal is not to examine how one individual affects another (impact) or how two or more individuals come to understand one another (intersubjectivity). The goal is not to understand how an autonomous individual manages contradictory needs or how two parties achieve their goals through jointly managing contradictions. The theoretical and analytic quest is to understand how the play of discourses constructs meaning.

As such, RDT aligns itself much more readily with the alternative to effectiveness that Deetz (1992) advanced by which to determine the heuristic value of a communication theory: participation. In the context of the study of discourses, participation focuses on which discourses can be voiced in a given social moment, and by implication, which discourses are marginalized or silenced. True to its dialogic roots, RDT focuses on how meanings are wrought from the interplay of centripetal-centrifugal struggle, a question that squarely merits evaluation not by any effectiveness criteria such as impact, intersubjectivity, or goal accomplishment but rather by the criterion of participation, understood as the interanimation of discourses.

Thus, RDT scholars should be critiqued if they fall back on language in which competing discourses are presented as individual needs, because this presupposes a monadic individual. The interplay of competing discourses cannot productively be viewed as a matter of strategic management, as if competing discourses exist "out there," independently of communication, and toward which communication tactics are deployed in order to control the contradictory process. Competing discourses, like self-identities, are *of* communication, *not* outside it.

Reworking 4: The Inattention to Power

RDT positions issues of power squarely at the analytic center by taking seriously Bakhtin's concept of centripetal-centrifugal struggle. Power, in other words, is conceived as a relation between discourses.

Overwhelmingly, the RDT research to date has stopped the analytic project prematurely by simply identifying the competing discourses present in given texts, without examining their interplay. In taking the interplay of competing discourses seriously, it is difficult to presume that all discourses are equal in the play for meaning. In idealized dialogue, such equality of discursive footing is present. However, in everyday talk, a more likely scenario is that competing discourses are not equally legitimated. Some are centered (the centripetal) and others are marginalized (centrifugal). In the instance of monologue, all but a single totalizing discourse is erased.

This dialogic conception of power departs significantly from the conception that prevails in mainstream interpersonal/family communication. The mainstream approach locates power as a characteristic of individuals, not discourses. This is hardly surprising in light of the presumption in favor of the monadic individual discussed above. From this traditional perspective, power is a discretionary matter of scholarly interest: A scholar interested in studying power is free to do so (and many have), but a scholar need not feel required to study power. In short, from the traditional perspective, power-located-in-the-individual is but one of many potentially interesting variables worthy of scholarly attention. RDT makes it difficult to ignore power-located-in-discourse. Centripetal-centrifugal struggle is central to understanding the intertextuality of competing discourses, and thus the meaning-making process.

The centering of power in RDT may be off-putting to scholars who to this point have, for one reason or another, steered clear of critical approaches to interpersonal communication. In fact, Braithwaite and Baxter's (2008) content analysis of the interpersonal communication research suggested that only a scant 2.9% of research articles in communication journals from 1990 to 2005 were critical in orientation, a percentage only slightly higher in the research on family communication with 3.5% critical presence (Baxter & Braithwaite, 2006b). Historically, both interpersonal and family communication have been dominated by research that is postpositivistic in nature, a set of assumptions to which the critical project is antithetical. *i.e., contrasted*

But not all critical perspectives are the same, and the critical stance articulated in this iteration of RDT does not locate power in individual subjects or in social groups. Instead, the focus is on how relating parties are subject to the competing discourses that animate their talk.

Reworking 5: The Illusion of Relationships as Containers

The title of this book, *Voicing Relationships*, underscores that when we give voice to discourses, their interplay creates relationships.

However, this view stands against the grain of mainstream interpersonal and family communication scholarship. The most common image of relationships in the interpersonal and family communication literature is still that of a container. Relating parties communicate within the container of their relationship, and different kinds of containers (friendships, long-distance relationships, marriages, etc.) can be compared with respect to how communication is enacted. Certainly, relating parties bring to a current interaction the definition of their relationship built up over a history of prior interactions; they do not enter a current interaction *tabula rosa*. These discursive traces are just that, and they are far from finalized. The view presented in this book is that relationships are not static things—containers—in which communication takes place. Rather, the position of RDT, like that of many social constructionist views, is that relationships are constituted through the communication practices of the parties. The unique contribution of RDT is to argue that the engine of meaning making is the interplay of competing discourses. Relationships are, then, meanings rather than contextual containers. They are constructed in communication, rather than being mere settings in which communication occurs. Rather than studying communication in relationships, RDT would have scholars study relationships in communication (Baxter, 2004).

However, RDT moves beyond the container imagery in a second, arguably more profound, way. Because talk is conceptualized as an utterance chain, all talk can be viewed as relational communication. That is, any utterance is part of a dialogue in which it responds to prior discursive utterances and addresses anticipated discursive responses of others. The discursive voices of others are with us in our talk. The very concept of an utterance, thus, is relational.

These five reworkings represent what is at stake in this volume. Taken as a set, they provide us with an alternative way to make sense of relating from that found in the mainstream interpersonal and family communication literature. The issue is not whether this alternative way of seeing is falsifiable but rather, whether viewing relating through the alternative theoretical framework of RDT is heuristic—does it help us to see interpersonal and family communication in new ways that open up alternative understandings compared to what is available through other theories and through common sense.

❖ OVERVIEW OF THE CHAPTERS

The five reworkings that I have just previewed do not "map" in a neat and tidy one-to-one correspondence to the chapters that follow.

Instead, these reworkings infuse all of the chapters. So let me conclude this introductory chapter by providing you with a concrete map of the remaining chapters of the volume.

Chapter 2 provides an introduction to the life and work of Mikhail Bakhtin. It summarizes Bakhtin's work in chronological order, which is important because it was first made available to Western readers in almost a reverse chronological order and with a time lag of several decades. This chapter also introduces the key concepts in Bakhtin's theory of dialogism, which will be developed in subsequent chapters. The chapter also attempts to locate Bakhtin's theory of dialogism inside the broader intellectual conversation among scholars of interpersonal and family communication. In particular, I position Bakhtin's theory of dialogism according to its paradigmatic commitments and its social constructionist conception of communication. Finally, I position RDT within Bakhtin's dialogism project; many appropriations of dialogism exist throughout the social sciences and humanities, and each is somewhat different from the others depending on what is emphasized from Bakhtin's writings.

Chapters 3 and 4 are devoted to the central dialogic building block of communication: the concept of the *utterance chain*. The Bakhtinian conception of communication is decidedly one of interdependence of messages, a concept others refer to as *intertextuality* (Allen, 2000). These chapters elaborate on the kinds of intertextual discourses that are voiced in a given utterance. We can imagine an utterance as a chain of prior and anticipated utterances, all of which have a foothold in the construction of meanings at the moment. The utterance chain adds complexity to scholarly understanding of communication.

In particular, Chapters 3 and 4 point to four specific discursive sites in the utterance chain where competing discourses can be identified. The first of these underscores that relating gives life to culture; when relationship parties speak, they invoke systems of meaning that circulate in the broader culture. The second discursive site emphasizes that relating is the interplay of the relational past with the relational present; in every utterance, relationship parties engage in the constitutive acts of reproducing the relationship's past system of meaning and creating a new system of meaning, as well. The third discursive site focuses on the Self-Other relation. In anticipating the partner's response, relationship parties enter the discursive dance of negotiating similarity to, and difference from, one another. The fourth, and final discursive site brings us full circle back to culture as relationship parties anticipate the evaluative reactions of third parties—both particular family members and friends and the generalized other of society—to the relational actions of the parties. This site draws attention to the clash of competing visions of the ideal.

Chapter 5, on centripetal-centrifugal struggle, centers the process of interplay. In the dialectically centered research, the notion of interplay has often been ignored in the focus on the mere coexistence of binaries. Researchers, myself included, have too often used RDT to identify lists of paired oppositions, without examining how those opposing discourses struggle interactively. The action sits in the struggle, and Chapter 5 takes a clear process approach, emphasizing various ways in which competing discourses struggle. This chapter envisions a continuum of struggle whose endpoints are monologue and idealized dialogue. As introduced above, monologue is the presence of an authoritative discourse so dominant that other discursive positions have been silenced if not eliminated. Idealized dialogue, by contrast, features the give-and-take of discourses that are positioned as fully equal in value. The vast majority of utterances are probably situated somewhere in the middle of this continuum, involving the interplay of multiple discourses, some of which are more valued or central than others as the Bakhtinian terms *centripetal* and *centrifugal* suggest (Bakhtin, 1981d). This chapter thus positions the concept of power centrally.

Chapter 6 concludes the book by formalizing a qualitative or interpretive method by which to analyze utterances dialogically. Over time, my own RDT-based research has become more qualitatively oriented and less quantitatively oriented. Although I still think that quantitatively oriented approaches are useful in attempting to make statements about frequencies and patterns, in the end they privilege an oversimplified conception of discursive struggle and seek to finalize what is inherently unfinalizable. I have struggled over the past decade with the traditional qualitative tool kit, attempting to identify an approach consistent with the RDT theoretical lens. The product of my current thinking on methodology is addressed in Chapter 6, where I present *contrapuntal analysis*, a specific kind of discourse analysis that is compatible with the tenets of Bakhtin's dialogic perspective. I conclude this chapter with a sample contrapuntal analysis to concretize the method for the potential researcher.

❖ **ENDNOTE**

1. I would draw the interested reader's attention to five interrelated differences between RDT 2.0 and RDT 1.0 as articulated in Baxter and Montgomery (1996). First, this articulation of the theory underscores that contradiction—the unity of opposites—is a discursive struggle, not a conflict between individuals, and not a psychological tension within an individual between competing needs or motivations. *Discourses* are struggling. Thus,

utterances are studied for the discourses that are given voice instead of being positioned as representations of speakers' inner thoughts and needs. To be sure, individuals can align their respective viewpoints with given discourses, but the objects of analysis are the discourses not the individuals. To mark the centrality of discourses to RDT, this volume will use such phrases as "discursive struggle" and "competing discourses" instead of the term "contradiction" which frequented RDT 1.0. Although RDT 1.0 argued that the individual was a narrative artifact of a discourse of individualism, this book makes that point with what I hope is greater consistency and clarity. Second, an individual's utterance is conceived not as a psychological phenomenon but instead as a social unit in which discourses that are already spoken are in play with anticipated responses from real or imagined addressees of the utterance. An utterance is thus reconceptualized from an isolated sequence of words uttered by a speaker—a turn at talk—to an *utterance chain* in which multiple discourses (some already spoken and others not yet spoken but anticipated) can be identified. The utterance chain is the framework used in RDT 2.0 to situate different kinds of discourses in play with one another. Although the concept of the utterance chain was briefly mentioned in RDT 1.0, it is given a central place in this latest articulation of the theory. One upshot of this conceptual move to the utterance chain is that competing discourses can rightfully be studied in the utterances of individuals—for example in interview settings or in diary records—not just in the conversations between relating parties. Individual and relationship identities are constructed whenever and wherever we have uttered language. Third, it is the *interplay* of competing discourses where the action sits—the interplay of discourses is how meanings are made. RDT 2.0 devotes substantially more attention than RDT 1.0 to the ways in which discourses can interpenetrate. Of necessity, this requires a closer attention to the details of language use than was provided in the 1996 articulation of the theory. As a consequence of attending more microscopically to the details of uttered talk, RDT 2.0 reworks the concept of praxis introduced in RDT 1.0. Fourth, competing discourses are rarely on an equal discursive playing field; some discourses are typically more dominant or more central than other more marginalized discourses. This discursive inequality draws attention to the issue of *power*, conceived not as something individuals have but as a characteristic of discourses. Although RDT 1.0 extensively used the term *centripetal-centrifugal struggle*, that articulation of the theory did not attend to the implications of discursive inequality inherent in the centripetal-centrifugal distinction. Fifth, and last, RDT 2.0 elaborates on a qualitative or interpretive method by which to examine the interplay of competing discourses, a method labeled *contrapuntal analysis* after a term first used by Bakhtin (1984b). The first articulation of RDT was more ecumenical with respect to methods, arguing that all methods were potentially valuable. This volume favors more qualitative/interpretive work, and formalizes a particular kind of discourse analysis that may prove helpful to future researchers.

2

Mikhail Bakhtin, Dialogism, and RDT

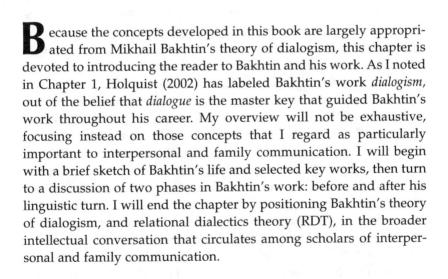

Because the concepts developed in this book are largely appropriated from Mikhail Bakhtin's theory of dialogism, this chapter is devoted to introducing the reader to Bakhtin and his work. As I noted in Chapter 1, Holquist (2002) has labeled Bakhtin's work *dialogism*, out of the belief that *dialogue* is the master key that guided Bakhtin's work throughout his career. My overview will not be exhaustive, focusing instead on those concepts that I regard as particularly important to interpersonal and family communication. I will begin with a brief sketch of Bakhtin's life and selected key works, then turn to a discussion of two phases in Bakhtin's work: before and after his linguistic turn. I will end the chapter by positioning Bakhtin's theory of dialogism, and relational dialectics theory (RDT), in the broader intellectual conversation that circulates among scholars of interpersonal and family communication.

Source: Chapter adapted from Baxter, L. A. (2007). "Mikhail Bakhtin: The philosophy of dialogism." In P. Arneson (Ed.), *Perspectives on Philosophy of Communication* (pp. 247–268). West Lafayette, IN: Purdue University Press.

Bakhtin is widely regarded as one of the most powerful and influential thinkers of the twentieth century (e.g., Clark & Holquist, 1984;
Emerson, 1997; Hirschkop, 1999; Holquist, 2002; Morson & Emerson,
1990; Todorov, 1984). Specialists in any number of fields have been
informed by his work, including literary critics, film scholars, classi-
cists, theologians, political scientists, anthropologists, and language
scholars, among others. Indeed, the "Bakhtin industry," as Holquist
(2002, p. 184) has referred to it, is thriving.

❖ BAKHTIN'S LIFE AND SELECTED KEY WORKS

Bakhtin's life and work are surrounded by a swirl of uncertainties, ambi-
guities, and confusions, in large measure the result of the Stalinist political
times in which he lived. His work was slow to gain publication in Russia
and even slower to reach English translation; later works were generally
more accessible in translation before earlier works, posing challenges to
understanding the chronology of his thinking; and the authorship of several texts is disputed. Before turning to the substance of his ideas, it is thus
worthwhile to take a brief biographical/bibliographical excursion.

Born in 1895 into a family of minor nobility with a banking-
executive father, Bakhtin spent his youth in the culturally and linguis-
tically diverse Russian cities of Vilnius and Odessa. (Or so the
dominant view goes. However, as Hirschkop (1999) suggests, the
minor nobility portion of this story may not be true.) Educated at
home, he was apparently familiar with ancient Greek, Hellenistic, and
modern European philosophy, including Buber and Kierkegaard. He is
reported to have studied classics, philosophy, and literature at
St. Petersburg University, although it is unclear whether he was formally enrolled and whether he received a degree (Hirschkop, 1999).
Bakhtin fled to the countryside in 1918 in the chaos of the Russian
Revolution. There, he met on a regular basis with other young intellectuals in a discussion group that subsequently became known as the
Bakhtin circle. This intellectual circle assumes importance because of
controversy surrounding the authorship of several disputed texts discussed below. Many members of this group subsequently moved to
Leningrad in 1924 and continued meeting until the government crackdown on unorthodox intellectuals at the end of 1928. Until near the end
of his life in 1975, Bakhtin was either in political trouble with the
Communist government or marginalized from the center of Russian
intellectual life because of those political troubles. It is hardly surprising that Bakhtin's critique of monologue, in which one perspective
dominates and silences all others (the Marxist regime in the Soviet

Union comes to mind as the obvious example), became the cornerstone of his intellectual project for the fifty years of his career.

Four essays in particular hold relevance in understanding dialogism from the 1919 to the 1924 period of the Bakhtin circle, where Bakhtin's energies were concentrated on the aesthetics of the creative act, consciousness, and ethics. In 1919, Bakhtin published in a minor provincial journal a two-page essay entitled "Art and Answerability," which was subsequently translated into English and published in a 1990 volume of the same title. An unfinished essay entitled "Author and Hero in Aesthetic Activity," thought to have been written between 1920 and 1923 and originally published posthumously in Russia in 1979, was also translated into English and published in the 1990 *Art and Answerability* volume. The 1924 essay "The Problem of Content, Material, and Form in Verbal Art," a critique of Russian formalism in literary criticism, remained unpublished in Russia until 1975 and appeared in the English translation in the *Art and Answerability* volume. The essay entitled "Toward a Philosophy of the Act," thought to have been written in the early 1920s, was published posthumously in Russia in 1986 and was translated into English in the published 1993 volume by the same name.

An important intellectual backdrop for the emerging articulation of dialogism was Freud's work. Bakhtin and the Bakhtin circle were critical of the inward focus of Freud, and his position was critiqued in a book *Freudianism: A Critical Sketch* authored by N. N. Voloshinov in 1927 (and published in English translation in 1987), yet widely attributed to Bakhtin. The essence of the critique was Freud's reliance on introspection as the key to psychic life and his apparent neglect of the role of the other and sociality more generally.

By the end of the 1920s, members of the Bakhtin circle evidenced a distinct linguistic turn, as they increasingly focused on the implications of Saussurean linguistics and recognized the role of language in social life. Particularly important in this later articulation of dialogism was an essay published under the name of a fellow member of the Bakhtin circle, Valentin Voloshinov, the 1929 *Marxism and the Philosophy of Language* (available in English translation in 1986). However, this text, as well as some of the work of fellow Bakhtin circle member P. N. Medvedev (and the *Freudianism* text discussed above), has been widely attributed to Bakhtin.

Medvedev was arrested and shot in 1938, and Voloshinov died of tuberculosis in 1936, so they were unavailable when the authorship question surfaced in the 1970s. Similarly, other Bakhtin circle members had died by the 1970s. Bocharov (1994), on the basis of conversations with Bakhtin late in his life and testimony of others, including Voloshinov's widow, builds a persuasive argument for Bakhtin's authorship of the disputed texts. However, definitive proof of authorship of these disputed texts does not exist. Hirschkop's (1999) distillation of the dispute surrounding authorship is that the intellectual life of the Bakhtin circle was one of interdependence of ideas, and that the only issue of dispute among Bakhtin scholars is the specific form this interdependence took in finished products: "The fact of collaboration is agreed by all, though its exact form—rewriting, composition based on discussion, dual authorship—is in dispute" (p. 139).

Under his own name, Bakhtin published in 1929 his important *Problems of Dostoevsky's Creative Art*, a revision of which became available in English translation in 1984 under the slightly revised title, *Problems of Dostoevsky's Poetics*. This is arguably Bakhtin's most detailed treatment of texts, including insight into the interplay of competing discourses, and it provides what few insights we have from Bakhtin about how to perform a dialogic analysis, something he referred to as *contrapuntal analysis* (Bakhtin, 1984b, p. 221).

The period from 1929 to 1941 was one of personal uncertainty and intellectual productivity for Bakhtin. In 1929 Bakhtin was arrested, probably as part of a larger crackdown on unorthodox intellectuals. He was first sentenced to a work camp in Siberia, but this sentence was subsequently reduced to one of exile for a 5-year period to the remote Kazakhstan, where he taught bookkeeping to cover expenses and continued his intellectual interests, albeit at the margins of intellectual life, until 1936. He then moved to Saransk, where he taught literature at the Mordovian Pedagogical Institute for a year before fleeing to Savelovo during the 1937 political purge. During this period, Bakhtin completed several important essays on the novel as a dialogic genre, although these were not published in Russia until 1975 and not available in English translation until 1981. The most important of these to communication scholars is arguably "Discourse in the Novel," published in the 1981 English translation *The Dialogic Imagination: Four Essays by M. M. Bakhtin*. Other essays from his period on the novel, including "Epic and Novel," "From the Prehistory of Novelistic Discourse," and "Forms of Time and of the Chronotope in the Novel," were also included in *The Dialogic Imagination*. Although one might wonder what his work on the novel has to do with communication, several of these essays are rich in insights about the struggle of competing discourses and how a text of any kind, including interaction, can be examined for its monologic or dialogic inclinations. These essays underscore the significance of narrative.

Bakhtin also penned what is purported to be his most definitive statement on the genre of the novel during this period (Hirschkop, 1999). Unfortunately, it was never published in its entirety, although it was reportedly accepted for publication by a publishing house but subsequently destroyed in a German bombing raid. The story (Hirschkop, 1999) is that Bakhtin, an addicted smoker, gradually smoked away all but a fragment of his only remaining copy of the manuscript in his desperation for cigarette papers during the Second World War!

During this period, he also completed a dissertation on Rabelais for submission to the Gorky Institute of World Literature, but it was not accepted until 1947, not published in Russia until 1965, and unavailable in English translation until 1984 under the title, *Rabelais and His World*. The significance of this book lies in its insight into the second genre that fascinated Bakhtin, in addition to the novel—carnival rituals. The study of the carnivalesque—interaction forms that are carnival-like—informs us about one way the struggle of competing discourses can take form, as well as shedding light on the role of parody and humor in the interplay of different discourses.

The period from 1941 until 1963 saw steady employment for Bakhtin, although his work remained hidden from the mainstream Russian intellectual community. After the German invasion of Russia in 1941, Bakhtin was allowed to teach German and Russian in a Savelovo high school. When World War II ended, Bakhtin was recalled to Saransk where he became a university professor of Russian and world literature. Probably the most substantial work from this post-WWII period is the essay, "The Problem of Speech Genres," written in the 1950s, published posthumously in Russia in 1979, and available in English translation in 1986 in an edited book bearing the title *Speech Genres & Other Late Essays*. This essay introduces us to the very important dialogic concepts of the utterance chain and genre.

In 1963, Bakhtin was rediscovered by intellectuals at the Gorky Institute, who were impressed with his works on Dostoevsky and Rabelais and pleased that he was still alive, unlike many other intellectuals of his generation. They worked on behalf of the republication of Bakhtin's work, and Bakhtin became an intellectual sensation. He was brought to Moscow, where he worked for the most part on the republication of his earlier works until his death from emphysema in 1975. It is thus not much of an exaggeration to claim that half a century separates the creation from the consumption of much of Bakhtin's work. With this overview of Bakhtin's life and work in hand, let me turn to a summary of the main ideas from the two rather distinct phases in the evolution of dialogism.

❖ **BAKHTIN'S DIALOGISM 1919 TO 1924**

RDT is grounded largely in the later Bakhtin after his linguistic turn in 1924. However, selected concepts from the earlier phase have influenced

my thinking. In particular, we will see in subsequent chapters the influence of Bakhtin's commitment to the prosaics of everyday life, his view
that Self is socially constructed, the centrality of difference in meaning
making, and the aesthetic moment. The early Bakhtin had not yet
landed on language and discourse, as will become apparent as you proceed through this section of the chapter where I summarize Bakhtin's
focus on aesthetics, ethics, and consciousness.

Bakhtin argued that art and life are not discrete domains of human-
ity; everyday living is not free of creative activity and art should not
be "too high-flown" or "too exalted" for everyday life (Bakhtin, 1990a,
p. 1). In his focus on everyday living, Bakhtin initiated a lifelong theoretical commitment to the prosaic—the ordinary, taken-for-granted
process of living. Dialogism is widely accepted as a philosophy of the
ordinary in its focus on prosaics (Morson & Emerson, 1990, p. 23).

Life and art are united as aesthetic or creative acts in their answerability, or responsibility, to an Other (Bakhtin, 1990a, p. 1). In conceiving
life (and art) as an act—a deed—of answerability to an Other, Bakhtin
articulated his view of human consciousness based on otherness. The aesthetic or creative act, in all of its forms, is a relation that Bakhtin referred
to with varying vocabularies in his writing from this early period:
I-and-other, I-for-myself and I-for-another, spirit-and-soul, author-and-
character (hero), artist-and-work. In his later work, this relation in its
most general sense would be referred to as a dialogue of voices—that is,
different positions, points of view, ideologies, or discourses.

Bakhtin argued that consciousness is impossible without an Other.
We can never see ourselves as a whole; the Other is necessary to give
us—to author—our sense of self. Bakhtin (1990b) expressed it this way:

> [A] human being experiencing life in the category of his own *I* is
> incapable of gathering himself by himself into an outward whole that
> would be even relatively finished. . . . In this sense, one can speak of a
> human being's absolute need for the other [in] producing his
> outwardly finished personality. This outward personality could not
> exist, if the other did not create it. (pp. 35–36)

This key dialogic principle—that consciousness is a relation of one
person and an Other—was remarkably resilient throughout Bakhtin's
corpus of work. In the revision of his *Dostoevsky* book we encounter the
same thought:

> I am conscious of myself and become myself only while revealing
> myself for another, through another, and with the help of another. The
> most important acts constituting self-consciousness are determined

by a relationship toward another consciousness. . . . A person has no internal sovereign territory, he is wholly and always in the boundary; looking inside himself, he looks into the eyes of another or with the eyes of another. (Bakhtin, 1984a, p. 287)

What about Otherness enables consciousness? In dialogism, it is outsideness, or an excess of seeing in relation to the other that enables mutual creation of consciousness:

> When I contemplate a whole human being who is situated outside and over against me, our concrete, actually experienced horizons do not coincide. For at each given moment, regardless of the position and the proximity to me of this other human being whom I am contemplating, I shall always see and know something that he, from his place outside and over against me, cannot see himself: parts of his body that are inaccessible to his own gaze (his head, his face and its expressions), the world behind his back, and a whole series of objects and relations, which in any of our mutual relations are accessible to me but not to him. (Bakhtin, 1990b, pp. 22–23)

In dialogism, self is a relative event constructed out of the relation of two perspectives. Self and other do not exist as separate entities but as a relation of similarity and difference. Consciousness is the ongoing, situated action of relating.

The being of self thus is the activity of co-being in which neither person has an alibi from the deed or act of answerability. People bear an ethical obligation to participate in the activity of co-being. It is the activity of relating between persons that gives each consciousness meaning in the moment. To be human entails the obligation to answer—to act toward—the other, thereby participating in the joint action of creation (Bakhtin, 1993, p. 40). In the act of answering, or authoring as Bakhtin (1990b) also referred to it, the self gains consciousness, as does the person doing the authoring:

> An author is not the bearer of inner lived experience, and his reaction is neither a passive feeling nor a receptive perception. An author is the uniquely active form-giving energy that is manifested not in a psychologically conceived consciousness, but in a durably valid cultural product. (p. 8)

In his later work, this cultural product becomes language use; however, in this early work, answerability is conceived more vaguely as an act that creates another. In the act of mutual authoring, selves become.

The act of authoring is aesthetic when we act toward the other as a whole being. However, in living everyday life, we often respond only to parts and pieces of the other. We engage only a part of the store clerk, the bank clerk, the neighbor girl who mows the lawn. Bakhtin (1990b) stated the distinction between aesthetic and nonaesthetic acts in the following way:

> In life, we are interested not in the whole of a human being, but only in those particular actions on his part with which we are compelled to deal in living our life and which are, in one way or another, of special interest to us. In the work of art, on the other hand, the author's reactions to particular self-manifestations on the part of the hero are founded on his unitary reaction to the *whole* of the hero. . . . What makes a reaction specifically aesthetic is precisely the fact that it is a reaction to the *whole* of the hero as a human being. (p. 5)

When a person answers to the whole of the other, the other is said to be consummated. However, this aesthetic consummation is never finalizable because the human being is always "yet-to-be" (Bakhtin, 1990b, p. 13). Only death brings finalized consummation; in life, consummation is a fleeting aesthetic moment against a larger dynamic of ongoing openness. Dialogism is a theory predicated on the assumption of unfinalizability. Order (meaning) is an accomplishment to be achieved out of the ordinary messiness of everyday life; it is constituted in fleeting moments of consummation.

Aesthetic activity is a three-part process, according to Bakhtin (1990b). First is empathy: "I must experience—come to see and to know—what he experiences; I must put myself in his place and coincide with him as it were" (p. 25). Second, is a return to one's outsideness: "My projection of myself into him must be followed by a return into myself, a return to my own place outside . . . for only from this place can the material derived from my projecting myself into the other be rendered meaningful" (p. 26). Third, and last, is answerability in which we respond to the other's wholeness—consummation. These three aspects of aesthetic activity do not function chronologically; instead, they are "ultimately intertwined and fuse with one another" (p. 27) in living experience.

Undeveloped in this first period of Bakhtin's work is a conception of how it is that persons concretely accomplish creation/authoring/answerability. In this early period, dialogue is a key concept for Bakhtin but only in a metaphorical sense. Just as any dialogue or conversation can be understood as the unity of different voices, so human existence and consciousness can be understood as a metaphorical dialogue, or relation of difference, between one embodied person and an embodied other. However, by the late 1920s, after Bakhtin's linguistic turn, dialogue is decidedly conceived as language use. Dialogue is a key concept not only at a metaphorical level but in reference to the interplay of disparate discourses, whether written or spoken.

❖ BAKHTIN'S DIALOGISM POST-1924

The Linguistic Turn

When the Bakhtin circle migrated to Leningrad in 1924 or thereabouts, the intellectual world was abuzz with Ferdinand de Saussure's work and the linguistic turn it represented (Saussure, 1983). Saussure's *Course in General Linguistics,* the text put together from his lectures by two of his students, was first published in 1916 and marked the beginning of modern linguistics. Saussure shifted the study of language from a focus on the history of languages to one focused on living languages. He distinguished *langue*—the structural system of language—from *parole*—individual instances of uttered language—and argued that the latter was too chaotic to be the focus of linguistics, favoring instead a discipline of linguistics built on the scaffold of language structure alone. He argued that language structure was a self-contained system that was simply deployed by individualized language users. The relationship between a sign (e.g., the word *bat* in English) and its referent (the flying nocturnal creature) is an arbitrary one; each language has its own word to refer to the same referent. Instead, English speakers understand the sign *bat* based on the structural system of phonemes (sounds such as the voiced bilabial sound we make to enunciate *b* as distinct from the unvoiced bilabial sound to enunciate *p*), morphemes (combinations of phonemes, for example, in English, *q* and *t* do not generally follow one another), and larger grammatical combinations of words (phrases, clauses, sentences). According to Saussure, the science of linguistics should be focused on the structural systemic features of languages.

Bakhtin and his fellow intellectuals applauded the shift to living languages, away from the dead languages studied by historical linguistics. In language, Bakhtin landed on the process by which the act of mutual authoring—answerability—is performed:

> There is no such thing as experience outside of embodiment in signs. . . . The location of the organizing and formative center is not within . . . but outside. It is not experience that organizes expression,

but the other way around—*expression organizes experience.* Expression
is what first gives experience its form and specificity of direction.
(Voloshinov, 1986, p. 85)

In other words, argued Bakhtin, language (expression) is constitutive
of the human experience. It is through language that the simultaneity
of differences is realized.

However, although Bakhtin joined the intellectual groundswell to
focus on language, his understanding of language was decidedly dialogic (Hirschkop, 2001). In particular, in *Marxism and the Philosophy of
Language,* Bakhtin took issue with two trends he identified in contemporary philosophy of language—abstract objectivism and individualistic
subjectivism—and in so doing articulated a dialogic conceptualization of
language (Voloshinov, 1986, pp. 45–46).

Bakhtin associated abstract objectivism with Saussure. Although
he applauded the move to study living language, he took issue with
Saussure's focus on the abstract system of language that governed all
phonetic, grammatical, and lexical choices of speakers. Such an emphasis conceptualized language as a closed system, one in which creation
was logically impossible: "From the point of view of [abstract objec-
tivism], meaningful language creativity on the speaker's part is simply
out of the question" (Voloshinov, 1986, p. 53). Bakhtin favored the
study of language use—*parole.* In moving from the study of language
as an abstract system to the study of language-in-use in everyday life,
Bakhtin continued his early theoretical commitment to prosaics.

At the same time, however, Bakhtin was critical of the opposite
extreme position, or what he called individualistic subjectivism in the
study of language; that is, the view that uttered speech is nothing more
than the product of an intact, monadic self:

Individualistic subjectivism is wrong in ignoring and failing to
understand the social nature of the utterance and in attempting to
derive the utterance from the speaker's inner world as an expression
of that inner world. The structure of the utterance and of the very
experience being expressed is a *social structure.* (Voloshinov, 1986, p. 93)

By social structure, Bakhtin meant that the utterance is performed
in a concrete situation between socially embedded speakers who are
mutually answerable:

Orientation of the word toward the addressee has an extremely high
significance. In point of fact, word is a two-sided act. It is determined
equally by whose word it is and for whom it is meant. As word, it is

precisely the product of the reciprocal relationship between speaker and listener, addresser and addressee. Each and every word expresses the "one" in relation to the "other." I give myself verbal shape from another's point of view, ultimately, from the point of view of the community to which I belong. A word is a bridge thrown between myself and another. (Voloshinov, 1986, p. 86)

Rather than conceptualizing language as either an abstract, closed system or a matter of individual psyches, Bakhtin argued that language should be viewed as the dialogue (understood in both metaphorical and nonmetaphorical ways) between the one and the other.

The critique of individual subjectivism shadows the earlier critique of Freudianism, published in 1927 under Voloshinov's name. Bakhtin argued that Freud's psychoanalytic theories relied on subjective introspection, neglecting the role of the social, specifically the other, in shaping the human being. Although they were attracted to the struggle and conflict that characterizes Freud's view of the individual psyche, they were otherwise critical of what they viewed as his nonsocial perspective, which understood the human as a set of essentialist instincts and drives:

The abstract biological person . . . does not exist at all. . . . What is needed, as it were, is a second birth, a social birth. . . . Only this social and historical localization makes him a real human being and determines the content of his life and cultural creativity. (Voloshinov, 1987, p. 15)

Thus, Bakhtin (1986b) moves us from the study of language structure (Saussure) and the study of individual psyches (Freud) to a focus on language use. It is historically significant for the communication studies discipline that Bakhtin referred to this subject of study as "speech communication" (p. 84).

Bakhtin's view of meaning is, thus, more complex than that of language structure, as Saussure argued, or individual dispositions, an argument attributed to Freud. We create meaning not only based on the structural features of language or the motivations and predispositions of individuals, but additionally, we grasp language as something a particular other says to us in a specific temporal, spatial, and social situation. Rarely is language use an equal playing field; some utterances pack more authority than others, based on cultural norms or social stratifications along lines of gender, race, and class, among others. And utterances mean different things based on the relationship that the parties bring to the interaction moment. In short, meaning is not just about linguistic structure and individual psychology; it is a decidedly social process, a joint undertaking of meaning making between interactants. Nor is meaning making a mere transmission process from one person to another; instead, it is the interplay of multiple, different voices or discourses, as the concept of the utterance suggests.

The Utterance Chain

The central analytic unit in language-as-dialogue is the utterance. Bakhtin's use of the term *utterance* invokes a meaning far more complex than our contemporary understanding of an individuated act by an autonomous speaker. To Bakhtin (1986b), an utterance is a link in a "chain of speech communion" (p. 93), a link bounded by both preceding links and the links that follow. These links provide a given utterance its "dialogic overtones" (p. 92). In this sense, utterances are interdependent with one another. Utterances always respond in some way to prior utterances. As Bakhtin indicated,

> Each utterance refutes, affirms, supplements, and relies on the others, presupposes them to be known, and somehow takes them into account. . . . Therefore, each utterance is filled with various kinds of responsive reactions to other utterances of the given sphere of speech communication. (p. 91)

Some of an utterance's preceding links are quite distant and remote in space and in time; for example, cultural habits and practices that have been enacted by others long before the immediate interaction event. Other utterances in the chain of speech communion are more immediate; for example, the immediately prior utterances in the conversation. Utterances do not merely repeat the past. Speaking, as a concrete and embodied act, is always performed in a unique time and space, a concept Bakhtin discussed as a *chronotope* (Bakhtin, 1981b). An utterance is always inflected with the speaker's chronotoped tone. As Morson and Emerson (1990) have expressed it, "Tone bears witness to the singularity of the act and its singular relation to its performer" (p. 133). More or less like the proverbial claim that one can't step twice in the same river, prior dialogic overtones are always new because the circumstances of their use are always different.

An utterance also sits at the dialogic boundary of the said and the unsaid. To some extent, speakers share the immediate situation in which they enact speech communion. In addition, speakers may swim in speech communities in which certain discourses are shared and thus do not need to be expressed explicitly. Shared speech community membership may also give speakers a shared understanding of the kind of speech-communication event, or genre (Bakhtin, 1986b, p. 78), that they are enacting. These shared meanings can function as taken-for-granted utterances in the chain of speech communion, unsaid but certainly not absent.

A given utterance also is laced with the dialogic overtones of conversational utterances that are anticipated to follow. When a speaker is constructing an utterance, he or she is taking into account the immediate addressee's possible response. Because the human experience is one of answerability, "an essential (constitutive) marker of the utterance is its quality of being directed to someone, its *addressivity*. As distinct from *i.e., listener* the signifying units of a language—words and sentences—that are impersonal, belonging to nobody and addressed to nobody, the utterance has both an author . . . and an addressee" (Bakhtin, 1986b, p. 95). Speakers orient their utterances to the addressee in anticipation of his or her response. An addressee can be distant, as well—an addressee who is not a fellow participant in the immediate conversation but who may respond to the utterance at a future time and place. This distant addressee can be thought of as a superaddressee "whose absolutely just responsive understanding is presumed, either in some metaphysical distance or distant historical time" (Bakhtin, 1986c, p. 126). The presence of a superaddressee creates a loophole in which meaning is forever unfinalizable, as Coates (1998) has noted:

> There is neither a first nor a last word. The contexts of dialogue are without limit. They extend into the deepest past and the most distant future. Even meanings born in dialogues of the remotest past will never be finally grasped once and for all, for they will always be renewed in later dialogue. At any present moment of the dialogue there are great masses of forgotten meanings, but these will be recalled again and given new life. For nothing is absolutely dead: every meaning will someday have its homecoming festival. (p. 39)

At some point in the future, an utterance spoken in the past can become part of some superaddressee's dialogue with its unique emergent meanings. In other words, meanings are not fixed.

The addressivity of an utterance—the anticipated responses from the immediate addressee and from the superaddressee—precludes ownership by an individual speaker. The expression of an utterance is constructed as much by the anticipated listener as by the particular speaker. In this sense, an utterance can never be owned by a single speaker but instead is jointly owned by the speaker and its (super)addressees.

In short, dialogism's utterance is far from an individual act. It isn't even a duet between two speakers. It is more of an ensemble in which the simultaneous interplay of multiple different utterances produces meaning at the moment (Baxter & Montgomery, 1996, p. 29). This fleeting unity of differences is Bakhtin's conception of dialogue. It is also what he means when he describes the *heteroglossia* of language (Bakhtin, 1981d, p. 271).

Bakhtin's post-1924 work often uses the term *voice* to stand for *utterance*, reminding us of the chronotoped embodiment of communication. But he also means utterance/voice in a more general sense as well, to refer to any specific point of view, worldview, value, or ideology constituted in the uttered word (Bakhtin, 1981d, pp. 291–292). I am using the term *discourse* to capture this sense of voice.

Dialogue

Bakhtin's conception of dialogue is far from our contemporary idealization of the term to mean a smooth and seamless consensual exchange between equals (Deetz & Simpson, 2004). Bakhtin's (1981d) dialogue is envisioned as a rough-and-tumble affair:

> The word, directed toward its object, enters a dialogically agitated and tension-filled environment of alien words, value judgments and accents, weaves in and out of complex interrelationships, merges with some, recoils from others, intersects with yet a third group: and all this may crucially shape discourse. (p. 276)

Put simply, dialogue is counterpoint among multiple competing discourses, or systems of meaning. Although Bakhtin believed in the importance of understanding the situated particularities of a given instance of speech communion, he also advanced a more general claim about all dialogic discourse. Dialogue, according to Bakhtin (1981d), is a process in which unity and difference, in some form, are at play, both with and against one another:

> Every concrete utterance of a speaking subject serves as a point where centrifugal, as well as centripetal forces, are brought to bear. The processes of centralization and decentralization, of unification and disunification, intersect in the utterance. . . . It is possible to give a concrete and detailed analysis of any utterance, once having exposed it as a contradiction-ridden, tension-filled unity of two embattled tendencies in the life of language. (p. 272)

It is important to appreciate that Bakhtin's use of the term *contradiction-ridden* in this excerpt does not commit him to a dialectical view in the narrow Hegelian-Marxian sense that dominated his sociopolitical world. In fact, late in his life Bakhtin wrote a harsh critique of this brand of dialectics as too abstract and removed from concrete experience; too mechanistic in its either-or logic that moved from thesis, to antithesis, to synthesis, in contrast to the both/and interplay envisioned in dialogue; and too biased in favor of finalizable synthesis, in contrast to the ongoing interplay of unity-and-difference that characterizes dialogue (Bakhtin, 1986a, p. 147).

Some genres of communication actualize dialogue more readily than others. Bakhtin valued the former for their dialogic potentials and criticized the latter for their monologic tendencies. Bakhtin wrote in particular about two dialogic genres: the novel and the medieval carnival. The novel, in contrast to other literary genres such as epic or poetry, is characterized by a polyphony of voices, according to Bakhtin (1981a). This is particularly so, argued Bakhtin, under the skilled pen of Dostoevsky (Bakhtin, 1984b). Dostoevsky had the ability to write double-voiced discourse; that is, he wrote without merging his voice as author with the voices of his characters. In Dostoevsky's double-voiced discourse, another label for dialogue, the reader experiences "not a multitude of characters and fates in a single objective world, illuminated by a single authorial consciousness; rather a plurality of consciousnesses, with equal rights and each with its own world, combine but are not merged in the unity of the event" (Bakhtin, 1984b, p. 6).

In analyzing Dostoevsky's works, Bakhtin (1984b) provides a typology of possible ways of orienting toward another's utterance that holds relevance to any form of communication, whether written or oral (p. 199). In general, the typology advances a continuum from more monologic to more dialogic utterance types. Toward the monologic side, we have single-voiced discourse, that ignores the other's voice in its expression of the speaker's position as the ultimate semantic authority (p. 199). For example, official or institutional discourse (the discourse of the Stalinist regime comes to mind) is monologically inclined. Toward the dialogic side, we have various degrees of double voicedness in which the voice of the other is engaged in some way. For example, quoting someone else's voice for purposes of advancing one's own argument is more double voiced than merely asserting one's position using one's own authoritative voice. But because the other's words are positioned as a servant to one's position, this act is less double voiced than a rejoinder in a conversation in which the other's position is responded to on its own terms.

Bakhtin had earlier introduced the concept of *reported speech*, a similar concept to double voicedness (Voloshinov, 1986, pp. 115–159). In this earlier work, the concept had been used to discuss the ease, or difficulty, with which different languages such as Russian or French enabled a speaker to contain another's utterance in one's own. The later articulation of double voicedness represented in *Problems of Dostoevsky's Poetics* (Bakhtin, 1984b) presents a more sophisticated and concrete return to reported speech, reconceptualized as a feature of utterances rather than of languages.

The second genre identified by Bakhtin for its dialogic prospects is the carnival, exemplified in the medieval carnival (Bakhtin, 1984c). In reflecting on carnivalistic life in general ("in the sense of the sum total of all diverse festivities, rituals and forms of a carnival type," Bakhtin, 1984b, p. 122), Bakhtin (1984b) observed these characteristics:

> The laws, prohibitions, and restrictions that determine the structure and order of ordinary, that is noncarnival, life are suspended: What is suspended first of all is hierarchical structure and all the forms of terror, reverence, piety, and etiquette connected with it—that is, everything resulting from socio-hierarchical inequality or any other form of inequality among people. . . . All distance between people is suspended, and a special carnival category goes into effect: free and familiar contact among people. . . . Carnival brings together, unifies, weds, and combines the sacred with the profane, the lofty with the low, the great with the insignificant, the wise with the stupid. (Bakhtin, pp. 122–123)

The carnivalesque, then, is a moment where centripetal hierarchy is temporarily decrowned (Bakhtin, 1984b, p. 124). Eccentricity—in its many centrifugal forms—rules the event as life is drawn out of its usual rut (p. 124).

Bakhtin's discussion of the carnival is arguably as close as he comes to explicit treatment of power relations at the analytic level of the genre, beyond his general critique of all monologically inclined discourses. However, the carnival event may not be a permanent shift in the discursive landscape of circulating ideologies and the institutionalized hierarchies they construct and sustain. The decrowning of hierarchy may be temporary; upon carnival's end, the usual rut of life may return. Although Bakhtin's dialogism recognizes power inequality in its differentiation of centripetal (at the center) and centrifugal (at the margins) discourses, it does not examine systematically whether or how it is that once centrifugal voices become centripetal, and vice versa, in any manner other than in the fleeting moments of the carnivalesque.

Bakhtin's career spanned a half century. His philosophy of dialogism generated a wealth of insights about the human experience, especially the place of speech communion in that experience. Communication scholars have much to gain from conversing with Bakhtin's dialogism.

❖ LOCATING BAKHTIN'S THEORY OF DIALOGISM IN COMMUNICATION RESEARCH

It is ironic that the theorist who privileged "speech communication" (Bakhtin, 1986b, p. 75)—real-life dialogue with the utterance chain as its core unit of analysis—has been relatively slow to gain recognition among communication scholars. A number of scholars engage in dialogue studies, drawing upon a wide range of relevant theorists other than Bakhtin (see Anderson, Baxter, & Cissna, 2004, for an introduction to some of the primary dialogue scholars in communication). Some communication scholars interested in communication and ethics have employed Bakhtin's pre-1924 dialogism work (e.g., Conquergood, 1985; Friedman, 2001; Murray, 1999). A number of rhetorical scholars have employed Bakhtin's post-1924 dialogism to examine a variety of communication texts in the public sphere (e.g., Bialostosky, 1992; Bruner, 2005; Conway, 2003; Diamondstone, 1997; Farmer, 1998; Garvey, 2000; Grano, 2007; Halasek, 1992; Hariman, 2008; Janack, 2006; Jasinski, 1997; Murphy, 2001). Performance studies feature a range of Bakhtin-informed work (e.g., Bergman, 2004; Bruner, 2005; Conquergood, 1985; Fenske, 2004; Hoy, 1994; Rogers, 1998; Strine, 2004). Scholars of mass media also have drawn upon Bakhtin's work (e.g., Brown, Stevens, & Maclaran, 1999; Curnutt, 2009; Druick, 2009; Fiske, 1986; From, 2006; Martin & Renegar, 2007; Newcomb, 1984; Olbrys, 2006; Pitcher, 2006; Sarch, 1997; Sobchak, 1996). Bakhtin's dialogism is characterized by a more muted, but nonetheless vital, presence in other areas of communication scholarship, including: health communication (e.g., Geist & Dreyer, 1993; Thatcher, 2006); interpersonal communication (e.g., Shotter, 1993a, 1993b, 2000); language and social interaction (Holt, 2003; Taylor, 1995; Yael, 2002); and organizational communication (e.g., Barge & Little, 2002; Bathurst, 2004).

True to the dialogic spirit, an important part of understanding Bakhtin's dialogism is to position it in conversation with and against other intellectual projects that can be identified in interpersonal and family communication. I am going to locate Bakhtin's dialogism by anchoring it in two ways. First, I will position Bakhtin's dialogism according to its underlying paradigmatic assumptions about reality and how one comes to know it, relying heavily on Deetz's (2001) framework of basic paradigmatic assumptions. Second, I will position Bakhtin's dialogism by locating it more particularly according to its assumptions about communication, linking it explicitly to social constructionism.

Paradigmatic Location

At the level of paradigms, or basic assumptions about reality and how knowledge claims are made, it is useful to position dialogism in reference to a framework that Deetz (2001) originally used to describe organizational communication but which holds currency, as well, for interpersonal and family communication. Deetz presented two underlying dimensions of contrast in which four basic paradigmatic approaches can be positioned, one of which fits the perspective of Bakhtin's dialogism. I prefer Deetz's framework to more traditional paradigmatic frameworks that focus on only three paradigms (post-positivistic, interpretive, and critical; e.g., Bochner, 1985) for reasons that become apparent as I summarize his four quadrants.

The first dimension of contrast that Deetz (2001) identified is anchored by the endpoints of *local/emergent* as opposed to *elite/a priori* and refers to the origin of concepts and problem statements studied by researchers; the core question that orients this dimension is that of whose concepts are used (p. 12). The local/emergent endpoint favors situated knowledge claims, in contrast to the search for large-scale empirical generalizations that characterize the elite/a priori endpoint. The role of theory for researchers who favor the local/emergent approach is to guide or sensitize the researcher while sustaining an openness to emergent knowledge that surfaces during the process of research. The local/emergent approach values the perspective of participants, who are envisioned as research partners of the researcher. By contrast, the role of theory in the elite/a priori approach fixes concepts and issues in advance of data collection; research participants are observed from the researcher's perspective and are subjects of study rather than collaborators of knowledge production. Given the discussion of language use as a chronotoped process of unfinalizability, it is not surprising that Bakhtin's dialogism fits comfortably near the local/emergent endpoint of this first dimension of contrast.

The second dimension of contrast identified by Deetz (2001) is *consensus* versus *dissensus*, focusing on "the relation of research to existing social orders" (p. 14). The consensus endpoint endorses a view of research as a discovery enterprise in which a researcher's goal is to mirror or represent the natural or social world by identifying its underlying stable and orderly patterns. In the consensus view, deviance, conflict, and fragmentation are viewed as problematic; researchers' attention is focused on how natural or social systems maintain order, predictability, and stability. By contrast, the dissensus view provides an intellectual home to researchers who view conflict, fragmentation, struggle, and disorder as normal. Achieved order, coherence, and stability in the social world are regarded as power-filled dynamics rather than natural outcomes. Given dialogism's view of the meaning-making enterprise as a struggle of competing discourses, its fit is near the dissensus endpoint of this second underlying dimension.

When the two dimensions are considered together, four basic research orientations, or paradigms, can be identified. The approach that occupies the vast majority of research activity in interpersonal/family communication is what Deetz (2001) labeled the *normative* approach; other commonly used terms to describe this set of assumptions are *postpositivism*, *logical-empiricism*, or the *scientific approach* (Bochner, 1985; Baxter & Braithwaite, 2006b; Braithwaite & Baxter, 2008). This approach is marked by its commitments to the elite/a priori and consensus views. The goal of research from this approach is to discover basic lawlike patterns between observed phenomena or variables. Research is evaluated by its fidelity in representing an objective world, thus research methods are favored that regulate the subjectivities of both the researcher and participants, often replicating the preferred methods of the natural sciences including experimental design and precise quantitative measurement. Generally, communication is viewed either as a mechanism of persuasion or as information transfer in the normative model. An objective reality preexists communication in this approach. Clearly, Bakhtin's dialogism is a poor fit with this approach to scholarship, and efforts to evaluate it against normative standards are misguided.

A distant second in paradigmatic approaches to interpersonal/family communication research is what Deetz (2001) labeled *interpretive* (a label shared by others, for example, Baxter & Braithwaite, 2006b; Bochner, 1985; Braithwaite & Baxter, 2008). The interpretive perspective values local/emergent and consensus views. The goal of much interpretive work is to show "how particular realities are socially produced and maintained through ordinary talk, stories, rites, rituals, and other daily activities" (Deetz, p. 23). Deetz argued that much interpretive work has a consensus view in its focus on shared values and common practices within a given community or culture. Interpretive work is local/emergent in its commitment to understanding the multiple social realities and their particularities. Interpretive researchers value the subjective perspective of those who are studied, seeking to understand a community from the native's point of view. Within the interpretive project, communication is regarded as more than information transmission; instead, it is a key means by which meaning is produced and maintained. Methods are valued that afford the richest and deepest understanding of the particularities of a given culture or community, focusing on what native members must know, believe, and do to be regarded as culturally competent. Participant observation and in-depth interviewing thus frequent the methodological toolkit of interpretive researchers. Theory is used as a sensitizing mechanism, but the researcher remains open to interpretations that emerge inductively from the data collection process. Deetz argued that interpretive work in communication studies is evolving, with some interpretive work challenging a consensual view, thereby becoming more dialogic, and some interpretive work is showing interest in issues of power, thereby becoming more critical (p. 25). If we were denied Deetz's fourth approach, described below, Bakhtin's dialogism could fit in the interpretive perspective, especially its more recent turn toward viewing culture as fragmented. However, a better fit can be found, as described below in the fourth approach.

Deetz (2001) identified a third paradigmatic perspective at the intersection of the dissensus and the elite/a priori endpoints on the two dimensions of contrast. As noted in Chapter 1, the *critical* perspective is barely on the radar screen of interpersonal and family communication (Baxter & Braithwaite, 2006b; Braithwaite & Baxter, 2008). Critical researchers view the condition of the social world as one of struggle and power relations. Their goal is to demonstrate and critique forms of domination, thereby liberating the oppressed (women, people of color, lower social classes) from the grip of these power relations. Ideological critique is particularly prominent in the critical perspective. The analysis of ideology focuses on reification (the ways in which a socially or historically constructed world becomes framed as necessary and natural) and suppression (of conflicting interests and perspectives). A method frequently employed by critical researchers in communication studies is textual analysis of one kind or another, with the researcher's task that of interrogating discourse for its implicit or explicit ideologies. Critical researchers begin with a priori theoretical commitments that "aid them analytically to ferret out situations of domination and distortion" (p. 26). One might argue that Bakhtin's dialogism could fit in the critical fold, given its critical concern with monologue and the value it attaches to dialogue. However, let's continue on to the fourth perspective identified by Deetz, where we will encounter an even better paradigmatic home for Bakhtin's dialogism.

The fourth, and final, paradigmatic approach identified by Deetz (2001) is what he labeled *dialogic*. From the label alone, it is evident that we have come to the best home in which to locate Bakhtin's dialogism. But it is important to recognize that Bakhtin's theory of dialogism is but one member of this growing paradigmatic family. Deetz's dialogic perspective sits at the intersection of the dissensus and local/emergent endpoints along the two dimensions of contrast. Several themes characterize the dialogic perspective identified by Deetz. First, researchers from this perspective give a central place to discourse, or the systems of meanings by which social realities are shaped. In embracing fully the linguistic turn initiated by Saussure and others, dialogic scholars break from normative and interpretive traditions, as Deetz explained:

> The linguistic turn enabled a critique of normative research's claim of objectivity through examining the processes by which objects are socially constituted and the role of language in that process and simultaneously a critique of interpretive research through demonstrating the fragmentation of cultures and personal identities and removing the psychological subject from the center of experience. Focusing on language allowed a conception of social constructionism that denied the normative claim of certainty and objective truth and the interpretivists' reliance on experience and neutral cultural claims that led them to miss the social/linguistic politics of experience. (p. 32)

Second, the dialogic perspective is committed to a view of identity as fragmented, which functions to decenter the autonomous individual self that is valued by normative, interpretive, and critical scholars. In normative interpersonal and family communication, the autonomous self can most readily be identified in the rationalist view that communicators make strategic communicative choices in response to their inner goals. In interpretive interpersonal and family communication, acceptance of the autonomous self rests in the presumption of a seamlessly coherent consciousness in the individual subject. Critical researchers tend to view personal identities as fixed or unitary, e.g., one's identity as a woman or as a member of the working class. By contrast, argue dialogic scholars, identities are fragmented and always in flux because they are discursive productions and always emergent in the competing discourses of a given moment.

According to Deetz (2001), the dialogic perspective focuses on power but in a manner different from the critical perspective. In contrast to the predefinition of groups and forms of domination that characterize the critical perspective, we encounter a more fluid conception of power:

> Dialogic studies focus more on micropolitical processes and the joined nature of power and resistance. Domination is seen as fluid, situational, and without place or origin. Even group and personal identities cannot be seen as fixed or unitary. The attention is to reclaim conflicts suppressed in everyday experiences, meaning systems, and self-conceptions. (p. 31)

Power resides not in top-down structural systems and their predetermined group memberships. Instead, power resides in discourses—the systems of meaning that produce and maintain these social constructions.

The goal of dialogic research, argued Deetz (2001) is "not to get it right" (p. 37), whether "rightness" is cast as accuracy in discovering the underlying causal order of the objective world (the normative perspective), descriptive adequacy in representing the native's point of view (the interpretive perspective), or exposing the actual power relations that are often ideologically masked (the critical perspective). According to Deetz, the goal of the dialogic project instead is to reclaim conflict, to "challenge guiding assumptions, fixed meanings and relations, and reopen the formative capacity of human beings in relation to others and the world" (p. 37). That is, dialogic work is committed to the unfinalizability of discursive struggle and the value of opening up new discursive possibilities.

Like their interpretive cousins, the role of theory in the dialogic quadrant is that of providing a sensitizing guidance to the research enterprise. Like interpretive and critical researchers, dialogic researchers pay close attention to language use, based on a social constructionist belief that language use produces and maintains social realities. However, unlike interpretive researchers, language use is not examined in order to identify its coherences and common practices; rather, the focus is on the ruptures, struggles, and fragmentation seen to characterize language use. Like critical researchers with an interest in ideology, dialogic researchers are especially interested in interrogating language use for insights into its discursive formations—that is, attention to the systems of meaning by which realities come to be taken-for-granted. Unlike critical research, however, the process by which some discourses gain dominance is not understood as a top-down consequence of structural power relations but instead is understood as the fluid and emergent result of the situated clash of different, often competing, systems of meaning.

In discussing paradigms, I have hinted that dialogism aligns with a social constructionist conception of communication. Given the growing significance of the social constructionism perspective in interpersonal and family communication research and theory, it is important to elaborate on this point.

Bakhtin's Dialogism and a Social Constructionist Conception of Communication

A growing commitment among both interpretive and dialogic scholars of interpersonal and family communication is that of social constructionism. Actually, as Burr (2003) usefully reminds us, there is no single social constructionism but instead a set of related theoretical perspectives sharing a family resemblance to one another. According to Burr, family membership in social constructionism involves a commitment to four basic assumptions. First, the social constructionism family involves "a critical stance toward taken-for-granted knowledge" (p. 2). This assumption challenges a view that our knowledge of the world is based upon objective, unbiased observation. Thus, this assumption challenges Deetz's (2001) normative approach, discussed above. Reality, as we know it, is socially constructed through language use or communication. As such, reality is neither natural, nor objective. This assumption thus takes an anti-essentialist stance; no essences inside people or objects make them the way they are. Communication is conceived as constitutive of social reality, rather than representing a world that is preformed prior to communication. By contrast, a representational view of communication begins with the assumption that the world exists out there, and that effective communication describes it accurately. More formally, the representational view of communication is known as the correspondence theory of language among philosophers (Gergen, 1999). The so-called "crisis of representation" (Gergen, p. 19) that has assaulted the social sciences over the past couple of decades has profoundly challenged the representational view of communication, shifting a growing number of scholars to a constitutive conception.

The remaining assumptions flow from the first core assumption. Second, family membership in social constructionism requires a commitment to "historical and cultural specificity" (Burr, 2003, p. 3). As a logical consequence of the first assumption, our knowledge of the world depends on our culture and the historical times in which we live. Third, social constructionists share a belief that "knowledge is sustained by social processes" (p. 4). We fabricate our knowledge of the world through the daily interactions we have with others. Communication is the essential tool by which social processes are enacted. Finally, social constructionists believe that "knowledge and social action go together" (p. 5). Our knowledges of the world are integrally linked to power relations in that our constructions of reality produce and reproduce some knowledges and practices and function to exclude others.

Although these assumptions are common to all strands of social constructionism, differences are also evident among the various family members. Pearce (1995) has provided a map of the social constructionism territory that summarizes several basic differences among social constructionist approaches. In particular, he proposed a conceptual scheme organized around three underlying dimensions. The first dimension is anchored by the endpoints of a monadic social world versus a pluralistic social world (p. 94). Although all social constructionists take issue with the notion of a natural world, social constructionists vary in their focus on processes of socially constructing, as opposed to a focus on the products that are socially constructed. The pluralistic-social-world endpoint features social constructionist work that foregrounds process: the situated, interactional patterns—the communicative practices—of meaning making. Here, the focus is on "constructing social realities" (p. 94). Social constructionist work centered at this end of the continuum celebrates the fluidity of meanings and the multiplicity of realities that potentially are, or can be, constructed in the interactional moment. In Deetz's (2001) framework, these social constructionists would probably align with the dialogic approach in light of their commitments to the fragmentation of culture and its resulting multitude of social realities. By contrast, the monadic-social-world endpoint features social constructionist work that foregrounds products; that is, the meanings that are made—"the social construction of reality" (Pearce, 1995, p. 94). Social constructionist work that is centered at this end of the continuum tends to focus on the symbols, structural forms, and meanings that are reproduced and come to be taken-for-granted as natural. Social constructionists that align with this end of the continuum probably fit best in Deetz's interpretive approach.

Other social constructionist work tends to sit closer to the middle of this continuum, focusing on both issues of process and product. Bakhtin's dialogism is process centered in its focus on the unfinalizability of meaning in the struggle of competing discourses and in the value it attaches to dialogue over monologue. However, its distinction between centripetal and centrifugal discourses recognizes that dominant discourses often have a semantic edge and are likely to be reproduced unless centrifugal discourses can gain a sufficient foothold in the meaning-making process. Thus, Bakhtin's dialogism is positioned near the center of Pearce's (1995) first dimension of social constructionism but with clear allegiance to the pluralistic-social-world endpoint.

The second dimension identified by Pearce (1995, p. 98) is bounded by the endpoints of spectator knowledge versus participant knowledge. The endpoint of spectator knowledge emphasizes the cognitive process of knowing the world; it foregrounds individual perception. By contrast, the endpoint of participant knowledge emphasizes the social action implicated in creating the world. Social constructionists located at both endpoints concur that we construct our social worlds. However, those at the spectator end of this dimension believe that this construction happens more individually as we develop a mental map and then act on the basis of that map, whereas those at the participant end of this dimension believe that this construction happens socially, between communicators, as they participate in the construction of social worlds. Linking this dimension to Deetz's (2001) framework, the spectator-knowledge endpoint probably feels better to interpretive scholars, whereas the participant knowledge endpoint probably feels better to dialogic scholars.

In its decentering of the autonomous self, Bakhtin's dialogism clearly aligns with the participant knowledge endpoint of this second dimension identified by Pearce (1995). From early in his career, Bakhtin's focus was on the creative act, conceived not as an individual action but as a joint process that creates, or constitutes, meanings, including consciousness.

The third dimension identified by Pearce (1995, p. 102) in sorting out different approaches to a social constructionist conception of communication is marked by a quest for certainty versus an exercise of curiosity. As social constructionists move to the quest-for-certainty endpoint of this dimension, they experience "a strain toward closure; it is a motivation to inquiry which will, at last produce certainty" (p. 102). By contrast, the exercise-of-curiosity endpoint celebrates the impossibility of certainty and thus the ultimate futility of seeking it. As Pearce indicates, "The exercise of curiosity by social constructionists consists of an affinity for paradox and irony, a certain playfulness about our own actions that take into consideration the fact that we make the world that we describe" (p. 102). Pearce notes that the strands of social constructionism that align with the monadic-social-world endpoint from the first dimension and the spectator knowledge endpoint from the second dimension are not likely to partake in the exercise of curiosity, instead feeling more comfortable with the quest for certainty.

Bakhtin's work can be understood as a celebration of dialogue and its unfinalizability of meaning. It evidences clear anxiety about the potentiality for monologue in the form of dominating centripetal discourses. Monologue produces certainty, and Bakhtin's project was not to seek it but to resist it. Thus, Bakhtin's theory of dialogism can be regarded as an exercise of curiosity. However, Bakhtin's theory of dialogism nonetheless recognizes that meanings are created, and he celebrates the aesthetics of meaning making in which emergent meanings are formed out of the spontaneous combustion of competing discourses. However, the meaning-making process envisioned by Bakhtin is fluid, with meanings in the moment potentially up for grabs in the next interactional moment. The certainties valued by Bakhtin are ephemeral; they emerge in the moment and resist calcification.

Of course, placement of Bakhtin's theory of dialogism with respect to this third dimension is profoundly humbling to me as an author. A book, by its very nature, can be regarded as a form of calcification, an effort to fix meaning—in this instance, an attempt to fix an interpretation and application of Bakhtin's theory of dialogism. The irony of being the single author of a book about a theory that is committed to process, co-constructed meaning making, and unfinalizability does not escape me! I ask for your indulgence as you progress through the book's remaining chapters.

❖ LOCATING RDT IN BAKHTIN'S DIALOGISM

This chapter has been devoted to the life and work of Mikhail Bakhtin with the goal of providing the reader with a sense of the whole of the dialogism project. Perhaps you noticed that RDT is barely mentioned in the pages of this chapter. RDT is an extension of Bakhtin's theory of dialogism to understanding familial, social, and personal relationships. Whereas Bakhtin focused his intellectual energy on language, culture, and the novel, RDT takes the core concepts and principles of dialogism in a different direction, that of understanding how communication makes meaning in the everyday prosaics of relating. Although dialogue is the central concept in Bakhtin's theory, he ironically failed to examine the everyday talk of people as they enacted their acquaintanceships, friendships, romantic relationships, and family relations, focusing instead on the novel. RDT is the theoretical bridge that brings Bakhtin's dialogism to the study of interpersonal and family communication.

But why come up with a different name to begin with? Why not simply call this Bakhtin's dialogism theory? Labels do important work. In adopting the label, *relational dialectics theory,* this extension of Bakhtin's dialogism is marking its differences from other appropriations of Bakhtin's dialogism, which are numerous throughout the social sciences and humanities. The work performed by the term *relational* signals that this appropriation of Bakhtin's dialogism privileges Bakhtin's (1986b) essay "The Problem of Speech Genres," in its focus on the intertextuality of the utterance chain; an utterance is always interdependent with "already-spokens" from prior interlocutors and with anticipated "not-yet-spokens" from "super"addressees. The term *relational* also marks the theory's focus on relating, thereby differentiating itself from more literary-based appropriations of dialogism and from appropriations seeking to understand public-sphere communication.

But why is the theory labeled relational *dialectics* theory, especially in light of Bakhtin's harsh critique of what he understood as Hegelian-Marxist dialectics? In 1996, Barbara Montgomery and I (Baxter & Montgomery, 1996) chose to name the theory the way we did because our use of the term *dialectics* was not the simplistic thesis-antithesis-synthesis version that Bakhtin criticized. Instead, we used the term dialectics in a general way, best captured by Murphy (1971): a worldview that centers change through conflict and thus is "destructive of neat systems and ordered structures, and compatible with the notion of a social universe that has neither fixity or solid boundaries" (p. 90). Thus, to us, the term dialectics emphasizes the struggle of competing discourses, and it is this feature that we foreground from Bakhtin's dialogism in emphasizing his essay "Discourse in the Novel" (Bakhtin, 1981d). RDT narrows the domain of intertextuality from a more benign focus on differing discourses to the more combative focus on competing discourses.

i.e., gentle.

3

Discursive
Struggles of Culture

Let me begin this chapter with an utterance from a 46-year-old man who was being interviewed about his voluntary kin, that is, those persons he regarded as family although they were unrelated to him according to the mainstream cultural metrics of biological bonds or legal ties. The interview participant was describing his relationship with Jim, a pseudonym for a member of his second family:

> Well, sometimes it's difficult and challenging when they're [the members of his voluntary kin family] going through some very difficult times. Sometimes they make decisions that you wouldn't make for yourself. . . . For example, Jim, you will notice that I didn't include his partner Ron as my voluntary kin, but obviously Jim is there, Ron is there. But I think that it is a bad relationship and that's a very difficult thing to have to go through. But obviously I would never let those feelings out because Jim is an adult and can make his own decisions. But it's difficult to see people you love and support in clearly bad relationships. But all you can do is support the process. (Baxter, Braithwaite, & Bach, 2009, Interview 52)

The study participant was constructing a certain meaning for his relationship with Jim as he talked about it to the interviewer. It is, the interviewer is told, like all of his voluntary kin relationships in that it is effortful and challenging because he feels that he can't interfere when those fictive kin are experiencing difficult times that result from poor decisions. From a dialogic perspective, this participant's utterance can be conceptualized as an utterance chain—an utterance riddled with potentially competing discourses of a variety of kinds. In this chapter, I concentrate on discourses that circulate in the broader culture and that animate speaker talk as resources to help speakers and listeners (relationship partners if the utterance is part of a conversation between the two partners or, as in this instance, third parties such as interviewers) construct the meaning of that talk. As we shall see shortly, these discourses are referred to as *distal already-spoken* because they were spoken by many other cultural members in utterances that long predated either the participant's familylike relationship with Jim or the participant's relationship with the interviewer formed at the time of the interview.

The participant's talk invokes a discourse of connection in his mention of enduring "love and support" during the "difficult" process of watching Jim experience a "bad relationship" with Ron. The participant is constructing his own relationship with Jim as one of loyalty and commitment for the long haul despite its challenging nature at the time of the interview. The participant's talk invokes a second radiant in a discourse of connection by informing the interviewer that Ron is not part of his own voluntary kin network; instead, we get the sense that the participant is willing to make a sacrifice and put up with Ron's presence when he accompanies Jim. According to a discourse of connection, the participant is appropriately willing to make sacrifices on behalf of his relationship with Jim.

What makes this relationship with Jim challenging for the participant is rendered sensical by a discourse of individualism. Jim is "an adult who can make his own decisions," and voluntary kin members should respect this independence, even when it is apparent to the participant that Jim has made a poor decision in choosing Ron as his romantic partner.

This participant's talk also is animated by a discourse of discretion, one in which the decision to withhold opinions is legitimized as a positive relational act that protects Jim's right to make his own decisions. However, the participant suggests, through his use of *but*, that such discretion is frustrating for him, a frustration that makes sense to fellow cultural members who swim in a discourse of expression, in which parties have a right to express their thoughts freely, and a discourse of rationality, in which open talk is often viewed as a means to solve problems.

Although this excerpt from a much longer interview is fairly short, it underscores the point of this, and the next, chapter: Utterances are intertextual acts—utterance chains—riddled with a myriad of competing systems of meaning that are resources that enable meaning making. According to dialogism, the utterance chain is the central building block by which meanings are made.

This chapter elaborates on the general concept of the utterance chain, distinguishing four constituent types of links in the meaning-making chain. In this chapter, I will focus in depth on one of these links—what I refer to above as the distal already-spoken link, that is, those competing discourses that originate in the culture at large and that are given voice by speakers in the process of constructing meanings in the moment. This chapter underscores that relating is a profoundly sociocultural process, in contrast to dominant approaches to interpersonal communication that tend to view relationships as isolated dyads or small groups driven by internal relational dynamics, largely psychological in nature. From a dialogic perspective, an utterance should be analyzed for the competing discourses that circulate in it instead of being understood as a window to the speaker's internal motivations, feelings or cognitions. Utterances that refer to such internal conditions are intelligible to us only through the discourses that give them meaning. In the next chapter I will examine in depth the remaining three kinds of links in the utterance chain. Throughout these two chapters, I will use the utterance chain as the organizing scaffold for discussing the major discursive struggles that can be identified in existing dialectically positioned scholarship.

❖ THE UTTERANCE CHAIN

Just as the sentence can be regarded as the basic unit of language, so speech communication is built on the foundation of the utterance (Bakhtin, 1986b, p. 73). Put simply, a single utterance is bounded by a change of speaking subjects; it is a turn at talk. However, from a dialogic perspective, an utterance is not conceptualized as an isolated communicative act that bears a one-to-one correspondence with a speaker's inner motivations, thoughts and feelings.[1] It is, instead, conceptualized as an utterance chain, and thus theoretical attention shifts from the utterance, per se, to the utterance chain.

Bakhtin's (1986b) rejection of the utterance as autonomous, or independent, from other links in the utterance chain is part of the Voloshinov/Bakhtin critique of Saussure's (1983) work, discussed in Chapter 2. As Bakhtin (1986b) expressed it (this time writing under his own name):

> [T]he single utterance, with all its individuality and creativity, can in no way be regarded as a *completely free combination* of forms of language, as is supposed, for example, by Saussure (and by many other linguists after him), who juxtaposed the utterance (*la parole*) as a purely individual act, to the system of language as a phenomenon that is purely social and mandatory for the individuum [individual]. (p. 81)

By contrast, argued Bakhtin (1986b), the utterance is a profoundly intertextual social unit. Simply put, each individual utterance can be thought of as the site in the utterance chain where already uttered discourses voiced by others come together with discourses anticipated in others' responses (p. 91). Meaning making happens in the utterance chain—the "chain of speech communion" as Bakhtin (p. 93) called it. A given utterance "is filled with echoes and reverberations of other utterances to which it is related" (p. 91).

Baxter and Montgomery (1996), elaborating on Bakhtin's discussion, presented a typology of four distinct forms of utterance links that are implicated in a given utterance: *distal already-spokens, proximal already-spokens, proximal not-yet-spokens,* and *distal not-yet-spokens.* Distal versus proximal captures the temporal proximity of prior (and anticipated) utterances to the immediate utterance. Figure 3.1 presents a visual metaphor of the components of the utterance chain. This flowerlike visual metaphor presents the utterance as the center, interdependent with four kinds of petals that can be understood as the four kinds of links in the utterance chain. These petals are comprised of discourses that come together in a given utterance to construct its meaning.

The distal already-spoken link in the utterance chain refers to utterances circulating in the culture at large, which are given symbolic life when voiced by speakers. As we will see below, mainstream U.S. society, like all societies, is a swirl of systems of meaning—discourses—that cultural members voice in constructing meaning. For example, imagine someone describing to a friend a new romantic relationship in this way: "We had great chemistry right away, and we're spending a lot of time together, I guess, but I want to take it kind of slowly to make sure it's the real thing. I don't want to be hurt again." Many different cultural discourses inflect this utterance to make it understandable to the friend (and to us). The discourse of romanticism that circulates in mainstream

| Figure 3.1 | The Utterance Chain |

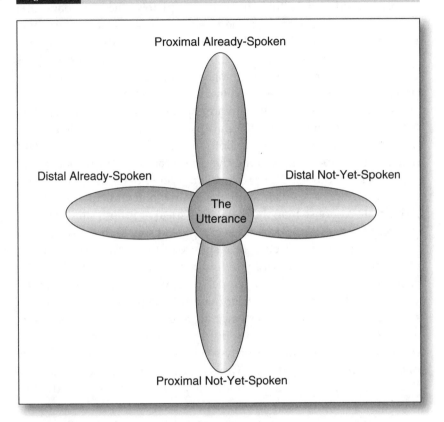

American society makes understandable the description of "great chemistry" and "the real thing." The competing discourse of rationality helps make intelligible the efforts by the speaker to proceed "kind of slowly." The discourse of individualism provides the backdrop against which the friend is positioned to understand the speaker's expressed desire to protect self from hurt that competes with the discourse of community through which the friend can understand the meaning of spending "a lot of time together." Considered as a whole, the speaker's utterance displays discursive struggle, most clearly marked by the use of "but" and the qualifiers "I guess" and "kind of."

The proximal already-spoken link is a discursive site in which the relationship's past meaning bumps up against the meaning of the relationship in the present. The relational meaning system—what kind of relationship the parties regard themselves as having—is always an inheritance from past interactions that serve as a backdrop for current interactions. With every utterance in a conversation, parties potentially act (consciously, or more likely unconsciously) to move the relationship to a new state. Oftentimes, the relational meaning system of the past is simply reproduced—although never completely; the old adage that you can never step into the same river twice holds true for relational rivers as well as literal ones! However, the relationship's meaning system potentially is up for grabs with more dramatic changes, perhaps even competing relational meanings. This discursive struggle of the past and the present is examined in the next chapter.

The contrast between the already-spoken and the not-yet-spoken focuses on utterances from the past as opposed to the anticipations of not-yet-spoken utterances. Both proximal not-yet-spokens and distal not-yet-spokens examine the role of anticipated response and evaluation by others. The proximal not-yet-spoken link focuses on the interaction of speaker with the hearer and anticipates a more immediate response than the distal. The speaker is both similar to, yet different from, the hearer. Whenever a person speaks, he or she potentially anticipates the reaction or response of this similar-yet-different other and has the opportunity to fold that anticipation into the utterance itself. For example, when a person says to the partner, "I know you won't like this idea, but hear me out," the partner's difference is salient, and the speaker is attempting to deflect it in how the utterance is expressed. Difference—the divergence of speaker-hearer meaning systems—is in play with similarity—the convergence of speaker-hearer meaning systems—in the proximal not-yet-spoken. I will examine this in depth in the next chapter as part of a discussion of identity construction in relating.

The distal not-yet-spoken link moves beyond the immediate conversation between speaker and hearer to an anticipation of how generalized others—Bakhtin's (1986b) superaddressee—will respond to an utterance. At this fourth kind of link in the utterance chain, discursive struggles usually emerge as variations of the struggle between competing discourses of the conventional and the ideal—that is, struggle between different systems of meaning with respect to what is normatively regarded as the prescriptive ideal by social network members and culture in general. For example, a couple who decides to define their relationship as one of cohabitation may bump up against friends and family who reject this as a legitimate relationship form. We can hear this struggle in one party's query to the partner, "Should we tell my family about our decision to live together when we go to the family picnic this weekend? They're pretty conservative, you know, and I don't want to make a scene." The discursive struggle of normative evaluation is discussed in depth in the next chapter.

❖ DISTAL ALREADY-SPOKENS OF CULTURE

Some dialogic echoes are from already-spoken utterances by cultural members other than the parties of a given relationship. Bakhtin (1986b) referred to such utterances as already spoken "cultural communication" (p. 93). Rare indeed, claimed Bakhtin, are moments in which speakers are "biblical Adams, dealing only with virgin and still unnamed objects, giving them names for the first time" (p. 93). We enter an utterance stream already embedded in a culture that long ago named objects and developed world views—what I call *discourses,* or systems of meaning.[2]

These distal already-spoken discourses are ever-present in the utterances of a given conversational moment. And of course, cultural communication, like all communication, is constantly in motion, as utterances in the moment function to reconstitute culture, perhaps reproducing it but also opening space for its systems of meaning to change and evolve. If you return to the conversation that opened Chapter 1, you will recall in my abbreviated analysis mention of the discourse of friendship with two strands—one that values similarity and one that values a friendship as a unique and private dyadic unit. The discourse of friendship—and the multiple strands of meaning of which it is comprised—is one system of meaning among many that collectively comprise mainstream Anglo European U.S. culture. Whenever relationship parties engage in communication with one another or with third-party others, these cultural discourses can be heard; there is no such thing as culture-free interpersonal communication. A dialogically informed analysis of relationship communication thus begins with an identification of the distal already-spokens that interanimate talk.

Bakhtin (1981d) understood language as inherently verbally ideological: "We are taking language not as a system of abstract grammatical categories, but rather language conceived as ideologically saturated, language as a world view" (p. 271). As such, one can never speak of **a** language, for this is a monologic conception of what a language is. Instead, Bakhtin understood language as inherently dialogic, a struggle among different ideological points of view, or what he called *heteroglossia* (p. 272). An utterance should not be analyzed as "a struggle between individual wills or logical contradictions" (p. 272). Instead, argued Bakhtin, an utterance is chained to heteroglot already-spokens:

> It is entangled, shot through with shared thoughts, points of view, alien value judgments and accents. The word, directed toward its

object, enters a dialogically agitated and tension-filled environment of
alien words, value judgments and accents, weaves in and out of
complex interrelationships, merges with some, recoils from others,
intersects with yet a third group: and all this may crucially shape
discourse, may leave a trace in all its semantic layers. . . . The living
utterance, having taken meaning and shape at a particular historical
moment in a socially specific environment, cannot fail to brush up
against thousands of living dialogic threads. (pp. 276–277)

Contrary to the traditional view of culture as a unitary and coherent system, contemporary theorists of culture "take cultural disjunctures and contradictions largely for granted" (Swidler, 2001, p. 12).
Bakhtin's (1981d) view of culture aligns with these contemporary theorists; culture can be understood as a process of interanimation of multiple, often competing, verbal ideological languages. Some verbal
ideologies reflect already-spoken traces from past historical epochs.
Other verbal ideologies are given life in the social standpoints at play in
a given conversation; that is, interaction between individuals who are
gendered, raced, and classed cultural members. These verbal ideologies
"are specific points of view on the world, forms for conceptualizing the
world in words, specific world views, each characterized by its own
objects, meanings and values" (pp. 291–292).

As a way to help us concretize the distal already-spokens, I will
discuss several basic discourses that circulate widely in mainstream
U.S. culture. Following Quinn and Holland (1987), these cultural discourses can be understood as

presupposed, taken-for-granted models of the world that are widely
shared (although not necessarily to the exclusion of other, alternative
models) by the members of a society and that play an enormous role
in their understanding of that world and their behavior in it. (p. 4)

On its face, a cultural discourse or model bears resemblance to the concept of schemata employed by scholars of interpersonal communication who take a cognitive approach. But there is one important
difference: A cultural discourse or model emphasizes the meaning constructions shared by cultural members, in contrast to the focus on the
purely personal model represented by schemata (Bachen & Ellouz,
1996; Shore, 1991).

The interplay among some of these discourses helps us to understand why certain discursive struggles keep popping up in the relational dialectics theory (RDT)-based research literature, which for the
most part is based on samples of middle class Anglo Americans.

My claim in this chapter is that the reason why some discursive struggles are apparently so pervasive in the research is because they voice
basic circulating discourses, or systems of meaning, in mainstream U.S.
society. RDT has never made a claim about the universality of dialectical tensions; in fact, there is every reason to expect that competing discourses will be culturally specific (Baxter & Montgomery, 1996). Let me
turn to some of the prominent cultural discourses that circulate in
mainstream U.S. society. The remainder of the chapter will be devoted
to a discussion of two families of discursive struggles that dominate
the dialectically based research: discursive struggles of integration and
discursive struggles of expression.

Some Prominent Cultural Discourses That
Animate Talk in and About Relationships

The Discourse of Individualism

Because this discourse is complex and a foundation for other deriv-
ative discourses, I will discuss it in greater depth than will be characteristic of my treatment of the other discourses. In seeking to
understand the habits of the heart of early Americans, Alexis de
Tocqueville (1835/1969) first used the term *individualism* to refer to
Americans' excessive self-interest that threatened a sense of community. Subsequently, several scholars have elaborated on the discourse of
individualism. Sampson (1993), borrowing from Macpherson (1962),
referred to this discourse as *possessive individualism*—a belief that the
person is a self-contained, autonomous entity, "the owner of one's own
capacities and self" (p. 33). Such a belief seems natural to those of us
socialized as members of contemporary mainstream U.S. culture, but it
is far from a universal understanding (Geertz, 1983). Habermas (1975)
argued that individualism grew hand in hand with the rise of bureau-
cratic state authority and capitalism. According to Sampson, individualism positions Self in opposition to Other:

> The more the other is involved in the life of the person, the less the
> person is involved in his or her own life. . . . Others are posited as
> potential thieves of one's personhood. The more others take priority,
> the less priority exists for the individual. (pp. 33–34)

Other is valued to the extent that he or she is serviceable to Self, serving the
individual's self-interests and sustaining his or her independence of action.
According to individualism, personhood is privately owned.
Cognitions, personality traits, motivations, and other psychological

concepts are located inside the person and thus controlled exclusively by him or her. Individualism is a discourse that serves as the theoretical backdrop for much of the research in interpersonal and family communication (Lannamann, 1992, 1995); the autonomous self is positioned nonproblematically as the central mechanism of communicative production. In this research tradition, self precedes communication, rather than being constituted in communicative practices between persons.

Bellah and his colleagues (Bellah, Madsen, Sullivan, Swidler, & Tipton, 1985) have elaborated on the discourse of individualism by identifying two interdependent strands: expressive individualism and utilitarian individualism. Common to both strands of meaning is the core belief in "an autonomous self existing independently, entirely outside any tradition or community" (p. 65). Expressive individualism, epitomized in the writings of the poet Walt Whitman, emphasizes the value of self exploration and self expression. It idealizes an autonomous self who acts free of constraints and conventions, a "life rich in experience, . . . luxuriating in the sensual as well as the intellectual, above all a life of strong feeling" (p. 34). Utilitarian individualism, epitomized in the writings of Benjamin Franklin, idealizes the vigorous pursuit of self-interest with a goal of individual self-improvement and achievement.

These two strands of individualism are woven together in the mainstream American culture through the metaphor of the manager-therapist (Bellah et al., 1985). The manager-therapist role combines the ideal of the contractual give-and-take of utilitarian individualism with the ideal of expressive openness featured in expressive individualism. Individuals relate to others on hedonistic grounds in order to have their individual needs actualized. Open disclosure is valued as a means to self-actualization through others' support. The discourse of individualism, then, values Other only because of his or her serviceability to self. Individuals choose to associate with others who are similar to oneself, in what Bellah and his colleagues referred to as *lifestyle enclaves* (p. 71), thereby celebrating narcissism (p.72) through therapeutic communicative practices of reciprocal support. If others cease to be serviceable to Self's needs, they are expendable with limited sense of commitment and obligation.

In the scholarship of cross-cultural communication, a number of scholars have identified individualism-collectivism as an underlying dimension of cultural variability, with mainstream U.S. culture high in individualism (e.g., Hofstede, 1980; Kluckholm & Strodtbeck, 1961; Triandus, 1995). Individualism privileges the needs, values, and goals of the individual over those of the group. This cultural dimension is not conceptualized as an absolute either-or; rather, both discourses circulate in all cultures, with one more dominant over the other (Hofstede). Thus, although the discourse of individualism is widely accepted as the dominant discourse in mainstream U. S. culture, it coexists with a discourse of collectivism.

The Discourse of Community

Bellah and colleagues (1985) have identified two interwoven strands of meaning in the mainstream U.S. cultural discourse of community: the biblical tradition epitomized in the writings of the Puritan John Winthrop, first governor of the colony of Massachusetts, and the republican tradition epitomized in the writings of Thomas Jefferson. The biblical tradition idealizes a person's obligations and responsibilities to his or her community in the service of what is morally just. This tradition values the interdependent whole in service of the collective best interests of all. Bellah and his colleagues quote from Winthrop's famous sermon, "A Model of Christian Charity" in which we are presented with the image of the "city set upon a hill" that he and fellow Puritans intended to found—a community in which "We must delight in each other, make others' conditions our own, rejoice together, mourn together, labor and suffer together, always having before our eyes our community as members of the same body" (p. 28). It is this archetype, for example, that renders intelligible a view of marriage as a lifetime commitment of obligation and responsibility for the collective good not only for the couple but for the larger institution of marriage itself and the function it serves in the broader societal order. The republican tradition underscores the person's identity as a citizen with corresponding civic obligations in the public sphere. Together, these two traditions argue for placing the needs of the communal group above those of the individual person.

The Discourse of Privacy

One offshoot of the discourse of individualism is the discourse of privacy—the belief that the autonomous individual owns information and should have the right to control access to that information as she or he sees fit. In fact, this discourse provides the backdrop to Petronio's (2002) communication privacy management theory, which is devoted exclusively to understanding how persons embedded in a variety of social systems coordinate disclosure and privacy. The position of RDT is that there are many discourses that can inform the meanings surrounding acts of expression and nonexpression, including but not limited to the discourse of privacy. For example, a pair's joint effort to sustain certain topics as "taboo," that is, off limits for discussion, could be rendered

meaningful through the discursive logic of privacy ("it's none of my partner's business, and so we don't talk about it"), or it could be rendered
meaningful through alternative discourses, for example, a discourse of
caring ("We will only hurt each other if we talk about these issues"), or a
discourse of pragmatism ("We only repeat the same old arguments and
don't get anywhere, so why bother talking about it?"). The discourse of
privacy, in short, is only one discourse that makes meaningful our acts of
nonexpression. In mainstream U.S. society, where individualism is so
dominant, the discourse of privacy may be the baseline discourse from
which communicators operate. Cultural members take for granted the
rights of individual ownership of information; this discourse makes
understandable statements such as "It's none of your business," "It's my
secret and you can't tell it," or "I plead my Fifth Amendment rights."

The Discourse of Rationality

Because members of mainstream U.S. society swim in a discourse of
individualism, the discourse of rationality is taken for granted as the
natural way to understand human action. Stated simply, this discourse
presumes that if a person wants or desires something, believes that a
given action is a means to attaining that something and is capable of
engaging in the action, then the person will undertake the action
(Rosenberg, 1988). Human actions, then, become intelligible through a
means-end logic: understanding wants (the desired end) and the
actions that can fulfill those wants (the means). The value attached to
certainty is high in the discourse of rationality. In order to understand a
person's actions, we need certainty about the person—a capacity to predict their wants and desires. We also need certainty in predicting the
person's beliefs about which actions are appropriate in a given situation. The individual person values certainty, as well; he or she needs to
be confident that outcomes predictably follow from actions. From inside
the discourse of rationality, it seems only natural to speak of the importance of having goals, making plans to accomplish those goals, making
wise choices, and understanding that actions have consequences.

The Discourse of Romanticism

The discourse of romanticism is a system of meaning "in which the
affective component is regarded as primary and all other considerations
are excluded from conscious reflection" (Spanier, 1972, pp. 481–482).
This discourse makes sense in tandem with individualism, for it presumes an autonomous individual who is free to make romantic choices
based on his or her internal feeling states. According to Schwartz and
Bilsky (1987), the self-direction, achievement, and individual enjoyment

values of individualism are fully compatible with the discourse of romanticism, in contrast to the collectivist values of other orientation, conformity, and group-based security. Five constituent beliefs of romantic love have been identified for mainstream U.S. culture: (1) a belief that love conquers all, (2) a belief that there is for each person one and only one true love match, (3) a belief that the beloved will meet one's highest ideals, (4) a belief that love at first sight is possible, and (5) a belief that we should follow our hearts rather than our minds when choosing a partner (Knee, 1998). The discourse of romanticism, it is fair to argue, values the excitement and spontaneity of adventure. According to the discourse of romanticism, each romantic relationship is unique, never replicable. The discourse of romance also values total openness between the two soul mates as part of their totalizing immersion in one another.

Various Relationship-Specific Discourses

Discursive templates circulate throughout mainstream U.S. culture for any number of commonly identified relationships—same-sex platonic friendship, opposite-sex platonic friendship, the long-distance couple, "friends with benefits," relationships at various stages of romantic involvement, marriage, extramarital affairs, and family, to list only a few. For the most part, scholars with a psychological orientation have studied these at the individual level of analysis and under a variety of conceptual labels, including *schema, prototypes,* and *lay theories,* among others. When approached at the individual level, the issue of cultural commonality is ignored, as is the issue of how these discursive templates are voiced by persons in constructing meanings.

Consider the discursive template of the "real family," often invoked by members of stepfamilies to foreground their idealization of what a family is and thereby to construct their own stepfamily as somehow artificial, feigned, or otherwise not "real" (Baxter, Braithwaite, & Bryant, 2006). The "real family" is based on biology and law (Schneider, 1980) and is idealized to have open and honest communication that flows among all family members (Baxter, Braithwaite et al., 2006). Against this discursive construction, the stepfamily inevitably falls short, unless an alternative discursive template of family is constructed, perhaps one based on mutual affection or shared fate (e.g., Galvin, 2006). Just as the discursive construction of family is subject to competing ideologies—blood and law versus alternatives, for instance—so are the discursive constructions of other relationship types. Furthermore, discourses often clash with one another. For example, as the movie *When Harry Met Sally* suggests, a man and a woman can't be both friends and romantically involved (or can they?). A culture's discursive templates of relating provide a backdrop of distal already-spokens that are rife with potential for dialogic struggle in the moment as parties undertake the business of defining their relationships to themselves and to third-party outsiders.

And So Forth

This short list of cultural discourses is far from exhaustive; obviously, anything about which culture speaks is part of distal already-spoken systems of meaning. My goal in this section has been simply illustrative, suggesting that whenever persons come together communicatively, they are not "biblical Adams," but instead speak with cultural traces that animate the meaning-making process with respect to relationships and individual identities within those relationships. Let's turn to two families of discursive struggle that are likely to emerge when several of these cultural discourses are put in play with and against one another: integration and expression. These two families of struggle are arguably the most frequently identified in the RDT-informed research literature. However, two caveats are necessary before I proceed.

Researchers are embedded in the cultural discourses that circulate in the society, and as I have noted above, the interpersonal communication literature is steeped in the discourse of individualism (Lannamann, 1992, 1995). Thus, it is accepted as natural to write unproblematically about individual motivations, needs, and wants, rather than discourses. In the next two sections, I have taken the liberty of translating this research literature from a heavily psychologized vocabulary to the discourses that render such references intelligible. For example, when I encountered a statement in the research such as "Participants reported feeling a tension between a desire for more time alone and a simultaneous desire for time together," I engaged in a translation process of sorts. Reference to "tension between" marks a competition. Reference to "a desire for more time alone" makes sense within a discourse of individualism, in contrast to the discourse of community that makes intelligible the reference to "a desire for time together." This translation work is more than a superficial exercise in which one vocabulary set is substituted for another. As discussed in the first two chapters, dialogism and RDT are committed on theoretical grounds to the study of the discourses that animate language use and meaning making. Reports of parties' feelings or cognitive states are intelligible to us only when they can be framed within the appropriate systems of meaning.

The second caveat is an observation about methods. In general, the dialectically informed research literature discussed in the next two sections of this chapter has drawn heavily on individual self-reports, either in surveys (the quantitatively oriented work) or in interviews (the qualitatively oriented work). Self-reports, especially when produced through qualitative methods, can be analyzed productively as utterance chains, and I do so in the pages that follow. However, it is fair to say that the bulk of this research has tended to position self-report data as mere representational conduits for speakers' inner thoughts and feelings, rather than framing them as utterance chains. Furthermore, underrepresented in research to date are utterance chains that are implicated in the conversational exchanges between relationship parties. Reliance on self-reports overemphasizes meaning making to third parties (researchers) and provides us with limited insights into the meaning making that unfolds in the moment between relationship parties.

❖ THE DISCURSIVE STRUGGLE OF INTEGRATION

Bellah and his colleagues (1985) regarded the discourse of individualism as the first language of Americans, who speak in more muted ways in the second language of community (p. 20). Their discussion of these first and second languages nicely exemplifies Bakhtin's (1981d) notion of centripetal-centrifugal struggle between competing discourses. The discourses of individualism and community circulate as distal already-spokens in the interpersonal communication of persons socialized in the mainstream Anglo-American culture. Thus, it is hardly surprising to see traces of the discursive clash of these two verbal ideologies in RDT-based research conducted with members of this cultural group.

A number of researchers have identified a struggle of integration that elsewhere I have labeled *autonomy-connection* (Baxter, 1993): the discursive struggle between individual partner autonomy or independence, and relational connection or interdependence. This struggle clearly shows the salience of the distal already-spoken cultural discourses of individualism and community. A second discursive struggle that implicates the tension between individualism and community is what I have elsewhere labeled *inclusion-seclusion* (Baxter, 1993). In contrast to autonomy-connection, which locates the struggle internally within the boundaries of the relationship, inclusion-seclusion addresses the pair's independence from (and integration with) the social network. The more secluded a dyad is from the social network, the more the pair legitimates their dyadic autonomy and the discourse of individualism; the more embedded a dyad is with the social network, the more the pair legitimates their dyadic connection and the discourse of community. Research on these two contradictions and other variations of the discursive struggle of integration has been studied both deductively and inductively. I will organize my discussion (and translation) of the research findings by these two approaches, for they lead us in slightly different directions.

Deductively Oriented Research

Several researchers have examined in a deductive manner what I am translating as the discursive struggle of autonomy-connection, starting with researcher-defined conceptualizations and operational-izations to which relationship parties react in an open-ended and/or a closed-ended manner. When used to solicit open-ended data, relationship parties have been presented with a description of the struggle and asked whether it was present and how it was experienced. In soliciting closed-ended data, relationship parties have been presented with a description of the struggle and asked to rate its importance on a Likert-type scale. This deductive approach has marshaled claims about the relative frequencies and importance of the autonomy-connection struggle compared to other deductively based struggles.

Consistently, the autonomy-connection struggle is reported to be both frequent and important, although its salience appears to vary by temporal issues related to where the relationship is in its developmental course and by communication event. In particular, the autonomy-connection struggle has been reported more frequently than other deductively defined struggles for romantic relationships (Baxter, 1990), marital relationships (Pawlowski, 1998), and postdivorced pairs (Graham, 2003). Furthermore, the autonomy-connection struggle has been perceived by relational partners as highly important in both romantic relationships (Baxter & Erbert, 1999) and marital relationships (Pawlowski). Among romantic pairs, the frequency of the autonomy-connection struggle appears to increase as a relationship's development progresses (Baxter), although for marital partners the frequency of this struggle appears to be greatest in the beginning stages of relationship development (Pawlowski). Autonomy-connection appears to be a common, and important, underlying theme as parties make retrospective sense of a variety of types of turning point events—events that function to propel the relationship toward, or away from, closeness (Baxter & Erbert). In addition, autonomy-connection appears to be an underlying theme in many marital conflicts (Erbert, 2000).

A smaller body of research has examined the inclusion-seclusion struggle in a deductive manner that parallels the study of the autonomy-connection struggle. Although Pawlowski (1998) found that her married participants reported frequent struggles with inclusion-seclusion and rated the importance of inclusion-seclusion at a level comparable to autonomy-connection, Baxter and Erbert (1999) found that romantic partners rated inclusion-seclusion important in only a subset of turning point events in their relationships' development. In particular, events that involved issues of external competition for the affection of the parties, dyadic quality time away from others, and making up events following conflict featured the salience of inclusion-seclusion struggle. Erbert (2000) found that inclusion-seclusion was salient for marital conflicts that involved decisions about holidays and time use.

Although I have authored studies in this deductive tradition early in my engagement with RDT, I have shifted over time to favor an inductive, qualitative approach to the study of this and other discursive struggles. I have been persuaded by two limitations with the deductive approach. First, although the descriptions of the integration dialectic are similar from study to study at an abstract level, they are far from identical at a particular level. Some wordings are more individually centered (descriptions of intra-individual tension), whereas others are more centered in the relationship (descriptions of shared tension or tension between relationship parties). Some wordings focus on the organization of time spent alone/together, whereas others emphasize identity constructions. There is substantial room for oversimplification when researchers gloss over these differences to infer more general claims about the autonomy-connection or inclusion-seclusion struggles. The inductive, qualitative work allows us to infer the various strands of meaning at play within the broader discourses of individualism and community. Furthermore, as I have noted above, both the deductive and inductive research in general positions the combatants in struggle as psychological characteristics (motivations, needs, and wants) rather than discourses. Thus, translation work was needed on my part to focus on the discourses that render such psychologized descriptions intelligible. I turn now to this cluster of inductively based work, because it underscores the multivocal ways in which the discursive interanimation of individualism and community organizes meaning making in talk.

Inductively Oriented Research

The bulk of the research has taken an inductive approach, examining issues relevant to the discursive struggle of integration in enacting a wide range of relationships. Heterosexual dating and romantic relationships among younger adults have garnered substantial research attention (Baxter, Braithwaite et al., 1997; Chornet Roses, 2006; Feeney, 1999; Feeney & Noller, 1991; Sahlstein & Dun, 2008), as have dating and romantic relationships among older adults (Aleman, 2003, 2005; Dickson, Hughes, & Walker, 2005). The discursive struggle of individualism and community can be identified in the dialectically informed research on the enactment of long-distance relationships (Sahlstein, 2004, 2006; Stafford & Merolla, 2007; Stafford, Merolla, & Castle, 2006), marital relationships (Baxter & Braithwaite, 2002; Hays, 1996; Hoppe-Nagao & Ting-Toomey, 2002; Kline, Stafford, & Miklosovic, 1996; Kvigne & Kirkevold, 2003; Medved & Graham, 2006; Pawlowski, 2006; Sahlstein & Baxter, 2001; Stafford & Kline, 1996), lesbian relationships (Suter, Bergen, Daas, & Durham, 2006; Suter & Daas, 2007), and relationships between ex-spouses (Graham, 1997, 2003; Masheter, 1994; Schrodt, Baxter, McBride, Braithwaite, & Fine, 2006). The discursive struggle of individualism and community can also be identified in the dialectically based work on the enactment of friendship among young adults (Bridge & Baxter, 1992; Johnson, Wittenberg, Villagran, M., Mazur, & Villagran, P., 2003; Rawlins, 1983a, 1989, 1992; Sias, Heath, Perry, Silva, & Fix, 2004) and the enactment of sociality for persons who reside in retirement communities (Aleman, 2001; Williams & Guendouzi, 2000). The enactment of a variety of family relationships also appears to be animated by a discursive struggle of individualism and community, including parent-child relationships (Afifi, 2003; Afifi & Keith, 2004; Baxter, Hirokawa, Lowe, Pearce & Nathan, 2004; Braithwaite & Baxter, 2006; Braithwaite, Toller, Daas, Durham, & Jones, 2008; Miller-Day, 2004; Penington, 2004; Pitts, Fowler, Kaplan, Nussbaum, & Becker, 2009; Stamp, 1994; Stamp & Banski, 1992); grandparent-grandchild relationships (Erbert & Aleman, 2008), stepparent-stepchild relationships (Baxter, Braithwaite, et al., 2004; Cissna, Cox, & Bochner, 1990), relationships with in-laws (Prentice, 2009), and voluntary or fictive kin relationships (Baxter, Braithwaite et al., 2009).

Taken as a whole, these studies underscore the importance of appreciating subtle differences in how the discursive struggle of individualism and community plays itself out in constructing meaning. Rather than present a detailed treatment of this body of work organized by relationship type, I emphasize instead a more selective discussion of some studies in order to illuminate the various radiants of meaning (Baxter & Montgomery, 1996) in the struggle between discourses of individualism and community. Although the discursive struggle of integration can be reduced to a simple binary (as the deductively oriented work demonstrates), it is important to appreciate that the discourses of individualism and community interpenetrate along multiple radiants of meaning. I have identified nine different radiants of meaning in the research relevant to the discursive struggle of integration.

Individual Identity Construction
Surrounding Physical (In)Dependence

The discursive struggle of individualism and community surfaces in some of the research as a matter of identity construction in relating, specifically, the extent to which one's personal identity is that of an autonomous, independent being as opposed to a personal identity as someone who is physically dependent upon others. Clearly, constructing an identity as an autonomous being draws upon the discourse of individualism. An identity as a dependent being implicates the discourse of community in that the individual is understood as inherently interdependent with others rather than independent from others. This radiant of meaning features prominently in the dialectically based research with older adults who are experiencing physical decline associated with advanced aging or the loss of independence associated with major illness.

For example, this radiant of meaning can be identified in Williams and Guendouzi's (2000) study among older residents of a retirement community. With respect to relationships outside of the community—family and friends who did not reside in the retirement home—elderly residents constructed an identity of autonomy; these social network members were no longer actively involved in providing day-to-day care, which liberated the residents' identities to emphasize self as an independent adult. At the same time, the physical decline of their bodies constructed identities of dependence with staff members within the residential home. Residents thus had multiple identities depending on the person with whom they were relating, and even exchanges with staff members were sensitive to the importance of sustaining an identity of independence in residents to the extent possible.

Two dialectically informed studies have focused on older survivors of stroke (Kvigne & Kirkevold, 2003; Pawlowski, 2006) in which struggles of meaning unfolded with respect to identity construction as independent versus dependent beings. Stroke victims experienced physical problems that required very concrete forms of assistance from their spouses and other caregivers in order to function on a daily basis, yet this bodily dependence struggled with a competing identity as an independent adult; stroke victims did not wish to be seen as burdens on their families or as helpless persons. The support from caregivers was seen as an act of love, but it risked at the same time the prospect of threatening the victim's identity as a functioning, contributing adult member of the family.

Individual Identity Construction
as Coupled or Free of Commitment

This radiant of meaning implicates individual identity construction as (in)dependent, but the basis of that (in)dependence is emotional and social rather than physical. The studies in which this form of the discursive struggle of individualism and community can be identified also implicate the discourse of romance and tend to be concentrated in the dating research, although not exclusively so.

An example from the dating research is a study of later-life women by Dickson and her colleagues (2005). The researchers found that their sample of women cherished their identities as independent women, and they expressed fear of losing monetary independence and assuming the burdens of a caretaking role if they became too interdependent with a later-life man. The women found themselves resisting their dating partner's desire for marriage, preferring instead a companionship without long-term commitments. These identity concerns make sense to us from the perspective of the discourse of individualism. Yet at the same time, these women were attracted to the idealization of romance and expressed a desire for interdependence and the affection, intimacy, and companionship it afforded. Discourses of community and romance make these women's feelings comprehensible to us.

Identity as part of a couple features as a radiant of meaning in the marital research, as well. For example, the selection of a surname upon marriage—wife adopts husband's last name, wife keeps her own surname, or the couple adopts a hyphenated surname—appears to implicate discourses of individual identity and couple identity for women more so than men (Kline et al., 1996; Stafford & Kline, 1996). Women who elect to keep their own surname are concerned about their autonomous identity independent from the spouse. Ironically, for some women, that autonomous identity from the husband is constructed by drawing upon a discourse of community in which they keep their maiden names as a way to honor their own family heritage.

Individual identity can also be identified as a radiant of meaning in the discursive struggle of individualism and community among mothers and daughters. As Miller-Day (2004) has eloquently expressed, the relationship between mothers and daughters is one of "velvet chains" (p. 3), "a loving one that seems to bind women together across generations, even while they pursue separate identities" (p. xii). Miller-Day's study of three generations of women found that the process of developing an identity that is differentiated from the mother while still remaining emotionally close to her is a life-long project riddled with many dangers that range from the inability to separate (enmeshment) to emotional and behavioral estrangement.

Voluntary Versus Involuntary Interdependence With a Relational Other

The discourse of individualism presumes that individuals have full choice in their selection of relational partners. However, the discourse of community emphasizes membership in a larger social group where choice may be constrained. This radiant of meaning is emphasized in research on nonvoluntary relationships (Hess, 2000, 2002) such as families. In instances where family members don't necessarily like one another, they are still stuck with each other.

This discursive tension between choice and constraint in the selection of others with whom one is interdependent can be heard in the talk of ex-spouses (Graham, 1997, 2003; Masheter, 1994) who continue to grapple with issues of behavioral interdependence involving coparenting. Although the marriage is voluntarily dissolved, the mutual biogenetic or adoptive link to the child is ongoing, and thus so is the coparenting relationship between ex-spouses.

This voluntary/nonvoluntary radiant of meaning can also be heard in the talk of stepfamily members. For example, Cissna et al. (1990) identified a basic discursive struggle between the marital and stepparent relationships. The adults voluntarily entered into their marriage, and they emphasized the importance of establishing the solidarity of that relationship, including communicating to the children that their marriage would come first in the family. At the same time, the marriage event created a nonvoluntary relationship between the stepparent and the stepchild. This relationship was regarded as very challenging, as efforts to create a legitimated bond of trust between stepparent and stepchild bumped up against the forced status.

Emotional Distance and Closeness

The discursive struggle of individualism and community also is played out on an emotional plane with separation and integration framed, respectively, in terms of emotional distance and closeness between relating parties. Although emotions are represented as internal states of individuals in this research, what renders them intelligible to hearers is their framing within discursive systems of meaning.

An example of this emotional radiant of meaning can be found in a study by Baxter and her colleagues (Baxter, Braithwaite et al., 2004) in which they sought to understand the stepparent-stepchild relationship from the stepchild's perspective. The researchers identified a dialectic of integration framed around issues of emotional distance and emotional closeness. On the one hand, stepchildren spoke of an awkward emotional distancing from the stepparent that purportedly was the result of several factors, including the stepparent's outsider status to the family, a felt loyalty to the nonresidential parent, and a feeling that the stepparent was a wedge between them and the residential parent. On the other hand, stepchildren spoke of desired or actual emotional closeness to the stepparent that resulted from the observation that the stepparent had provided them with parent-like care giving and had made the residential parent happier.

Self-Interests Versus Others' Interests

In some dialectically informed research, the discursive struggle of individualism and community is evident in a radiant of meaning surrounding priority to one party's self-interests as opposed to giving priority to the partner's interests. Giving priority to the individual's self-interests is an act legitimated within a discourse of individualism, whereas an other-orientation that gives priority to the needs and interests of the other is intelligible from a discourse of community.

An example of this radiant of meaning comes from a study by Baxter and her colleagues (Baxter, Hirokawa et al., 2004) among a population of low-income, rural Iowan women in their decision making about alcohol consumption during pregnancy. These women were socialized to a cultural discourse of individualism that values individual choice in how to think and act, including a pregnant woman's decision about whether to drink alcohol. Because this decision was an autonomous one, it was deemed inappropriate for others to interfere and try to influence her drinking. The discourse of individualism underscored self-interest, allowing a pregnant woman a discourse of justification of her choice to drink during her pregnancy because of the benefits it provided to her (e.g., a release from stress). Competing with the discourse of individualism was a discourse of responsible motherhood, grounded in the cultural discourse of community. According to the discourse of responsible motherhood, motherhood begins with the pregnancy. With motherhood comes the moral obligation and responsibility to place the fetus's needs as primary. A mother who fails to do everything possible to protect her unborn baby from risks (e.g., fetal alcohol syndrome) is being selfish and irresponsible. According to the discourse of responsible motherhood, a mother is socially accountable for her actions, and others are given social license to hold a mother accountable for her actions.

A second illustration of self-interests versus other-interests comes from a study of successive generation planning among farming families (Pitts et al., 2009). On the one hand, the senior generation is drawn to a discourse of individualism in seeking to maximize their profits in the sale of the farm, thereby assuring their retirement income. At the same time, the discourse of community renders intelligible the competing interest of selling low in order to maximize the affordability of the farm to the younger generation family member(s).

Competing Individual Rights

This radiant of meaning is similar to the self-interests/other-interests radiant just discussed, in that the issue is whether self will be privileged above other. However, competition of self and other is made meaningful in a vocabulary of rights as opposed to a vocabulary of needs and wants, benefits and rewards, and sacrifices and costs, as typifies the radiant of meaning surrounding self versus other interests. The rights radiant implicates talk of entitlements, prerogatives, infringements, and (in)justice.

This struggle can be heard, for example, in ex-partner talk about the meaning of the divorce decree (Schrodt et al., 2006). Some ex-partners emphasized their individual rights in coparenting, invoking a meaning of the divorce decree as a legal contract that can be invoked as a mechanism to protect those rights and interests. Other ex-partners emphasized their ongoing interdependence with the former spouse as a member of a co-parenting team; these ex-spouses were more likely to invoke a meaning of the divorce decree as a heuristic guide to coparenting decisions but to be used with flexibility in response to the needs of the individuals involved. The coparenting team is a construct that is meaningful from within a discourse of community.

Competing Demands on Time and Energy

The discursive struggle between individualism and community often is defined as a competition between competing demands for time and energy for the relationship parties. The discourse of community privileges spending time and investing energy in the relational partner, whereas the discourse of individualism privileges a decision by a person to honor the other demands on his or her time and energy.

Illustrative of this meaning strand within the discursive struggle of integration is the work by Stamp and his colleague (Stamp, 1994; Stamp & Banski, 1992) on the transition to parental status in married couples. Whereas the spouses could devote their relational energies exclusively to the marriage before the birth of the baby, the baby's birth presents a competing focus of time and energy as spouses enact the labor-intensive role of parent. Paradoxically, execution of the parenting role requires increased coordination efforts and interdependence between the adults as parents, yet at the same time limits their interactions as husband and wife. The partners construct their parenting roles and their spousal roles as a matter of competing demands on their time and energy in a zero-sum manner; time devoted to their individual role as a parent is framed as time away from the dyadic community of their marriage.

Also illustrative of this radiant of meaning is the research on competing demands for time and energy in fulfilling both home and work obligations. As the demographic profile of the American family increasingly evidences workforce participation by both spouses, the married couple faces the discursive struggle of sustaining both private life (marriage and family) and work outside the home (Hays, 1996). Individual achievement is valued and expected in the world of work, yet, especially for women (Medved & Graham, 2006), this is often in competition for the communal liens on time and energy associated with enacting spousal and parenting roles on the home front.

Time together versus time apart also is a core radiant of meaning in the enactment of long-distance relationships. In analyzing couple talk about their long-distance romantic relationship, Sahlstein (2004) identified complex ways in which separation from the partner was in play with and against proximal togetherness. Partners legitimated their time apart from within a discourse of individualism, emphasizing how alone time serviced their individual life commitments such as work and embracing their own individual interests without regard to the partner's preferences. However, the absent partner was a social ghost of sorts, ever-present and sometimes complicating social network relations for individuals as they conducted their separate lives. Togetherness was legitimated from within a discourse of community; it was a time to emphasize couple time, yet the ghost that was ever-present for the partners was the realization that they each had another, independent life.

Competing Loyalty Demands

A related radiant of meaning in the discursive struggle of individualism and community is that of competing expectations of loyalty. Often, how a person spends his or her time and energy is regarded as a marker of loyalty, but loyalty is enacted (and violated) in ways other than time/energy expenditure. For example, Baxter and her colleagues (1997) identified, among both platonic friends and romantic partners, a struggle surrounding "taking sides." On the one hand, the discourse of community implicates an expectation to defend one's partner in the presence of criticism or opposition from others; yet, at the same time, embedded in the same discourse of community, those others similarly expect loyalty to them and thus taking their side. Rather than privilege the discourse of individualism, in which the individual is legitimated for taking positions and sides based on his or her own autonomous decision-making process, the person is caught in the privileged discourse of community, with all parties feeling betrayed because loyalty to one person is framed as disloyalty to another.

Participants in this study gave voice to a second kind of loyalty struggle with respect to whether to form a relationship with a third party that would garner the disapproval of the current relationship partner. On the one hand, according to the discourse of individualism, partners cannot monopolize one another's autonomous decision about who is in or out of their respective social networks; yet, within the discursive frame of community, parties feel comfortable making claims about others with whom the partner affiliates.

Dyadic Segregation and Integration

In contrast to the prior eight radiants of meaning—in which the interplay of autonomy from, and connection with, the relational partner is centered—this final radiant of meaning constructs the boundary between the relationship as a unit and others outside of that unit by focusing on the independence or connection of the relationship pair with others. Whereas the first eight radiants of meaning are relevant to Baxter's (1993) autonomy-connection struggle, this radiant corresponds to the inclusion-seclusion struggle.

Illustrative of this struggle is Prentice's (2009) study of relationships between married couples and their in-laws. Intelligible within a discourse of individualism, married couples expressed a desire to spend time alone as a couple, free of obligations to the in-law relations. Yet at the same time, these married couples attended to a cultural discourse of community that makes sense of their feelings of responsibility to the larger extended family beyond the boundary of their nuclear family unit. At once separate from, yet integrated with, the larger familial unit of in-law relations, these couples reported ongoing balancing between these competing commitments.

Cultural Variations

We have limited insight into cultural variations in the discursive struggle of integration. An interesting exception is a study of platonic friendships among Taiwanese international students studying in the United States (Chen, Drzewiecka, & Sias, 2001) in which the researchers identified a knot of discursive struggles, many evidencing the culture-specific nature of friendship. Because the Taiwanese culture emphasizes friendship within the group of a larger social circle, the study's participants voiced tensions that related to group membership. Interdependence among friendship group members involves an expectation to provide mutual aid and care, called *gan qing,* and often implicates the related concept of *ren qing,* the asking and giving of favors. Although these participants benefitted personally from *gan qing,* they also articulated constraints imposed by the expected interdependency and its social obligations. Some participants expressed resentment because their group membership tied them to features of Taiwanese culture that they didn't like and were trying to escape from; yet, at the same time, the group was a source of the familiar and thus comforting. Participants also spoke of feeling caught between various dyadic friendship disputes that could erupt in the larger group, thereby requiring complex negotiations of loyalty to multiple individuals at the same time.

Fitch's (1998) in-depth ethnographic study of interpersonal connection in Colombia underscores, as well, the cultural variability that surrounds the discursive struggle of integration. In Colombia, Fitch argued, persons are defined in large measure through their web of connections; in this cultural discourse of community, individuals are evaluated based on how well they sustain and show the importance of their connections. Because people have a large number of varied types of connections, inevitable struggles emerge in which responsibilities to one relationship conflict with the expectations of other relational partners. While this struggle of loyalties appears similar to struggles identified in the U.S.-based research with respect to how a given relational pair integrates with the social network, it is culturally different because the very identity of the Colombian person is built on a scaffold of connection in a way that is quite different from the American discourse of individualism. In fact, argued Fitch,

> When describing relational *partners,* Colombians seemed often to envision a larger cast of participants than North Americans do. Friendship seems to happen more commonly in groups than in dyads, for example, and references to "my family" almost certainly include extended family in most cases. Even romantic partnerships and

marriage may be less intrinsically conceptualized as dyadic arrangements in Colombia. . . . It could be that the dyadic emphasis of much personal relationships research in the United States is a further reverberation of individualistic bias. (pp. 178–179)

Once the conception of a relationship as a dyadic phenomenon is problematized, struggles of integration and separation between two partners and with the larger social web take on very different meanings.

Summary

I have devoted substantial space to the discursive struggle of integration because of the size and scope of the relevant research to date. This struggle varies by culture, as the Chen et al. (2001) and Fitch (1998) research studies nicely illustrate. For members of mainstream U.S. society, the struggle of individualism and community probably occupies the primary discursive motif that organizes all of our communicative practices; its pervasiveness cannot easily be ignored in the meaning-making process. Although this discursive struggle can be studied at an abstract level, where subtle nuanced differences are glossed, I have emphasized the polysemy of this struggle in identifying nine different radiants of meaning.

My treatment of the discursive struggle of integration has been oversimplified in its suggestion that individualism and community can be isolated from a larger discursive web. From a dialogic perspective, communicative life is riddled with a myriad of discourses, all in play with and against one another at the same time. This web or knot of discursive multiplicity is important to appreciate and understand. I turn next to the dialogic struggle of expression, which is often at play with individualism and community, because parties' communicative actions to regulate information are a frequent way in which individualism and community are negotiated.

❖ THE DISCURSIVE STRUGGLE OF EXPRESSION

I start this section by drawing upon the distinction between a twitch and a wink, as described by Geertz (1973, p. 6), who asked his reader to consider

two boys rapidly contracting the eyelids of their right eyes. In one, this is an involuntary twitch; in the other a conspiratorial signal to a friend. The two movements are, as movements, identical; from an

I-am-a-camera, "phenomenalistic" observation of them alone, one could not tell which was twitch and which was wink, or indeed whether both or either was twitch or wink. Yet the difference, however unphotographable, between a twitch and a wink is vast; as anyone unfortunate enough to have had the first taken for the second knows. (p. 6)

The twitch-wink distinction is one of meaning; while the wink is a meaningful communicative gesture of a conspiratorial nature, a twitch is meaningful merely as an involuntary movement.

Similarly, we can engage in a parallel analysis of a communicator's action to express or to refrain from expression. When a communicator refrains from expression, its meaning can be varied. It might become meaningful through the discourse of privacy, in which case the gesture of nonexpression is understood as an instance of protecting one's rights to privacy. However, refraining from expression can also be made meaningful through the discourse of rationality; not everything needs to be made explicit, and some thoughts can most efficiently and effectively be communicated through taken-for-granted unsaid elements in the communication situation. Other efforts to refrain from expression can be rendered meaningful through the discourse of community; in enacting discretion, parties can protect one another's face and sustain their often fragile social connection. Still other instances of nonexpression become intelligible through the discourse of utilitarian individualism; an individual may refrain from expression in order to serve his or her self-interests in some way, for example, preventing a past mistake in judgment from coming to light.

And what about acts of expression? They, too, can be made meaningful in different ways, depending on the salient discourses within which they are framed. Some acts of expression implicate the discourse of expressive individualism, manifesting one's right to freedom of expression through catharsis. Some acts of expression implicate a discourse of utilitarian individualism—intelligible to us as acts of impression management in which parties attempt to put forth a positive image of themselves for others' consumption. Other acts of expression can be rendered intelligible within the discourse of community. For example, Bakhtin's (1993) notion of answerability, introduced in Chapter 2, argues that we are ethically bound to respond to one another and give them the gift of our otherness—our excess of seeing. For example, a parent may feel obligated to give advice to a child as a way to help him or her grow as an individual.

We could doubtless identify other discourses at play in the meanings associated with acts of expression and acts of nonexpression. However, true to the dialogic spirit, discourses often compete with one another, thereby resulting in dialogic struggles of expression. Research on *expression-nonexpression, openness-closedness, disclosure-privacy,* among other terms frequently invoked by researchers, has often ignored these differences in meaning; for all intents and purposes, research on the discursive struggle of expression has reduced it to a behavioral dilemma: to be open or not. This glossing of possible differences in meaning can be understood as the equivalent of conflating a twitch and a wink, focusing on the behavior of (non)expression rather than viewing the act as a meaningful symbolic gesture.

My early quantitatively oriented work was guilty of this conflation, as is other deductively oriented, quantitative work on expression-nonexpression. I will organize the research findings related to the discursive struggle of expression in a manner parallel to the discussion of integration above.

Deductively Oriented Research

Baxter (1990) tackled the expression dialectic in developing romantic relationships by differentiating openness-closedness from revelation-concealment. The former referred to what relationship parties say and what they don't say to one another. By contrast, the revelation-concealment dialectic focused on what a couple says and doesn't say about their relationship to outsiders. She solicited participant open-ended recollections of the openness-closedness dialectic between partners by asking participants to focus on their individual behavioral choices between talking openly and not talking openly. Results of the 1990 study indicated that this dialectic was present throughout the development of a romantic relationship, but it was especially frequent during the initial stage of formation. Although this study informs us about frequency of a behavioral dilemma for participants, it fails to address expression-nonexpression as a discursive struggle—that is, a symbolic act that contributes to meaning making.

Baxter and Erbert (1999) followed up on this study by soliciting turning points of relationship development for romantic partners, asking participants in their study to indicate on 1–5 scales the importance of a variety of dialectics at each identified turning point. As with the Baxter (1990) study, they presented participants with a definition of openness and closedness that focused on behavioral dilemmas rather than struggles of meaning. When this contradiction of expression manifested itself as a matter of how open to be with persons outside the relationship, a contradiction of revelation and concealment, it was similarly described as a behavioral dilemma.

Respondents reported that openness-closedness was a pervasive dilemma in participant retrospective accounts of the development of their romantic relationships. However, results were suggestive of possible differences in the meanings attached to nonexpression. For example, closedness in the turning point of quality time—occasions when the partners went off by themselves, apart from others, to experience intensive couple time—appeared to be framed as celebrations of the unsaid beauty of the moment. This hints at discourses of rationality and of romance in which words are regarded as unnecessary and arguably damaging to the romance of the event. By contrast, closedness in the turning point of external competition—when at least one party faced competing demands on time and resources—was commonly framed through discourses of community (other-oriented protection) or utilitarian individualism (self-interested protection). Network interactions—turning points in the relationship's development that were driven by interactions with third party outsiders (e.g., advice from friends, pressure from family)—were likely to be important developmental points for the revelation-concealment dialectic, but the study does not inform us about how this tension functioned as a discursive struggle of meaning.

Although these researchers suggested the value of shifting from behavioral dilemmas to struggles between meaningful symbolic acts, especially in light of their findings with respect to the different meanings of closedness depending on the type of turning point, the study failed to advance much beyond the behavioral choice to talk or not to talk.

Pawlowski's (1998) study of marital partners' accounts of their relationship's development at beginning, middle, and developed stages focused on both openness/closedness and revelation/concealment dialectics, modeling the description of these contradictions after Baxter's (1990) study. That is, expression-nonexpression was presented as a matter of behavioral choice. She found that openness/closedness was evident across all developmental stages, but it was most frequently reported during the middle stage of relationship development. Overall, openness/closedness was rated by her participants as the most important of all of the contradictions studied. Revelation/concealment, by contrast, was relatively infrequent among her participants; however, wives rated this contradiction of greater importance than did husbands.

Erbert's (2000) study of marital couple's conflicts presented participants with a priori definitions of contradictions in order to discern their centrality to reported conflicts during the past year of marriage. He modeled his definitions after those employed in the Baxter and Erbert (1999) study, finding that openness/closedness joined autonomy-connection as the two most central contradictions that animated marital conflict.

The last of the deductively oriented studies to be discussed is Graham's (2003) study of the frequency with which several basic contradictions were identified in the turning points retrospectively identified by participants in their postmarital relationships. Graham modeled her a priori definitions of contradictions after Baxter's (1990) study; that is, expression-nonexpression was presented as a behavioral dilemma of talking or not talking. Openness/closedness was not as salient as the other two contradictions under study. Graham's examples hint at the possible discursive struggles that underpinned the behavioral dilemma of talking or not talking, but we lack systematic understanding of the meanings of these behavioral choices. For example, the discourse of rationality appears to underpin her participants' discussion of safe and pleasant conversations and how these functioned to bring an end to having the same fight (p. 209). Her quoted examples also hint at the discourse of privacy as a framing of closedness, as partners sought to establish their new identities apart from their former partners. However, in the end, this study failed to move beyond the behavioral dilemma of talking or not talking, consistent with the other deductively oriented work reviewed in this section.

Substantial deductively based, quantitative work has examined the phenomenon of topic avoidance, that is, respondents' self-report of the frequency with which they avoid talking about certain topics with specified recipient-targets (e.g., Afifi & Burgoon, 1998; Afifi & Guerrero, 1998, 2000; Baxter & Wilmot, 1985; Dailey & Palomares, 2004; Golish, 2000; Golish & Caughlin, 2002; Guerrero & Afifi, 1995a; Guerrero & Afifi, 1995b; Roloff & Ifert, 1998, 2000; Sargent, 2002). From the dialogic perspective of RDT, this body of work can be criticized on two counts. First, it fails to examine the struggle between expression and nonexpression, focusing exclusively on nonexpression in the form of topic avoidance. This is analogous to one-handed clapping, in that it ignores the other hand—expression in this instance. Low reported frequencies of topic avoidance cannot be regarded as the equivalent of expression. Second, this body of work shares with other deductively oriented research discussed in this section a focus on avoidance as a behavioral choice rather than a meaningful symbolic act.

Some of this research has examined motivations for topic avoidance (e.g., Afifi & Burgoon, 1998; Caughlin & Afifi, 2004; Guerrero & Afifi, 1995a), finding that individuals report a variety of motivations for topic avoidance, including self-protection, other-protection, relationship-protection, partner unresponsiveness, conflict avoidance, desire for privacy, lack of closeness, and social appropriateness. These motivations are relevant to some of the underlying discourses identified above. Self-protection and social inappropriateness, for example, make sense inside a discourse of utilitarian individualism; protection of the other party and of the relationship appear relevant to a discourse of community; and partner unresponsiveness and conflict avoidance seem to invoke a discourse of rationality. Other research in the topic avoidance tradition is framed using Petronio's (1991) communication privacy management theory, which implies an underlying motivation of privacy and its obvious link to a discourse of privacy (e.g., Caughlin et al., 2000); but much of this research presumes privacy as the underlying system of meaning when, in fact, the data are only self-reports of behaviors of openness or closedness.

The work on reasons for topic avoidance joins a larger research tradition in which reasons for disclosure and reasons for concealment have been examined (e.g., Derlega & Grzelak, 1979; Derlega, Metts, Petronio, & Margulis, 1993; Rosenfeld, 1979; Rosenfeld & Kendrick, 1984). However, motivations or reasons, which reside inside individual minds, are not the same as symbolic acts that are enacted socially. What motivates a given speaker's action may play a role in rendering it meaningful, if that motivation becomes known to, or is inferred by, the listener as a reason for that action. In fact, Caughlin and Afifi (2004) have found that attributed motives for topic avoidance on the part of self and by the partner mediate relationship satisfaction. But being motivated in a certain way doesn't necessarily result in meaning that will be legitimized for the action as communication unfolds. Although Partner A may intend to protect his or her right to privacy, an instance of topic avoidance may be heard instead as a self-interested act designed to protect A from criticism. Thus, the topic avoidance research, in general, fails to inform us about the meanings of topic avoidance in the communication between interlocutors. Of course, some individuals may be so artful at avoiding topics that their interaction partners are oblivious that an act of avoidance is being attempted. However, if partners perceive that a topic is being skirted, topic avoidance becomes a meaningful act between the parties and subject to meaning making. The same argument can be advanced with respect to disclosure—it can be rendered meaningful between parties as an act of catharsis, a self-interested matter of impression management, delivery of a relational obligation, and so forth.

In addition, the work on motivations/reasons is from a researcher's point of view; open-ended qualitatively oriented work holds greater potential for insights about the reasons for behavioral choices from the perspective of the relationship parties themselves. Nonetheless, the deductively centered work on reasons for topic avoidance/disclosure is a step in the right direction toward understanding how expression and nonexpression could be rendered meaningful by parties as they communicate.

In contrast to the body of deductive and quantitative research summarized in this section stands more inductively based qualitative work. To a much greater extent, this body of work informs us about the discursive struggle of expression and nonexpression—at least how relationship parties construct that struggle to third-party interviewers, and I turn to a discussion of it next.

Inductively Oriented Research

Insights into the discursive struggle of expression can be gained from the dialectically informed research on dating and romantic relationships (Baxter, Braithwaite et al., 1997; Baxter & Widenmann, 1993; Chornet Roses, 2006; Derlega, Winstead, & Folk-Barron, 2000); long-distance romantic relationships (Sahlstein, 2004); married couples (Baxter, Braithwaite, Golish, & Olson, 2002; Braithwaite & Baxter, 1995, 2006; Hoppe-Nagao & Ting-Toomey, 2002; Stamp, 2004); lesbian relationships (Suter et al., 2006; Suter & Daas, 2007); parent-child relationships (Braithwaite et al., 2008; Miller-Day, 2004; Pitts et al., 2009); grandparent-grandchild relationships (Erbert & Aleman, 2008); in-law relationships (Prentice, 2009); stepparent-stepchild relationships (Baxter, Braithwaite, et al., 2004); friendships (Bridge & Baxter, 1992; Rawlins, 1983b, 1989, 1992); and social network relationships more generally (Baxter, Hirokawa, et. al., 2004; Ford, Ray, & Ellis, 1999; Foster, 2005). Five discourses can be heard in (non)expression understood as a meaningful symbolic act: individualism, community, romance, rationality, and privacy. In many instances, these discourses are competing with one another in the valenced meaning that is constructed for expression and nonexpression. However, quite frequently, a single discourse ruptures, and it appears to compete with itself. That is, a disjuncture erupts within a discourse and renders meaningful both acts of expression and acts of nonexpression. Discursive disjunctures can be identified in the research relevant to integration, as well, but they are much more common in the discursive struggle of expression. They productively remind us that a discourse may not function as a unitary system of meaning characterized by seamless coherence. Instead, as noted by Billig and his colleagues (1988), discourse may "contain its own negations" (p. 23). "Discourse," they claimed, "which seems to be arguing for one point may contain implicit meanings which could be made explicit to argue for the counter-point" (p. 23). In this section I will continue the practice I employed in reviewing (and translating) the research on integration, opting for illustrative studies to discuss rather than providing an exhaustive summary of all of the research.

Disjuncture Within a Discourse

Discursive disjunctures are especially prominent in the research in which the discourse of individualism is in play, especially the radiants of meaning surrounding rights and interests. However, discourses of community and rationality also feature disjunctures. An illustration of such semantic fragmentation is found in Foster's (2005) moving autoethnographic analysis of the discourses about motherhood that circulate in the public sphere and in the private sphere; a discourse of self-interested individualism appears to legitimate both secrecy and disclosure. The researcher observed that the canonical narratives of motherhood that circulate in both public and private spheres legitimate a woman's secrecy with respect to her experiences with pregnancy, particularly personal experiences with unanticipated loss through miscarriage and unanticipated pregnancy. Such silencing of talk about these personal experiences is legitimated, in part, through the discourse of utilitarian individualism—the belief that a woman could experience hurt and nonsupport from others if she made her miscarriage known, or if she failed to muster sufficient elation at the prospects of an unanticipated pregnancy. (Additionally, Foster argued for a legitimizing discourse of privacy, that is, the belief that a woman was entitled to her right to privacy about her pregnancy, but I will not elaborate on this discourse given the focus of this section.) Paradoxically, observed Foster, such silencing actually functions to undermine the self-interests of women who have these experiences, functioning to isolate them from others who are having similar experiences. Her argument for public and private expression surrounding pregnancy experiences draws upon the value of women gaining affirmation of their experiences through communication with others, thereby better serving their individual interests.

A second example of a fragmented discourse with respect to expression and nonexpression can be found in the research on post-divorce children who are caught in the middle between their divorced parents (Afifi, 2003; Braithwaite et al., 2008). Children are exposed to a variety of kinds of parental disclosures that position them awkwardly—for example, details of marital infidelity that led to the divorce or financial details (Afifi, McManus, Hutchinson, & Baker, 2007). On the one hand, these disclosures recognize that children are not mere objects of custody but rather directly affected parties who are entitled to information about events that affect them and whose self-interests are served by knowledge; individualistic discourses of rights and self-interests clearly make such disclosures understandable to us. At the same time, however, such information often tells children more than they want to know about their parents, often jeopardizing subsequent interactions with them. Children apparently appreciate being kept in the information loop with respect to the current interactions between their parents, yet at the same time they feel as if this positions them to be used as informational conduits or conflict mediators, burdens they do not embrace because they are not rewarding. Thus, the self-interests legitimated in the discourse of individualism warrant both parental candor and parental discretion with respect to their children.

A more complex discursive web that animates the meanings of expression and nonexpression is one in which a given discourse both fragments internally, competing against itself in legitimizing both expression and nonexpression, and competes with another discourse at the same time. A rich example of this complex web can be found in a study by Ford and her colleagues (1999) that examined the experience of adult incest survivors. The key radiant of meaning making for this struggle was on moral terms with the potential good of making known the perpetrator's actions struggling with the potential risks to the victim of disbelief, blame, or ostracism, and risks to the entire family of irreparable disruption. Continued secrecy, of course, risked continued personal tragedy for the victim as well as ongoing risks to fellow family members with the continued presence of the perpetrator. Thus, the discourses of community and utilitarian individualism were invoked in positioning both disclosure and secrecy as morally good and bad.

Competing Discourses: Individualism in Play

Typically, the discourse of individualism competes with the discourse of community in constructing the meaning of (non)expression. What varies from study to study is which discourse is aligned with which communicative act. However, occasionally the discourse of individualism also is positioned in play with discourses other than community.

An example of the discourse of individualism making sense of expression in contrast to the discourse of community legitimating non-expression is a study by Baxter, Braithwaite et al. (2002) involving interviews with older wives whose husbands lived in residential facilities because of their diagnosed adult dementia (usually Alzheimer's disease). Wives talked of substantial uncertainty and frustration about information openness with their spouses. Husbands purportedly were saddened and upset when their wives talked about issues related to home and children, thus framing discretion by the wives as a positive communicative practice that protected the best interests of the husband. This meaning of nonexpression is intelligible from within a discourse of community, where interests of the other party are given priority in making sense of action. At the same time, however, these wives longed for the presence of their "real" husbands—the husbands of their memory prior to the onset of the dementia. They reported despondency, sadness, and frustration because of their status as married widows (Braithwaite, 2002; Rollins, Waterman, & Esmay, 1985). The wives reported that they did share information about home, children, and other personal matters as a way to affirm the return of their marriages, no matter how fleeting the experience. Wives admitted that they selfishly longed for these encounters, for it reduced their loneliness and sense of loss. Thus, openness for these wives was made sense of through the self-oriented discourse of utilitarian individualism.

Individualism in play with the discourse of privacy can be identified in Prentice's (2009) study of in-law relationships. During the courtship stage in which a child was dating the person who would become their son-in-law or daughter-in-law, parents spoke of feeling constrained not to express their liking for the person. Such discretion is intelligible through a discourse of privacy; the parents did not wish to be seen as interfering in the private relationship business of their child and thought that expressing their opinion of the person being dated might be regarded as an invasion of the child's privacy. However, parents felt frustrated by such discretion because it constrained their right to engage the person on their own terms. Such frustration is understandable to us from the individualistic right to expression.

Competing Discourses: Community in Play

As noted above, the discourses of individualism and community are often interdependent in constructing the meaning of (non)expression. However, the discourse of community is also put into play with and against other discourses.

An illustration of the interplay of individualism and community, but a counter example in which the discourse of community legitimizes expression against the individualistic legitimation of nonexpression, can be found in a study by Derlega and his colleagues (2000) on disclosures of positive HIV/AIDS status. The researchers found that intimates engaged in disclosure of their status out of a sense of duty or obligation to the partner and to the relationship, a sensemaking of expression through the lens of a discourse of community. Concealment of health status was rendered sensical by intimates through either the discourse of privacy or utilitarian individualism—the right to privacy and the desire to sustain a positive self-presentation to others, respectively. Both privacy and the avoidance of negative reactions from others are self-serving, legitimized within a discourse of utilitarian individualism.

The discourse of community in play with another discourse, in particular the discourse of rationality, comes from the study by Pitts and his colleagues (2009) on planning for the generational succession in ownership of the family farm. On the one hand, many family members gave voice to a discourse of rationality in opining that it wasn't necessary to have explicit communication and planning surrounding the generational succession issue; such succession would just happen naturally as it had for several generations, from father to son, or it was spelled out in the will, thus making communication about it unnecessary. Competing against this sense making was a discourse of community in which family harmony and issues of fairness to all of the children were regarded as important and were served by explicit talk.

Competing Discourses: Rationality in Play

The discourse of rationality often legitimizes either expression or nonexpression, usually in play with additional competing discourses. In general terms, the discourse of rationality involves beliefs that (non)expression is (in)effective, (in)efficient, and/or (un)necessary to successful understanding between relational partners.

An example of the discourse of rationality in play with other competing discourses can be found in the findings reported by Erbert and Aleman (2008) in their study of grandparents who engage in surrogate parenting of their grandchildren. In part, the researchers found that grandparents felt that they needed candor in their relationship with their grandchildren for reasons that make sense within a discourse of rationality. For example, grandparents needed information about the whereabouts of the grandchild so that they could enact proper supervision and thus enact good parenting practices. However, the expressed need for complete information from the grandchild risked alienation from the grandchild, who felt overly controlled by parenting practices that had too few degrees of freedom; such a response from the grandchild potentially violated an effort to build a bond of trust between grandparent and grandchild, an important ingredient in relating from within the discourse of community. Grandparents also felt that candor with the grandchild was important with respect to the circumstances of the absent parent. As one grandparent expressed it, "That's the only kind of relationship you have where it can work" (p. 684). This perspective is comprehensible from within a discourse of rationality; candor was deemed efficacious. However, at the same time, grandparents often reported that they felt that the truth about the absent parent hurt the grandchild; to know that a parent was missing because they were in jail or in rehab may have been truthful but nonetheless damaging to the grandchild. Such concern for the grandchild's welfare rings true within a discourse of community in which the desire to protect the other is valued.

Competing Discourses: Privacy in Play

Although the discourse of privacy is invoked to legitimize nonexpression, it does not emerge as the most frequent discourse that animates the discursive struggle of expression. Further, it is interwoven with other discourses in a complex web of meaning.

An example of one such web of meaning is Braithwaite and Baxter's (1995) interview study of the marriage renewal vows of older adults. On the one hand, participants talked about holding public renewal ceremonies so that others—family members and close friends—could witness their testimonials of love and commitment for the spouse. In other words, the act of public declaration is what rendered the testimonials meaningful to the parties themselves. In addition, the public testimonial of enduring commitment provided a sort of modeling for others to observe, especially adult children who were thought to benefit from seeing a successful marriage. The public declaration of commitment makes sense from a discourse of community, in which marriage was constructed as a socially embedded institution. At the same time, however, participants went to great length to describe the ways in which they and their respective spouses constructed a ceremony whose meaning was fully understandable only to the two spouses. Participants told of special rings whose meaning was known only to the married couple, and so forth. Participants argued that although marriage was a public institution, it was also a private relationship in which only the spouses could and should participate. The choice of ceremonial features that underscored marriage as private clearly draws upon the discourse of privacy in order to be intelligible.

Competing Discourses: Romance in Play

From the perspective of the discourse of romance, love is a totalizing experience in which parties should hold nothing back, including information about themselves. True love, according to this system of meaning, is finding one's soul-mate, and this requires complete openness. However, this discourse often competes with other discourses.

In his focus-group study of how some Americans make sense of dating, for example, Chornet Roses (2006) found that dating was often constructed from a discourse of romance; it was envisioned as a romantic journey in the search of one's true love, and such a quest featured total and complete psychological, emotional, and physical immersion between self and other, including open disclosure. However, bumping up against this image was the discourse of utilitarian individualism, in which dating was constructed as a risky business, and in which the parties could be hurt or forced into premature or unwelcome commitments that constrained individual freedom. As a consequence of this discursive tension, dating was widely constructed as something high in communicative ambiguity. Dating parties talked of performing a dance of ambiguity with one another largely for reasons of self-protection. Ambiguity was a safety net that protected parties while still affording them dating experiences, albeit of a more muted nature than idealized in the discourse of romance.

Cultural Variations

Fitch's (1998) ethnographic study of Colombian communication and relating usefully underscores how the discursive struggle of expression varies by culture. As noted above in the discussion of integration, the Colombian conception of personhood is not built on the cultural discourse of individualism the way it is in mainstream American culture; rather, Colombian personhood is a web of connections to others. This conception frames what can be said as well as what cannot be said in ways quite different from the cultural discourses that animate the mainstream U.S. experiences summarized above. Among Colombians, *confianza* gives license to sincerity, but this is not the same meaning of openness and candor that typifies mainstream American meaning making. *Confianza* is not animated by a logic of disclosure of an inner self. Although Colombians organize their close relationships by a logic of *confianza*, it is constrained by social expectations of respect for authority and hierarchy, which also animate close relationships. Authority and hierarchy entail behavioral expectations of formality in communication. To mainstream American cultural logic, disclosure and discretion occupy the heart of the discursive struggle of expression, whereas in Colombia, the struggle more centrally is between sincerity and formality.

The study of Taiwanese international student friendships by Chen and colleagues (2001) also reminds us that the discursive struggle of expression is culture-specific. On the one hand, the Taiwanese participants felt that friendship means that two people value one another enough to judge and criticize one another. In this way, friends can display caring for one another. On the other hand, friendship is built on acceptance of one another's faults, and exists in a more general cultural motif that favors harmony over criticism and conflict.

Summary

I have addressed at length the discursive struggle of expression in order to make an important point. Just as twitches cannot be equated with winks, so one act of (non)expression cannot be equated with another, except in the most abstract and general of ways as behavioral acts. Expression-as-rationality is not meaningful in the same way as expression-as-self-protection, which is different from expression-as-obligation, which is unlike expression-as-romance. Nonexpression as an enactment as one's right to privacy is not the same thing as nonexpression as self-interested protection, or nonexpression conceived as protection of the other or of the relationship. As our journey through the research has illustrated, the discursive struggle of expression takes on different meanings, just as we witnessed with respect to the companion discussion of integration in the prior section of this chapter. Taken as a whole, the research work published over the past decade strongly underscores Baxter and Montgomery's (1996) argument that contradictions have multiple radiants of meaning that should not be oversimplified.

❖ CONCLUSION

The research on the discursive struggle of expression often implicates discourses of individualism and community, which comprise the discursive struggle of integration. This is hardly surprising. As Baxter and Montgomery (1996) argued, contradictions rarely stand alone but rather are in multivocal conversation with one another. They described this conversation metaphorically as a knot of contradictions.

In addition, this knot is polysemic; both the discursive struggle of integration and the discursive struggle of expression have multiple radiants of meaning that interanimate in complex webs of meaning. Further, as the discussion of discursive fragmentation demonstrates, a given discourse easily can turn on itself and do counterpoint work in legitimizing opposing actions.

I have argued in this chapter that discursive struggles of integration and expression are pervasive in the dialectical literature because relationships are not isolated from the larger cultural streams in which they swim. Discourses that circulate throughout a culture are given communicative life in the interactions in and about relationships. The first link in the utterance chain is the site where culture and relationship meet.

Although substantial research has been generated over the past decade on the struggles of integration and expression, it can be criticized on several counts. First, very little work informs us about cultural variation. Since the core argument of this chapter is that relationships are embedded in cultural discourses, future research needs to take a comparative approach, identifying the dominant discourses that characterize given cultures and how their interpenetration animates meaning making.

Second, much of the work tends to be overly reliant on self-reports as a method. Although any utterance can be analyzed as an utterance chain—whether in the context of an interview or in a conversation between relationship partners—our understanding of how discourses compete in making meaning will be better served by a methodological tool kit that draws richly upon a variety of types of data, especially conversations between relationship parties as they construct their relationship, and their individual identities within that relationship, in the moment of interaction. Additionally, I have underscored in this chapter the value of open-ended qualitative approaches because they give us access to speakers' language use, and it is this detail that allows us to study discourses and their complex radiants of meaning.

Third, my treatment of the research literature in this chapter has gone through what I have called a translation exercise. Very little of the research has addressed directly the issue of discourses, and I have had to infer these by rereading the studies and asking myself the question "What system(s) of meaning make this statement intelligible?" Future researchers need to center this question in their analyses if they are using RDT as their theoretical framework.

❖ **ENDNOTES**

1. Although dialogism is unique in supplanting the notion of the utterance with the utterance chain, it is not unique in rejecting the utterance as an isolated act of an autonomous speaker. For example, conversation analysts have understood for quite some time that turn-taking, the parsing of one utterance from another, is a negotiated matter that requires careful coordination between speakers and hearers (Sacks, Schegloff, & Jefferson, 1974). Further, the negotiation of the utterance as a turn at talk is a culture-specific process. What is heard as a completed utterance in one culture can be regarded as incomplete to members of another culture (e.g., Philips, 1983). Some relationship scholars have also observed that the meaning of a given utterance can only be understood by embedding it in the larger conversational stream consisting of the prior utterance and the subsequent utterance (e.g., Rogers, 2006; Watzlawick, Beavin, & Jackson, 1967).

2. We might just as well refer to these distal already-spoken discourses as *ideologies,* in that they are patterns of belief, ideas, and values used to create meaning (Freeden, 2003). In a general sense, ideologies define what exists, what is good, and what is possible (Therborn, 1980). I prefer the term discourse to ideology to remind the reader that these cultural systems of meaning come to life in communicative action; they do not float out there as abstractions, nor do they reside inside of individualized psychologized minds. Their existence resides in communicative practices.

4

Discursive Struggles of Relational History, Otherness, and Normative Evaluation

"The moments of the past do not remain still."

—Marcel Proust, *Remembrances of Things Past* (1925)

"Self-absorption does not produce gratification; it produces injury to the self, . . . nothing new, nothing 'other' ever enter[s] the self. . . . The myth of Narcissus neatly captures this: one drowns in the self."

—Richard Sennett, *The Fall of Public Man* (1977)

"The world is full of judgment-days, . . . in every act [one] attempts, [one] is gauged and stamped"

—Ralph Waldo Emerson, *Essays, First Series* (1847)

In Chapter 3, I presented a brief discussion of the four links in Bakhtin's (1986b) utterance chain that productively organize the major types of discursive struggles animating the meaning-making process. The three epigrams that open this chapter mark, respectively, the remaining three links: the proximal already-spoken, the proximal not-yet-spoken, and the distal not-yet-spoken. The proximal-already-spoken focuses on how interactants' joint history interpenetrates with their present; to borrow from Proust, the relational past is not still in the present. The proximal-not-yet-spoken underscores the role of the other in constructing the self, an appreciation lost on the mythic Narcissus, as Richard Sennett reminds us. The distal not-yet-spoken centers on the role of evaluative judgment by others in the meaning-making process; as Ralph Waldo Emerson suggests, our utterances are always subject to praise or criticism through the prism of societal ideals and conventions. While the two proximal links direct our gaze toward communication between interactants in conversation, the distal not-yet-spoken puts us in contact again with culture, thereby making a full circle back to the discussion of culture that dominated Chapter 3.

Before I engage these three sites of the utterance chain, three overarching observations need to be made. First, the quantity of research informed by relational dialectics theory (RDT) is much more limited with respect to these links than with the distal already-spoken addressed in Chapter 3, especially so for the two proximal links. To some extent, this is a methodological artifact; research that is based largely on self-reports, especially in the context of interviews, is likely to provide us with insights into cultural discourses. Interviewers are cultural members who are virtual strangers to research participants, and participant utterances are reliant on common cultural discourses for their intelligibility to interviewers. Further, to the extent that the interviewer is regarded as a stand-in for other members of society and thus able to evaluate a participant's utterances for their normative conventionality, the distal not-yet-spoken may hold analytic currency. However, apart from relevance to the broader cultural discourses that are implicated in the distal already-spoken and the distal not-yet-spoken of the interview, it is the relationship between the interviewer and the participant that logically would become the focus of attention in the proximal already-spoken and the proximal not-yet-spoken; in this context, the proximal other is the interviewer. However, the purpose of an interview is generally not directed at understanding the interviewer-participant relationship but rather some other relationship of the participant.

Thus, my second observation is that existing work with respect to the proximal links relies too much on second-hand data. In order to make productive use of the proximal already-spoken and proximal not-yet-spoken concepts, future researchers will of necessity need to attend to interactions between relating parties more than they have to date. Until this shift in the research is achieved, we are left with second-hand self-reports by relationship parties about the two proximal links in the utterance chain. Such data are better than nothing, but they are obviously limiting.

Third, I underscore my continuing need in much of the RDT-informed research reviewed in this chapter to engage in translation work. Researchers to date have tended not to focus explicitly on the discourses— the systems of meaning—at stake, instead describing findings in psychologized terms such as motivations, needs, and wants of individuals. I have reread the research relevant to this chapter by asking the same analytic question that informed my discussion of research discussed in Chapter 3, namely, "What discourse makes this statement intelligible?"

With these three observations in mind, let me turn to the remaining three links in the utterance chain for their insights into relational meaning making. As was my practice in Chapter 3, I am selectively reviewing extant research, presenting examples in detail for illustrative purposes. Given my observations about existing research, this chapter of necessity is less of a review of literature than is Chapter 3 and more oriented toward setting an agenda for future research.

❖ THE PROXIMAL ALREADY-SPOKEN: DISCURSIVE STRUGGLES OF RELATIONAL HISTORY

Two bodies of research are relevant in understanding the analytic value of the proximal already-spoken: research on the micropractices of conversational coherence and repetition, which tends to be non-dialogic in its theoretical moorings, and RDT-informed research that tends to gloss the details of talk for a more abstract and general treatment of how discourses of the relational past and present are in play for relationship parties. I discuss each of these bodies of work separately, although future research could benefit greatly from marrying these two approaches.

The Micropractices of Intertextuality

Beginning with their second utterance, interacting parties have a history (Duck, 2002). This history encompasses not only prior utterances in the conversational exchange at hand but extends, as well, to their prior conversations together. The linking together of two proximate utterances illustrates intertextuality conceived as the sequencing of two speakers' utterances. Conversation analysts (e.g., Drew, 2005; Mandelbaum, 2008) have done an admirable job in examining the microscopic details of turn-taking and sequence organization in order to examine how two utterances are coordinated such that prior utterances are woven together with subsequent utterances to produce coherence.

Other scholars of the micropractices of talk have expanded the parameters of intertextuality to consider how utterance features from prior conversations between relating parties pop up in the utterances of a current conversation between the partners. For example, Tannen's (1989) work on repetition has examined how a variety of linguistic features, including word and phrase choices uttered by self and other in their past conversations together, are recycled in current interaction practices. She argued for the positive benefits of repetition, viewing it as a poetics of talk that enacts many useful functions for interacting persons, offsetting what she perceived as the conventional wisdom that repetition is negative. In particular, she argued that repetition is an efficient way to produce fluent talk, thereby saving the speaker from having to rediscover the proverbial verbal wheel. Repetition also enhances comprehension, according to Tannen, because it is high in redundancy. Additionally, repetition is an important verbal cohesive device that ties together current sentences, phrases and words with prior utterances. Last, she argued, repetition performs a bonding function between speakers, enhancing interpersonal involvement.

A negative view toward repetition can be found in the conflict research. Several scholars have examined topical intertextuality, that is, recurring topics or themes from one conversation to another in the conflicts between relationship parties (e.g., Roloff & Johnson, 2002; Tannen, 2006). Such serial or perpetual arguments are often viewed negatively by scholars, addressed as evidence that a relational pair carries baggage over from one conflict to another in a state of ongoing unproductive conflict management (e.g., Gottman, 1999).

Interactants face the inevitable struggle between the interplay of the given and the new—the utterances inherited as a legacy from their relational history in play with and against the new utterances of the moment. Meaning in the moment emerges out of the struggle of the old and the new, the predictable with the novel, the certain with the uncertain (Baxter & Montgomery, 1996). Thus, from a dialogic perspective, it is important to put repetition in play with its opposite in order to study how meaning emerges from this struggle. It is this dialogic view that is missing from much of existing work on the micropractices of coherence and repetition in talk.

From a dialogic perspective, however, the focus is on the utterance chain rather than the utterance, per se; thus, systems of meaning should be the focus of scholarly attention. The stockpile of past interactional encounters amassed by a relationship pair constitutes their relationship identity. Thus the meaning system of the relationship—the relationship's identity, or what the relationship means to the parties—is an historical trace that is brought by the parties to their subsequent encounters (Duck, 2002). Relationship parties enact the incumbency (Pomerantz & Mandelbaum, 2005) of what kind of relationship they have built historically through a myriad of interactional practices including reliance on taken-for-granted common joint experiences, referencing a common social network, and explicitly communicating about the past through ritualizing, storytelling, and informal reminiscing (e.g., Baxter & Pittman, 2001; Planalp, 1993; Planalp & Benson, 1992). To the extent that parties instantiate the incumbency of their historically built relationship identity, they are engaged in an exercise of *re*production, sustaining the given definition of their relationship as friends, lovers, enemies and so forth.

But the reproduction of the given relational system of meaning is inevitably in play with countervailing alternative systems of relational meanings, that is, alternative possible relational identities. The potentiality for *pro*duction, not just *re*production, is present in every new encounter between relationship partners; parties continue to construct the meaning of their relationship and through their adaptations in meaning, they construct new relationship identities. Although a focus on micropractices is valuable and dialogic work of the future could benefit substantially from greater attention to this level of conversational detail, most of the RDT-informed research to date has focused on a more abstract level of intertextuality.

Discursive Struggles of Relationship Identity

Taken as a whole, the research that refers to this family of discursive struggles in relationship-level meanings employs a variety of labels, including the *dialectic of stability-change, predictability-novelty, certainty-uncertainty, given-new, presence-absence, past-present, old-new,* and *reproduction-production*. Both deductively oriented and inductively oriented research begins to inform us about discursive struggles of relationship identity, albeit in general ways rather than through the careful study of the details of enacted talk between relating parties.

Deductively Oriented Research

Early, deductively oriented research investigated the salience of a tension between predictability and novelty. In general, this struggle was defined as tension among mystery, spontaneity, surprise, or uncertainty, on the one hand, and "knowing what is coming off in the relationship with some degree of predictability" (Baxter, 1990, p. 76) on the other hand. Baxter's retrospective study of romantic relationships found that parties reported experiencing this struggle in approximately two thirds of all reported relationship development stages, and that its prevalence increased with a relationship's length. The association between relationship length and prevalence makes sense; early on, relationship partners haven't amassed many interaction episodes upon which to establish a firm relationship identity; there is no salient incumbent identity yet in play.

The deductively based research on the marital relationship allows us to claim that predictability-novelty is a salient discursive struggle. Pawlowski's (1998) retrospective study of spouses' accounts of the development of their marriages identified predictability-novelty as the second most frequently reported dialectical struggle after autonomy-connection. Consistent with Baxter's finding, Pawlowski found that this struggle increased in frequency as the relationship developed. Graham's (2003) retrospective study of divorced partners also identified predictability-novelty as the second most frequently identified dialectical struggle after autonomy-connection. Partners reported struggling with the dysfunctionality of their old relational scripts, yet bemoaned the challenges of crafting alternative meanings for their newly reconfigured, postdivorce relationships.

The research discussed to this point has presumed that temporality features prominently in the discursive struggle of the given and the new. On conceptual grounds alone, time is, of course, central to any struggle of the past with the present. Baxter and Erbert (1999) centered time more prominently in suggesting that major points of transition or upheaval in a relationship's development—turning points (Bolton, 1961)—are occasions in which contradictions can be identified in bold relief. Their argument is that turning points are moments of major change in a relationship in which discursive competition of one kind or another will be especially prominent. Although relationship identities are always in flux to some extent in everyday interaction, turning points are potentially occasions of major identity shift in which the inherited relationship identity is upended in some significant way.

Subsequent research has followed up on the argument advanced by Baxter and Erbert (1999) in the study of a variety of turning-point events experienced by relationship parties. Although still in the quantitative mode, Erbert (2000), for example, focused on important conflict episodes experienced by marital pairs, finding that parties could identify salient discursive struggles in approximately one-third of their conflict events. The remaining work has adopted a more qualitative and inductive approach.

Inductively Oriented Research

Several studies have examined important life events in which a loss of some kind has been experienced by relating parties. This loss is constructed as a profound struggle in relational meanings between the old identity and the new identity, although it is important to appreciate the unique features of this struggle depending on the particular kind of turning-point loss.

Illustrative of this work are two studies that have identified a presence/absence struggle related to the turning-point event of the physical death of a loved one. Toller (2005), for example, interviewed parents who had experienced the devastating event of the death of a child. The child, although physically absent, still had a meaningful presence that was described on an emotional plane by the parents. When parents heard stories about their deceased child, visited spaces associated with the child, or encountered important anniversary dates, the emotional presence of the child was particularly salient. Parents used ritual events, such as celebrating the child's birthday, or symbolic memorabilia as a way to keep the memory of the deceased child alive, in spite of the pain involved and the discourse around them which beckoned them to move on. The parental efforts to keep their child symbolically alive evidenced the discursive power accorded to the old relational identity and resistance to the new family identity absent the child. Bryant (2006) also examined the turning-point event of death in her study of new stepfamilies in which one of the biological parents had formerly died. The deceased parent, although physically absent, lived as a social ghost in the stepfamily, whose presence was dealt with in a variety of ways by stepfamily members. Some stepfamilies incorporated the deceased biological parent into family rituals as a way to memorialize him or her. Other stepfamilies achieved denial in avoiding the symbolic commemoration of the person. Whether a family enacted homage to the deceased parent signals the relative power accorded to the old family identity versus the new stepfamily identity.

A different kind of loss—known as ambiguous loss (Boss, 1977, 1999)—is constructed when loss has been experienced but without a physical death (Baxter, Braithwaite, Golish, & Olson, 2002; Golish &

Powell, 2003; Powell & Afifi, 2005; Sahlstein, 2004, 2006). Illustrative is a study by Braithwaite, Baxter, and Harper (1998) on stepfamily ritualizing. Memories of the family of origin, the "old family," had ongoing salience for stepchildren in particular as they lived everyday life in their "new family." Rituals that paid homage to both the old and new family identities appeared to be evaluated favorably, but when either family meaning was privileged over the other in ritualizing, it was experienced as a negative communication event. But presence/absence is more than a matter of communicatively enacting collective memory, especially with respect to the nonresidential parent. From the perspective of the stepchild, the nonresidential parent has an ebb and flow physical and emotional presence and absence for them, which they often experience as disruptive (Braithwaite & Baxter, 2006).

Compared to the discursive struggles of integration and expression reviewed in the prior chapter, it is apparent that discursive struggles of past and present relational systems of meaning have been relatively understudied. Future research needs to examine relationship change from a dialogic perspective in which the relational meaning system of the past is in play with alternative relational meaning systems that are possible in the present. Existing work in interpersonal communication still tends to privilege relationship continuity to the relative neglect of discontinuity, and most importantly, to the neglect of the play of continuity and discontinuity in relational identity through time. In addition, existing research is not focused on the maintenance of relational identity, or systems of meaning; rather, it is focused on psychological or behavioral indicators. Let me turn to this body of work by way of critiquing it from a dialogic perspective.

Relationship Maintenance and Change From a Dialogic Perspective

Relationship maintenance research, which is now substantial in quantity, still persists in privileging maintenance as a process of continuity (e.g., Canary & Dainton, 2003). This bias can be detected in the very ways that maintenance is conceptualized. Dindia (2003; Dindia & Canary, 1993) usefully summarized four dominant conceptualizations of relationship maintenance. First, maintenance is conceived as keeping a relationship in existence; the relevant indicator of maintenance is staying together as opposed to terminating. This definition ignores the question of the relationship's meaning or identity and focuses broadly on the bottom-line outcome of a relationship's continued existence. Two people, or a family of persons, can continue to exist but with radically different relational meanings over time, yet this approach to maintenance ignores this potential fluidity in relationship identity.

The second definition of maintenance (Dindia, 2003) is to keep a relationship in a specified steady state such as closeness, commitment, and so forth. This definition potentially holds relevance for the system of meaning that constitutes a relationship; being close well might be part of partners' relational identity. However, these steady states could just as easily be conceived as psychological outcomes, not issues of meaning, and this is the common pattern in the research of this tradi-·tion. Furthermore, this conceptualization explicitly privileges the reproduction of the past as the marker of maintenance.

The third conceptualization of maintenance identified by Dindia (2003) is keeping a relationship in a satisfactory condition. Meaning is not addressed in this conceptualization; rather the focus is placed on the psychological outcome of partner satisfaction. This conceptualization allows for a relationship to change, so long as it stays intact and the changes sustain partner satisfaction.

The fourth conceptualization of maintenance (Dindia, 2003) is keeping a relationship in repair through both preventative and corrective actions by the partners. Implicit in the conceptualization of successful maintenance would be the outcome markers associated with any of the first three conceptualizations of maintenance. This conceptualization is a behavioral approach to maintenance, one driven by an implicit presumption toward reproduction of the past in the present.

All four of these conceptualizations, and the research programs associated with them, are biased in favor of *re*production activity. In addition, ignored in this research are the systems of meaning at play as partners ongoingly construct their relational identity from the past into the present. Change is generally positioned as a threat in these conceptualizations, something to be repaired, contained, and managed. It is useful to turn this conceptualization of maintenance on end and pose a question much friendlier to the dialogic perspective represented in this book: How do parties create new relationship identities from those inherited from their past? In turning the maintenance concept on end, we have posed a different metric for evaluating relationship continuity/discontinuity. Whereas existing maintenance research privileges continuity and positions discontinuity as a threat, my alternative question privileges discontinuity or creation, and asks how it results from interplay with past relational meanings. In this alternative dialogic conception, reproduction isn't conceived necessarily as the desired outcome; instead, it risks functioning as a force of semantic inertia, standing as a possible obstacle for relationship parties to craft new relational possibilities. Clearly, the discursive struggle of past and present holds potential for a range of alternative relational meanings in the moment, from total reproduction of the old relational identity to production of a radically new relational identity. It is this process that deserves attention from a dialogic perspective, in contrast to existing maintenance research in which only reproduction has garnered conceptual and empirical attention.

But what about the work in interpersonal and family communication that explicitly addresses relationship change? Stage-based approaches to relationship change are still common in contemporary relationship research (for a review, see Mongeau & Miller Henningsen, 2008). I won't repeat the details of my critique of stage theories advanced over a decade ago (Baxter & Montgomery, 1996), because I think it still stands. The main criticism is that stage theories are built on a presumption of linear progress toward some ultimate finalizable relational state. Thus, the kind of change allowed in stage theories is basically incremental, positively-valenced change, not qualitative or transformative change (Conville, 1991). The turning-points approach, discussed earlier, is envisioned as an alternative to stage-based approaches, and research suggests that, contrary to the presumption of progress that undergirds stage approaches, relationship change is often a volatile, up and down dynamic (e.g., Johnson, Wittenberg, Villagran, Mazur, & Villagran, 2003).

Even the turning-points approach to change can be criticized, however, for an underlying bias toward quantitative, rather than qualitative, change. The method employed to elicit turning points—the retrospective interview technique (Huston, Surra, Fitzgerald, & Cate, 1981)—asks informants to fill out a graph whose two axes are time (the X-axis, calibrated in months) and the metric of change (the Y-axis, usually marked in increments of 10 percentage points ranging from 0% to 100%). The metric of change has been defined a variety of ways, including the degree of commitment to the relationship, likelihood of marriage, degree of emotional closeness, extent of identification with other, and extent of feeling like a family (Baxter & Wolf, in press). However, in fixing the Y-axis to some unitary metric that can range only incrementally, from 0% to 100%, this research tradition constrains the kind of change that can be detected. In order to liberate the turning-point approach from this constraint, researchers will need to shift to a floating Y-axis, in which the informants identify for each turning point what the metric of change is. In this way, researchers will be able to detect qualitative, transformative change, not just incremental, quantitative change.

In this section, I have examined the proximal already-spoken; that is, how the meanings of a relationship inherited from the history of interactions between the parties interanimate with the current interactional moment in producing a relationship identity in the present. I have argued that the bias in existing research is on reproducing relationship identity rather than emphasizing the unfinalizable process of producing a new relationship identity. Let's now turn to the next link in the utterance chain, where we shift from the already-spokens of the relational past to the anticipation of responses from the future—the not-yet-spokens.

❖ THE PROXIMAL NOT-YET-SPOKEN: DISCURSIVE STRUGGLES OF OTHERNESS

The communicative act is a profoundly social enterprise; when words are uttered, they are addressed *to* someone (Bakhtin's concept of addressivity) and that someone responds (Bakhtin's concept of answerability). These features of addressivity and answerability are central to Bakhtin's (1986b) dialogism, as discussed in Chapter 2. In seeking to understand the construction of individual identities for relating parties, the proximal other of interest is the relational partner. Thus, my discussion of the third link in the utterance chain, the proximal not-yet-spoken, will be limited to the anticipated response of the partner(s) to the speaker's words and nonverbal gestures. Because utterances are acts of addressivity, they are, in one sense, never fully owned by the speaker alone (Baxter & Montgomery, 1996). Rather, from a dialogic perspective, it is more productive to think of them as jointly owned, for they sit between the speaker and the other who is addressed and who answers. Clearly, the kind of dialogic research needed to address this link in the utterance chain is talk between relational partners; however, as we shall see, this kind of work is in short supply. Thus, much of this section articulates a research agenda for future research.

Monadic Versus Decentered Conceptions of Self-Identity

The other who is addressed and who answers is both similar to, yet different from, the speaker. It is this dance of sameness and difference—a dialogue—that Bakhtin found so powerful throughout his career as a metaphor for all of social life. However, in this section, I will take dialogue at a more literal level in considering the exchange between self and other, enacted at the utterance site of the proximal not-yet-spoken. As discussed in Chapter 2, Bakhtin's early work focused on how the dance of self and other constructs the self-identities of the two parties. Thus, the meanings at stake at this link in the utterance chain are the social identities of the relating parties.

The dialogic belief that other is requisite to the ongoing construction of self is one that is still at odds with the presumptions of mainstream interpersonal and family communication, in which the self is, for the most part, still conceived as an autonomous, monadic unit. Hall (1992) labeled this the "enlightenment subject" which is "based on a conception of the human person as a fully centered, unified individual, endowed with the capacities of reason, consciousness and action, whose 'center' consist[s] of an inner core" (p. 275). In a similar vein, Sampson (1993) described the view of self to which we are acculturated in the ideology of individualism as a "bounded container":

> This inescapable cultural vise has given us—or, at least, the dominant social groups in the West—a sense of themselves as distinctive, independent agents who own themselves and have relatively clear boundaries to protect in order to ensure their integrity and permit them to function more effectively in the world. This describes the self-contained ideal. This ideal is supported by the twin pillars of a possessively individualistic understanding of the person (primarily, the male person) and the sense of the self as being like a container. (p. 32)

This self-contained notion of the self, the monadic self, was described by Bakhtin (1981d) as "a hermetic and self-sufficient whole, one whose elements constitute a closed system presuming nothing beyond themselves, no other utterances" (p. 273). From a dialogic perspective, such a conception of self is a cultural fantasy, because the other is essential in constructing the meaning of self: "I achieve self-consciousness, I become myself only by revealing myself to another, through another and with another's help. . . . Cutting myself off, isolating oneself, closing oneself off, those are the basic reasons for loss of self" (Bakhtin, as quoted in Todorov, 1984, p. 96). This alternative, dialogic view of self positions it as a relation between one person and another, a simultaneity of sameness and difference. At once, self and other are similar yet different. During interaction, the two occupy approximately the same time and space, what Bakhtin (1981b) referred to as a chronotope (literally time-space), yet they occupy this shared chronotope differently. Each individual has a unique outsideness or excess of seeing, as discussed in Chapter 2.

Of course, Bakhtin was not alone in articulating an alternative, dialogic conception of self identity. Hall (1992) referred to this alternative conception as a "decentered or postmodern subject" that is riddled with a struggle of competing social identities:

Within us are contradictory identities, pulling in different directions, so that our identifications are continually being shifted about. If we feel that we have a unified identity from birth to death, it is only because we construct a comforting story or "narrative of the self" about ourselves. (p. 277)

These contradictory identities come to us through encounters with difference, or alterity. In his articulation of dialogical self theory, Hermans (1996a, 1996b, 2001, 2002, 2004; Hermans & Kempen, 1993) similarly has underscored the multivoiced or dialogic self which is inevitable in these increasingly globalized times. Hermans and Demaggio (2007) have stated the following:

The other is like myself (ego), but at the same time, he or she is not like myself (alter). Dealing with differences in a globalizing world requires the capacity to recognize and respond to the other person or group in its alterity. Alterity, as a central feature of well-developed dialogue, is a necessity in a world in which individuals and cultures are confronted with differences that they may not understand initially but that may become comprehensible and meaningful as the result of a dialogical process. . . . [O]ther persons, groups, or cultures are parts of an extended self in terms of a multiplicity of contradictory voices or positions. . . . [A] decentralized conception of the self [is] multivoiced and dialogical. . . . [T]he dialogical self [is] a dynamic multiplicity of I-positions or voices in the landscape of the mind, intertwined as this mind is with the minds of other people. . . . The dialogical self is not only part of the broader society but functions, moreover, itself as a "society of mind" with tensions, conflicts, and contradictions as intrinsic features of a (healthy functioning) self. (p. 36)

Hermans and Demaggio's point is that the self of globalized times is riddled with the voices—perspectives—of different, often contradictory, others, which collectively constitute it.

To the extent that scholars in interpersonal and family communication attend to other in the construction of self, it is usually through the theoretical lens of symbolic interactionism. Thus, it is important to address differences between symbolic interactionist and dialogic perspectives.

Similarities and Differences Between Symbolic Interactionist and Dialogic Perspectives

Articulations of a decentered or dialogic self reveal important overlaps with a much older intellectual tradition—symbolic interactionism. Particularly prominent in communication circles is Mead's

(1934) articulation of self in what subsequently was labeled symbolic interactionism (Blumer, 1969). While Mead's argument is similar to Bakhtin's dialogic self, it is, in the end, different. The distinction is worth addressing in some detail, if for no other reason than clarifying the broader relationship of dialogism, and RDT, to symbolic interactionism on the matter of the self. Key to the similarity of the two is the joint belief by Bakhtin and Mead that language is the basis of society and of the individual; thought is conceived as inner speech with other. However, as Holquist (2002, pp. 55–57) has suggested, Mead's conception is basically that of pre- Saussurean (1983), Wundtian (1904) *Volkerpsychologie* in which language is viewed as a unified system by which a culture transmits a unified or consensual worldview to subsequent generations of speakers. By contrast, a dialogic conception of language is decidedly contentious, in which discursive struggles are inherent. Thus, according to Holquist, Mead's view is nondialogic because of how he conceptualizes language.

When the individual is viewed as a mere repository of culture through the transmission medium of language, he or she is positioned merely as a passive receptacle, a positioning rejected by both Mead and Bakhtin, but in different ways. Key to Mead's rejection of the individual as a passive receptacle was his distinction between the *Me* and the *I*. To Mead, the self involves two analytically distinguishable processes: the Me and the I. The Me represents the "incorporated other within the individual" (Meltzer, Petras & Reynolds, 1975, p. 61). It is the portion of the self that has internalized the attitudes, values, and norms of society. A person gains a sense of self through a process of introjection, in which he or she "can take [the] attitude of another and act towards himself as others act" (Mead, 1934, p. 171). To complement the passivity of the Me, Mead conceptualized the I, which represents "the initial spontaneous, unorganized aspect of human experience . . . the undisciplined, unrestrained, and undirected tendencies of the individual" (Meltzer et al., p. 61). The I is thus positioned to resist or conform to the Me, and it will be in harmony or disharmony with what is internalized from the social world. If there is tension in Mead's process of the self, it is in the potential opposition of the I with the Me. By contrast, as discussed in the prior paragraph, the dialogic Me is inherently riddled with tension; Mead's Me is far too unitary from a dialogic view.

But a dialogic view is also critical of Mead's conception of the I, which appears to sit mysteriously outside of sociality. Taylor (1991) has been especially pointed in his dialogic critique of Mead's I:

> Mead's I has no content of its own. It is a sort of principle of originality and self-assertion, which can lead at times to impulsive

conduct, or to resistance to the demands of society, but doesn't have an articulated nature. . . . What this description fails to capture is the way in which the I is constituted as an articulate identity defined by its position in the space of dialogic action. . . . [Mead] does not have a place in his scheme for dialogical action, and he can't have this because the impoverished behavioral ontology [of his theory] allows only for organisms reacting to environments. But this pushes toward a monological conception. (pp. 312–313)

Taylor's position is that the person's action (in the form of the I) sits outside of interaction—it is a reaction to it. But from whence does the I originate? Taylor rejects the Me-I bifurcation, adopting the Bakhtinian stance that self is a dialogic action, that is, a process of identity formation that emerges ongoingly through interaction with other. Through the dialogic action of anticipating the response of other (addressivity) and the obligation to respond to other (answerability), identity takes shape. According to Taylor, a dialogic self is joint action with another, not a mental process of introjection that is then either resisted or conformed to by an I whose origins sit outside of sociality.

Koczanowicz's (2000) differentiation of Mead and Bakhtin aligns with Taylor's (1991) position, for the most part. "Unlike Mead," Koczanowicz argued, "Bakhtin never concentrated on the psychological dimension of the relation with the other" (p. 60). In contrast to Mead, Koczanowicz argued, Bakhtin underscored the role of social action in self-identity. In the act of addressing another (addressivity) and in fulfilling one's obligations to respond to another (answerability), the self is formed. The other gives oneself the benefit of his or her "excess of seeing"—his or her difference—but self is not an internal reflexiveness about this social mirror; instead, self is one's act of response to other's similarity and difference in meaning systems. Actions of a person are always socially embedded in dialogism; they can never exist outside of sociality but are an integral part of it.

From a Bakhtinian perspective, then, self-identity is ongoingly constructed in the interactional dance of similarity and difference in systems of meaning between speakers. However, when we examine the mainstream project of interpersonal communication scholarship, we witness the containment, if not erasure, of difference.

The Bias Against Difference in Mainstream Interpersonal Scholarship

Elsewhere, I have critiqued mainstream scholarship that studies interpersonal communication in personal and familial relationships for its inattention to difference (Baxter, 2007). The containment, arguably even erasure of difference, is complex and emerges at many levels, beginning with the very definition of communication. Traditional scholarship in interpersonal/family communication positions communication in one of three interdependent ways, all of which are oriented toward unity at a sacrifice of difference. First, communication is envisioned as a mirror; the skilled interlocutor is the individual who can represent with fidelity an external, pregiven reality. Accuracy and clarity are valued qualities. Unity is sought between the preexisting reality and its representation in communication. Difference is represented by a disjuncture between reality and its representation, reflected in such communicative phenomena as deception and ambiguity. Second, and relatedly, communication is envisioned as a conduit that transmits (with fidelity and clarity) thoughts and feelings from one mind to another. Understanding is the key standard for efficacious communication in the conduit imagery. Unity is represented when one speaker's thoughts and feelings can be replicated in a listener's mind. In the conduit imagery, difference surfaces as misunderstanding and the absence of empathy—failed communication. Third, communication is envisioned as a control device. Through persuasive representations of reality, speakers can accomplish reproduction of values, attitudes, and beliefs: The listener not only understands the speaker but agrees with him or her. Unity is accomplished in the homogeneity of hearts and minds. In the control device imagery, difference is represented as evidence of ineffectiveness.

These constructions of communication are like old, comfortable shoes, and we have walked many miles in them. They are the pervasive conceptions of communication among laypersons and scholars alike in the U.S., and we readily take them for granted, reproduce them in our textbooks, and ground our programs of research in them. However, from a dialogic perspective, they privilege unity and position difference as a vexing problem.

A rejoinder might argue that interpersonal/family communication research *does* value difference. After all, the logical empirical tradition has as its goal the explanation of systematic differences along a myriad of variables: gender differences in communication, cultural differences in communication, communication in relationships of different types, and so on. The interpretive tradition celebrates difference and seeks to make the strange familiar by celebrating the unique strangeness of particular communities and situations. From a dialogic perspective, these two traditions can be described as monologues in parallel, not dialogues between. The interplay of different voices is missing in these programs of research.

But, the rejoinder might continue, a core question in interpersonal/ family communication scholarship is how different individuals form and maintain personal relationships. Surely, this is evidence of taking the interplay of difference seriously? Traditional scholarly approaches to the study of relationships are premised on the grand narrative of unity. The prototypical conception of a close relationship is one in which partner separation, autonomy, and difference evidence relational distance, not closeness (Baxter & Montgomery, 1996).

Interpersonal conflict is probably the research topic where difference features most prominently in the interpersonal/family communication research. Unfortunately, for the most part, difference is reduced to incompatibility (Roloff & Soule, 2002, p. 518) and is regarded as a rupture in, and problem for, the consensual social order—something which merits appropriate management. Deutsch's (1973) classic definition of conflict reveals the negative valence attached to difference-as-incompatibility: "Conflict exists whenever incompatible activities occur. . . . An action that is incompatible with another action prevents, obstructs, interferes, injures or in some way makes the latter less likely or less effective" (p. 73). When difference is reduced to incompatibility and conflict between persons, little room exists to conceptualize its positive, constructive role in meaning making.

The conceptual thread that weaves throughout the unity project in interpersonal/family communication is the centering of the sovereign, or contained, self, which is discussed above. The individual occupies the centerpiece of interpersonal/family communication scholarship. It is the primary unit of analysis, and difference is understood only as variations in the characteristics of individuals. Much of the research activity in interpersonal/family communication adopts a cognitive approach in which meaning making is located in the individual's sovereign mind. Individuals make sense of one another's communicative messages and react to those based on their prior states of mind (i.e., their expectations, mental models, and feeling states). Motivations and goals of individuals produce cognitive plans that are assembled within the individual mind and deployed strategically through the production of linguistic and nonverbal behaviors. Whether processing another's message or producing a message for other's consumption, the individual mind is the driver of the communication engine.

The other primary approach to the study of interpersonal/family communication—the so-called relationships approach—also privileges the sovereign individual. Much of this research views the relationship as a desired outcome of, or a context for, individual strategically deployed communicative activity. As noted elsewhere in this book, the still-dominant view of relationship development, a legacy from social penetration and other resource exchange theories (e.g., Altman & Taylor, 1973), frames the development, maintenance and disengagement of relationships from a rational choice perspective in which each individual engages in cost/benefit decision making and acts strategically in order to maximize social profits.

In sum, interpersonal/family communication overwhelmingly adopts a monologic orientation in its theoretical quest for unity. Difference becomes a vexing problem in need of containment, not an intellectual problem in need of serious theorizing. However, some limited scholarly attention has been given to difference on its own terms, and I turn to these few studies next for their insights into how other's difference is essential to the construction of self-identity.

The Dance of Similarity and Difference

As discussed in Chapter 2, essential to Bakhtin's notion of aesthetic activity in constructing another's self-identity is empathy combined with distance. Similarity in meaning systems positions an individual to answer another with empathy, whereas difference in meaning systems is a necessary prerequisite to distance in which the individual's excess of seeing is integral to answerability. However, as we will see below, this tidy analysis becomes complicated.

Scholars have devoted substantial research energy toward the study of similarity, to the relative neglect of difference. Similarity has been restricted to prior similarity, in contrast to what I have elsewhere labeled *chronotopic similarity* (Baxter, 2004), that is, the similarity of meaning systems that builds up between relationship parties as a function of spending time together. In newly initiated relationships, chronotopic similarity is limited and parties are left with only prior similarity. As parties build a history together, their chronotopic similarity increases. Research on prior similarity, largely defined in terms of sameness on attitudes, values, dispositional characteristics, and demographic features, has a long history (for useful reviews, see AhYun, 2002, and Baxter & West, 2003). Much of this research tradition examines the role of prior similarity in developing friendships and romantic relationships, to the relative neglect of its role in more established relationships. Difference is rarely studied on its own terms (for interesting exceptions see Felmlee, 1998, and Wood, Dendy, Dordek, Germany, & Varallo, 1994); instead, it is examined as the absence of similarity. However, parallel to my argument in Chapter 3 that the absence of expression cannot be interpreted as nonexpression, and vice versa, I would observe that the absence of similarity is not the equivalent of difference.

In any event, researchers for the most part have positioned similarity as an objective state that can be quantified, rather than as a meaning that is co-constructed between relating parties (Baxter & West, 2003). As Duck (1994) has observed, "By treating similarity as a drily mental comparison . . . research has left out the social power of the construction and management of similarity in everyday talk" (p. 101). The same point can be made with respect to difference.

However, two dialogically based studies have examined similarity and difference as meaningful phenomena (Baxter, Foley, & Thatcher, 2008; Baxter & West, 2003). This work is relatively rare in its study of talk between relating parties, and it is thus better positioned than the self-report tradition to inform us about the proximal-not-yet-spoken.

Baxter and West (2003) asked friends and romantic partners to jointly reflect on the meanings they attached to their similarities and differences. Across both types of relationships, parties articulated several bases of both similarity with, and difference from, the partner. Dispositional personality attributes, leisure time pursuits, demographic and family backgrounds, attitudes and beliefs, and communication style provided the grounds of both similarity and difference. Tidy distinctions between bases of similarity and difference were often blurred, however. Overall, approximately 85% of the study's pairs identified at least one characteristic that was both a basis of similarity and difference—what Baxter and West labeled *tight dialectical unity*. Tight dialectical unity took two distinct forms in partners' sense making.

Similarity and difference in the form of *quantitative/qualitative transformation* involved participants' realization that a similarity did not mean absolute equivalence. Rather, participants recognized that qualities or attributes were located in a zone or latitude of approximate similarity. So long as the actions of both parties stayed in this latitude of approximate similarity, slight differences were assimilated into a global perception of similarity. However, if one or both parties acted in a way outside this latitude of approximate similarity, a qualitative change of judgment occurred and the partners discursively reframed a contrast judgment in which similarity was transformed into difference. Thus, a pair could move in and out of similarity and difference with respect to a given feature, depending on whether action at a given point in time was within, or outside, the latitude of approximate similarity. For example, Baxter and West presented an example of two romantic partners who perceived that they were both open and honest with one another (a similarity), yet on occasion this went too far and became excessive honesty, which was reframed as a difference with respect to the partners' differing appreciation of the value of discretion.

The second form of tight dialectical unity enacted in participants' talk was what Baxter and West (2003) labeled *core-radiant interplay*. Relationship parties perceived themselves to be similar with respect to the core, or essence, of a characteristic. However, they simultaneously recognized differences along any number of dimensions, or radiants, of the feature. Baxter and West presented the example of two friends who perceived themselves similar in their musical tastes. But they then proceeded to discuss how they spent hours and hours disagreeing on a song or a band. Their basis of difference was how they liked the song or band, not that they liked it.

Participants in the Baxter and West (2003) study discussed several ways in which their similarities and differences were positive and negative. Again, this proved to be a complicated matter. In fact, a total of 98% of the relationship pairs identified at least one characteristic that was both positive and negative. Bases of similarity that were both positively and negatively valenced typically featured a characteristic that Baxter and West labeled *unstable valence*. A characteristic's valence was unstable in that it could take either a positive or negative turn, depending on specific circumstances at the moment. One friendship pair, for example, discussed that their mutual pursuit of drinking as a leisure time pursuit was a positive in their relationship, unless it was excessive, in which case it shifted to a negative factor in their friendship, producing arguments and hurt feelings. Bases of difference that were both positively and negatively valenced typically featured a characteristic that Baxter and West labeled *growth challenges*. On the one hand, relationship parties discussed how a given difference helped them to grow as individuals, yet the difference simultaneously functioned as a source of frustration and challenge, often in the form of conflict, jealousy, or envy.

Similarities were framed as positive factors by Baxter and West's (2003) participants for three primary reasons. First, similarities were discussed as *facilitators of communication*. Partners discussed how a given similarity resulted in comfortable and effective communication in their relationship, functioning to enhance partner understanding. This attribution by partners is fully consistent with the Bakhtinian argument that empathy (understanding) requires similarity. With less frequency, participants also framed their similarities as sources of *pleasure/fun* and as sources of *assistance/support*.

However, similarities were also framed as negative, in large measure because of their consequences for communication (Baxter & West,

2003). Problematic communication that resulted from similarity was of two types. Some similarities were framed as negative because they resulted in *conflict*. For example, one romantic pair discussed how their mutual stubbornness—a similarity—contributed to dysfunctional clashes characterized by anger and one-up actions. Other similarities were framed as negative because they resulted in non-conflictual *communication difficulty*. For example, one friendship pair discussed how they both liked to give people a hard time, which could result in hurt feelings when directed toward one another. Thus, similarity can be complicated, getting in the way of understanding.

The Baxter and West (2003) participants also framed their differences as positive and/or negative for several reasons. Most importantly, differences were framed as positive because of their potential for *individual growth*. Over and over, participants discussed how they learned and grew as individuals from one another's different personalities, interests, attitudes, backgrounds, and styles. This attribution is fully consistent with the Bakhtinian argument that the construction of self occurs through the other's excess of seeing—his or her difference. Secondarily, participants also framed their differences as *facilitators of communication*, largely through complementarity of styles.

Offsetting these positive factors were *conflict* and *communication difficulty* as reasons for negatively valuing differences. Differences—of any kind—purportedly increased the likelihood of conflicts and arguments, which were framed negatively by the study's participants. Communication difficulties unrelated to conflict were also attributed to differences, often through misunderstandings that resulted in discomfort, awkwardness, or felt ineffectiveness. Thus, difference, like similarity, takes on complicated meanings for relationship parties, with both similarities and differences being valenced positively and negatively.

However, in a follow-up study, Baxter, Foley, and Thatcher (2008) reexamined from a different perspective the same data used in the Baxter and West (2003) study, concluding that similarity and difference were not valued equally by the relationship partners. Whereas Baxter and West focused on the content of *what* partners said in their reflections about their similarities and differences, Baxter, Foley, and Thatcher focused on the details of talk in order to examine *how* participants talked about similarity and difference. The shift from what to how was illuminating in revealing that partners' talk functioned to contain and limit difference, whereas similarity was celebrated expansively and fully. Couples contained their differences in four primary ways.

First, partner talk functioned to mute difference, positioning it as a problem for the relationship to a much greater extent than was the case with similarity. Some participants muted difference by actively suppressing or refusing to acknowledge it. Participants enacted suppression by employing topic shifts when a difference was brought up; interrupting the partner when a difference was being introduced; actively denying a partner's assertion of difference; minimizing differences through qualifying terms such as "a little bit," "occasionally," "somewhat," and so on; and reframing difference as a similarity.

Second, partner talk functioned to mark difference as uncomfortable, in contrast to how similarity was discussed. Through nervous laughter, dysfluencies, and metatalk about how uncomfortable they were, partners indicated their discomfort in talking about their differences.

Third, partners actively framed their differences as negative to a greater extent than was the case with their talk of similarities, largely through their justifications and use of pejorative terms. By providing justifications for their differences, participants framed them as aberrant relationship phenomena that required an account. In contrast to similarities, which were simply discussed, differences tended to be accompanied by justifying accounts as a way to make them appear normal. Partners also employed a variety of pejorative terms in talking about their differences to a greater extent than characterized talk about similarities. These pejorative terms often made fun of differences by exaggerating or mocking them.

Fourth, and last, participants in the Baxter et al. (2008) study communicatively positioned difference as relationally distancing to a greater extent than characterized talk about similarities. For example, nonimmediacy cues were often used in discussing differences but not similarities. Reference was made to how "we are similar" while "you and I" are different. Whereas *we* marks immediacy, reference to *you and I* is a symbolic separation of the parties.

In sum, then, although parties recognized that both similarities and differences can be complicated and function positively and negatively for their relationship, how partners talked about their differences positioned them as decidedly unequal to their similarities. Through their talk, parties constructed difference as more dangerous, something that needed to be contained and regulated.

Participants in these two studies regarded dysfunctional conflict as the greatest threat posed by differences. As noted above, interpersonal scholars tend to conceptualize conflict as negatively valenced incompatibility, not unlike the participants in the studies just reviewed by Baxter and her colleagues (Baxter et al., 2008; Baxter & West, 2003). The difficulty with this conceptualization is that it allows little room to reclaim conflict (and difference more broadly) in positive ways. However, a number of dialogic scholars are attempting just that, and I turn next to a discussion of that work, which generally sits outside of interpersonal and family communication as that subfield has been commonly understood.

Dialogic Conflict: Reclaiming Difference (and Similarity)

Several dialogic theorists and practitioners have made progress in reconceptualizing conflict as a site for productive creativity. Much of this work draws on dialogic theorists other than Bakhtin. Stewart and Zediker (2000) made the distinction between descriptive and prescriptive approaches to dialogue, with Bakhtinian dialogism (and RDT) aligned with the descriptive approach, in which the assumption is made that all human life is inherently dialogic. According to Stewart and Zediker,

> These descriptive versions of dialogue urge theorists and practitioners to understand the human being as irreducibly dyadic or social. . . . Dialogue is characterized in these accounts as a prominent, pervasive, and consequential feature of the human condition that needs to be acknowledged, articulated, and integrated into understanding. . . . Their theorizing is grounded in a dialogic ontology that is a description of the universal human condition as relational. (p. 226)

They contrasted this descriptive approach with a prescriptive approach:

> Other widely cited accounts of dialogue treat the term more prescriptively, as an ideal to be striven toward or a goal to be achieved as an outcome of considered and ethically-freighted choices. . . . They emphasize the need to make principled choices to help the special kind of contact called dialogue to happen, rather than just acknowledging the already-given "dialogic" nature of human reality. (p. 227)

Prominent prescriptive theorists, according to Stewart and Zediker, include Buber (1970) and Bohm (1996). The philosopher Martin Buber's (1970) work, *I and Thou*, is probably the best known of the prescriptive approaches. He argued that people can respond to others in a variety of ways along a monologic (*I-It*) to dialogic (*I-Thou*) continuum. "Dialogue" for Buber references I-Thou relating, and he regarded it as a much needed antidote to excessive I-It (monologic) ways of relating. The physicist David Bohm developed a very different approach to dialogue, although it is still prescriptive. Motivated by his perception that communication breakdowns were rampant, Bohm developed a program of dialogic group functioning that promotes collaborative meaning making, or what he called "dialogue."

Much of the work in reclaiming conflict along dialogic lines grows from the prescriptive tradition (e.g., Ellinot & Gerard, 1998; Isaacs, 1999). To be sure, there are differences among prescriptive approaches (Pearce & Pearce, 2000), most particularly whether dialogue is being used to reference a quality of communication or a noun to describe a kind of group session. But this body of work is certainly compatible with the Bakhtinian view that communication is an opportunity to construct new meanings, not simply reproduce old systems of meaning.

Prescriptive work by communication scholars (e.g., Pearce & Littlejohn, 1997; Pearce & Pearce, 2000; Spano, 2001) affords rich insights into an alternative way that conflict can unfold, resulting in the creation of new meanings out of the dance of similarity and difference in systems of meaning among participants. Typically enacted under such rubrics as *public dialogue, participatory democracy,* or *deliberative democracy,* these how-to, applied training programs in alternative ways to conduct public conflict are rich in their implications for the conduct of private, interpersonal conflict, as well. Representative of these approaches is the Public Dialogue Consortium (PDC; Pearce & Littlejohn, 1997). Pearce and Littlejohn (pp. 200–204) have presented several key elements in the PDC effort to help conflicting parties shift to dialogic conflict. The first of these elements is systemic questioning. This involves the strategic use of questions to provoke "wonderings" (p. 201), that is, to invite disputants to think differently about their own interactions. This shifts the focus of attention away from individual wants and needs to a focus on the grammar of the unfolding interaction. The second element is appreciative inquiry. This involves a refocusing of the disputants' attention away from negativity to a search for "hidden virtues and positive resources" within the system. The final element is reflecting. This third element involves a "shared hypothesizing" (p. 203) in which disputants reflect on possible futures based on their responses to systemic questioning and appreciative inquiry. This element focuses on the opening up of space for new ideas and actions heretofore not contemplated because the parties have been embroiled in a view of their intractable differences.

Taken as a whole, the PDC effort does not smooth over or hide differences in systems of meaning; rather, the grammar of the conversation is shifted so that differences can be placed in play with similarities with the goal of emergent new insights and actions. If successful, a PDC intervention results in transcendence and transformative conversation:

If a conversation is transcendent, the participants must understand what they are doing in a new way. Old categories will not work for them. They will say that this conversation is somehow different from the conversations they had before. (Pearce & Littlejohn, 1997, p. 215)

Because of this brief description, I have done an injustice to the work on PDC intervention and other similarly prescriptively oriented approaches; they are complex, systemic interventions designed to change the conversation in profound ways, resulting in a complete reframing of the conflict. Paraphrasing Pearce and Littlejohn (1997, p. 105), dialogic conflict envisions outcomes that can be described as second-order changes in contrast to the first-order changes envisioned in traditional approaches to conflict. First-order change is change in which we take sides and fight for what we believe is right from our individual, partisan perspectives. By contrast, second-order change involves a transformation in the very structure of the conflict itself. The kind of conflict taken on by the PDC project is what Pearce and Littlejohn refer to as moral conflict, that is, perceived incommensurable value systems, where differences are pitched along evaluative lines of good and bad—"a deontic logic of 'oughtness'" (p. 56). This brings us to the final link in the utterance change, the distal not-yet-spoken, where discursive struggle implicates the conventional and the ideal through normative evaluation.

❖ THE DISTAL-NOT-YET-SPOKEN: DISCURSIVE STRUGGLES OF NORMATIVE EVALUATION

In this final section of the chapter, I turn to the fourth, and last, discursive site where one can locate discursive struggle: the distal-not-yet-spoken. This discursive site is a close cousin to the proximal-not-yet-spoken, in that it is concerned with the anticipation of Other's response to a speaker's utterance, thereby affecting what is actually spoken. However, unlike the proximal not-yet-spoken, the distal-not-yet-spoken focuses on the anticipated normative evaluation to be provided by a possible future listener who is not physically present when the utterance is voiced. This so-called third person—what Bakhtin (1986c, p. 126) referred to as the *superaddressee*—represents a perception that what one utters in the moment could be subject to later (re)evaluation. Whereas the proximal listener, Bakhtin's second speaker, is one's immediate conversational partner, this third party—not in an arithmetic sense but in some imagined "metaphysical distance or in distant historical time" (p. 126)—is the anticipated evaluation of one's utterance by outsiders: "God, absolute truth, the court of dispassionate human conscience, the people, the court of history . . . and so forth" (p. 126). This superaddressee, although imagined in some future time and space—is nonetheless present in the expression of a given utterance as parties pursue the business of constructing their personal and relational identities. Utterances are steeped in addressivity— they are addressed to both immediate listeners and absent listeners who may subsequently hear and evaluate a given utterance. Thus, speakers anticipate the evaluations of the superaddressee and adapt their utterances so as to garner responsive approval not just from immediate listeners but from these distal imagined listeners, as well.

In conceptualizing the superaddressee, Bakhtin centered the conventional and the ideal—benchmarks against which a given utterance can be evaluated. The conventional evaluates a given utterance against what is expected as normal or typical. The ideal evaluates a given utterance against what could or should be—the moral oughtness of an utterance. The conventional and the ideal are the normative evaluative backdrops against which both the content and the form of an utterance are subject to outsiders' evaluations.

This fourth site of the distal-not-yet-spoken brings us back full circle to where we began the utterance chain in the last chapter—cultural discourses. Notions of the conventional and the ideal are, of course, embedded in a culture's discourses. Further, as we realized in chapter 3, discourses are not totalizing but rather rupture internally and interanimate with competing discourses that are simultaneously present in the culture. What is conventional or ideal according to one discourse may be framed as unconventional or less than ideal according to an alternative system of meaning or a fissure within that discourse itself. Nonetheless, as Bakhtin's (1981d) distinction between centripetal and centrifugal discourses suggests, at any given moment, one discourse is arguably dominant over other, more marginalized, discourses. It is these dominant centripetal discourses to which superaddressee evaluations of the conventional and the ideal are anchored.

The distal-not-yet-spoken is understudied relative to the other sites of discursive struggle that have been discussed in this and the prior chapter. Nonetheless, we have some initial insights into the workings of this site of struggle. Early work informed by RDT focused on the struggle of conventionality-uniqueness. Baxter and Erbert (1999) described it this way to participants:

> Sometimes relationship parties deal with their desire, on the one hand, to be unique from all other relationships. On the other hand, partners experience the pressures to conform in conventional ways to

the expectations of the general society, or their friends and family, about how their relationship should be. (p. 556)

Other scholars have described this contradiction similarly. Pawlowski (1998), for example, described this discursive struggle as follows: "Couples want to be accepted by others by following the rules and norms of society, yet they also feel the need to be unique as a couple and not just a carbon copy of others" (pp. 415–416).

The limited research on the thematic frequency and rated importance of this struggle suggests that it is less salient to self-reporting research participants relative to other struggles (Baxter & Erbert, 1999; Erbert, 2000; Pawlowski, 1998). Baxter (1993) has argued that this contradiction is arguably one of the easiest for relational partners to negotiate in mainstream Euro-American culture. Although relationships are expected to be conventional in some respects, one of the key expectations of relationships is that they are somehow unique from all others. This contradiction may not be very salient to relationship parties when they are asked retrospectively to recall discursive struggles because it is so easily negotiated as a both/and: partners can fit their relationship inside conventional types (friendship, dating, marital, and so forth) yet do so in unique ways (e.g., the parties can hold a traditional wedding yet exchange uniquely crafted vows). In other words, the expectation to be unique is an important convention of mainstream relating in U.S. society.

When researchers shift from the a priori operationalization of conventionality-uniqueness just described to employ more open-ended qualitative methods, discursive struggles between competing discourses of superaddressee evaluation become more pronounced. Research has concentrated on two broad families of discursive struggle: the normative evaluations represented in the discourse of romance and those evident in the discourse of the "real family."[1]

Discursive Struggles of Romance

A number of scholars have documented the discourse of romance that circulates in mainstream U.S. society. I first introduced this discourse in Chapter 3, where it was identified as one of several salient discourses that animate communication in the mainstream U.S. culture. Holland and Skinner (1987) have identified several additional elements of this meaning system which are especially salient in the everyday experiences of adolescents and young adults: (1) physical attractiveness as symbolic capital in male-female relations; (2) male initiation of the courtship process; (3) the centrality of romantic love, emotional intimacy, and physical intimacy as important relational currencies; and (4) social worth or prestige predicated on one's capacity to attract and keep a romantic partner.

However, the meaning system of romance is a challenging one when competing discourses bump up against the romantic idealizations, or when it ruptures internally (e.g., the heteronormative ideal is ruptured by physical attraction between same-sex persons). Holland and Eisenhart's (1990) ethnography of how the discourse of romance animates college women's lives illustrates that it is fraught with competing discourses, including struggles to sustain autonomy in the midst of the gendered sexual manipulation that is perceived to accompany the enactment of romance, struggles of informational openness and closedness in the midst of gossip-driven social networks and impression management of oneself as successful in navigating romance, and the struggle for supremacy between discourses of romance and academic achievement.

But the discursive struggles implicated with the idealization of romance extend beyond the dating experiences of young adults. Stafford and her colleagues (Stafford & Merolla, 2007; Stafford, Merolla, & Castle, 2006) have identified the presence of a romantic idealization in long-distance romantic relationships that is particularly salient during the periods in which the partners are absent from each other. When apart, long-distance partners appear to idealize one another and their relationship, only to have those idealized bubbles burst when the parties are together. Unmet idealizations result in greater fragility for the relationship, with a greater likelihood of break up when compared to geographically proximate relationships.

A similar dynamic may account for why the likelihood of break up for romantic pairs appears to increase around Valentine's Day (Morse & Neuberg, 2004). Celebration of Valentine's Day is steeped in the idealizations of the discourse of romance, and the contrast between the everyday enactment of one's relationship, where competing discourses are at play, and the romantic ideal may serve as a catalyst for break up.

The discourse of romance is challenging across the lifespan, as Aleman's research on older persons suggests. In her ethnographic study of a retirement community, Aleman (2003) identified the salience of a code of romance for residents, in which there was an expectation to have a heterosexual companion and social prestige if accomplished. This code of romance contained three elements. First, the discourse of romance placed value on physical intimacy, yet a competing discourse of aging led residents to feel as if sexual intimacy was somehow inappropriate at their age. Second, the discourse of romance had a heterosexual bias to it, yet males in the retirement community were overwhelmingly outnumbered by women thereby reducing the likelihood of achieving male-female bonding while female platonic friendships were still positioned as somehow second class. Third, whereas male residents wanted commitment through remarrying, female platonic partners were more hesitant to commit to the long term, desiring instead the gratifications of the here and now. In her related study of a SeniorNet discussion board on the internet, Aleman (2005) identified narratives that both embraced and resisted the discourse of romance. Through their storytelling practices, seniors told idealized tales of the older woman's quest for romance that privileged heteronormativity yet challenged its asymmetrical relationships and male dominance. Instead, these senior women told tales in which they were not desperate for a man and resisted involvement for its own sake in the face of a dearth of "good men." The women presented themselves as deserving of love yet resistant to efforts that could constrain their independence and equality.

It is important to note the cultural specificity of the discursive struggles implicated in romance. Baxter and Akkoor (2008) have noted that the discourse of romance and romantic love is a cultural motif of contemporary mainstream U.S. society but holds less significance in many other cultures in the world. By contrast, they discussed so-called arranged marriages (Hatfield & Rapson, 1996) in which parents play a central role in mate selection and courtship. In examining Asian Indian conceptions of love and marriage, for example, Baxter and Akkoor identified an alternative discourse of love to the romantic love that organizes mainstream American practices of relating. In particular, arranged love was articulated with these meanings: (1) love as the ongoing accomplishment of respectful attention in which love is viewed as an action of respect, not a feeling of passion; (2) love as an emergent process that develops over time, after not before the marriage; and (3) love as ongoing effort, especially with respect to obligations to the extended families of the partners, which is not viewed as an impediment to self. Clearly, this alternative conception of love bumps up against the mainstream American conception of romantic love for second-generation Asian Indian immigrants to the U.S. and for Asian Indians in general as their culture becomes increasingly Westernized. Further, the Asian-Indian meaning of arranged love doubtless has its own discursive struggles. My point is that the discourse of romance, as it has been studied thus far, has a decided cultural bias, and subsequent researchers need to examine the discursive struggles that surround the relationship idealizations in other cultures.

Discursive Struggles of "Real Family"

Despite demographic trends away from the nuclear family household consisting of two parents plus their biological/adopted children, this model still captivates mainstream American culture as the idealization of the "real family." In a recent study, colleagues and I (Baxter, Henauw et al., 2009) replicated the classic study by Trost (1990) in which participants were asked to evaluate the family status of a variety of social groupings. We found, consistent with Trost's work, that social configurations were more likely to be legitimated as "family" to the extent that they were characterized by: (1) the presence as opposed to the absence of children; (2) the presence of intactness (in contrast to dissolved bonds); (3) marital as opposed to cohabitation status; (4) the presence of biological (blood) and legal ties over ties of affection (i.e., so-called fictive kin); (5) heterosexuality as opposed to homosexuality; and (6) sharing a household as opposed to being geographically dispersed. This idealization of the "real family" creates obvious discursive struggles in family forms that depart from these idealized characteristics.

Much of the RDT-based work in stepfamily communication, for example, has identified the discourse of the "real family" as a basis for criticism and delegitimation of, and disappointment with, the stepfamily. In established stepfamilies, stepchildren perceive "real" families to be characterized by all-channel, open communication between children and parents, and they find their stepfamilies lacking when evaluated against this standard (Baxter, Braithwaite, & Bryant, 2006). More specifically, stepchildren appear to suspect that the residential parent may have shifted loyalty to the stepparent (Baxter, Braithwaite et al., 2006), and they reject the stepparent as a real parent and resist his or her efforts at parenting (Baxter, Braithwaite, Bryant, & Wagner, 2004). In addition, communication with the nonresidential parent is criticized because he or she is insufficiently present in the child's everyday life, thereby challenging a legitimate claim to being a real parent.

More recently, colleagues and I (Baxter, Braithwaite, & Bach, 2009; Braithwaite et al., in press) have begun to examine voluntary kin— those people we regard as family even though they are unrelated by either blood or legal ties—for example, the close elderly neighbor who is treated as a grandmother figure, or the close family friend who is regarded as an "auntie," or the roommate who is like a brother. The mere existence of these close kinlike relationships functions to resist the nuclear family of origin as the cultural idealization. At the same time, however, when people talk about their voluntary kin members, they ironically invoke a discourse of the "real family" and thereby further instantiate its centripetal dominance in the ideological landscape of the mainstream culture. In particular, people's accounts of their voluntary kin relationships largely justified these relationships only because their own family of origin was somehow deficient in some way (Braithwaite et al., in press). The logical import of such justification is that if their own family met the cultural ideal, then voluntary kin relationships would have no reason to exist.

The societal debate surrounding the definition of marriage as a union between a man and a woman can be understood as a discursive struggle between competing discourses of family, one organized around a norm of heteronormativity and one not. Suter's work (Suter, Bergen, Daas, & Durham, 2006; Suter & Daas, 2007) with lesbian families productively examined how the discourse of heteronormativity functions in this alternative family form. The sample of lesbian couples both embraced and resisted heteronormative ideals. For example, some couples displayed symbols such as rings in a manner consistent with heteronormative conventions in order to gain recognition of their relationship, whereas other couples wore rings but in unconventional ways (e.g., wearing the ring on the right hand rather than the left). Other couples explicitly rejected heteronormativity and engaged in practices to challenge it, for example, making it known that they shared a single bedroom to foreclose a framing of the relationship as platonic roommates.

Relationships are enacted against myriad cultural conventions and idealizations represented by the imagined superaddressee. Dialogic scholars have barely begun the task of understanding how competing expectations are discursively enacted in personal and social relationships. Over a decade and a half ago, Rawlins (1992) identified the contradiction of the ideal and the real with respect to platonic friendship, yet his argument transcends this specific relational form and applies to all forms of relating. Compared to research located in the other sites of the utterance chain, discursive struggles surrounding normative evaluations have been relatively ignored.

❖ CONCLUSION

This chapter has completed the tour of the utterance chain begun in the prior chapter. The utterance chain is the basic building block from a dialogic perspective, and Chapters 3 and 4 have described in detail existing research that is situated at the four key discursive sites comprising the utterance chain: the distal already-spoken, where we put speaker talk in conversation with the cultural discourses which circulate; the proximal already-spoken, where we put a relationship's past identity in conversation with the parties' present construction of their relationship identity; the proximal not-yet-spoken, where self and other, the two relating partners, construct their identities through the dance of their similarities and differences in meaning systems; and the distal not-yet-spoken, where a speaker's current talk is placed in conversation with the anticipated evaluations of third-party others. Throughout Chapters 3 and 4, I have repeatedly observed that competing discourses interanimate—a process labeled *intertextuality*. In the next chapter, I turn to a more detailed treatment of what intertextuality look like, and the various forms of struggle that can be identified. Thus, I shift from a focus on the discourses that compete to a focus on the *process* of struggle.

❖ ENDNOTE

1. I use the word "real" in quotation marks to underscore that I am not legitimating any notion of an objective reality that can be marked by contrast to fictional imaginings. Furthermore, in the context of family communication in particular, research participants often invoke the term "real family" to distinguish some social structures from other presumably less legitimate family forms. From the social constructionist perspective of RDT, all constructions are the effect of language use and the marking of "real" from "not real" informs us about which discursive constructions are accepted as conventional or ideal.

5

Centripetal–Centrifugal Struggle

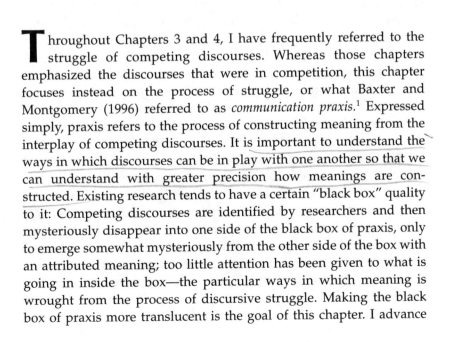

T hroughout Chapters 3 and 4, I have frequently referred to the struggle of competing discourses. Whereas those chapters emphasized the discourses that were in competition, this chapter focuses instead on the process of struggle, or what Baxter and Montgomery (1996) referred to as *communication praxis*.[1] Expressed simply, praxis refers to the process of constructing meaning from the interplay of competing discourses. It is important to understand the ways in which discourses can be in play with one another so that we can understand with greater precision how meanings are constructed. Existing research tends to have a certain "black box" quality to it: Competing discourses are identified by researchers and then mysteriously disappear into one side of the black box of praxis, only to emerge somewhat mysteriously from the other side of the box with an attributed meaning; too little attention has been given to what is going in inside the box—the particular ways in which meaning is wrought from the process of discursive struggle. Making the black box of praxis more translucent is the goal of this chapter. I advance three major points in attempting to accomplish this goal. First, I pay close attention to the power implications of the centripetal–centrifugal distinction noted by Bakhtin (1981d). In distinguishing centripetal from centrifugal, Bakhtin suggested that some discourses are centered whereas others are marginalized. Second, I argue that researchers need to pay greater attention to the details of uttered talk, and in so doing several different features of discursive struggle can be identified. Third, I argue that the interplay of competing discourses cannot be easily isolated from larger patterns of interaction, known as genres. As we shall see, genres vary in their dialogic potential. Whereas this chapter focuses theoretically, the next chapter provides a methodological companion in detailing a step-by-step primer on how to execute a dialogic analysis.

Two caveats are necessary before I develop these arguments. First, I continue to engage in translation work in this chapter. Researchers who frame their work in relational dialectics theory (RDT) often have referred to praxis as strategies through which parties manage contradictions. The term *strategy* implies that praxis is an individual's implementation of communicative action in response to some underlying needs or goals. RDT focuses on discourses not individual wants and needs. To be sure, discourses are given life through the embodied utterances voiced by communicators, but the focus is on discourse not individual inner states, motivations, or desires. Additionally, the term *manage* implies that contradictions, or discursive struggles, exist outside of communication. This positioning of communication implicitly conceptualizes it as a mere coping mechanism. As I have argued in Chapter 2, communication is constitutive of discursive struggle, not merely reactive to it. Thus, it is more consistent with RDT to refer to praxis patterns as different ways in which discursive struggles, and meanings, are constituted.

My second caveat bemoans the relative paucity of RDT-informed research that focuses on talk between relational parties. Instead, the heavy reliance on self-report data (whether in surveys or interviews) gives us talk about relationships rather than relationships in talk. Relationship meanings are under construction in any event. As I have indicated in Chapters 3 and 4, speaker utterances are animated by competing discourses whether they are addressed to a researcher or a relationship partner, but different links in the utterance chain are implicated.

❖ FOREGROUNDING POWER IN CENTRIPETAL–CENTRIFUGAL STRUGGLE

Locating Power in Discourse

Bakhtin (1981d) used the centripetal–centrifugal distinction to mark the inequality of discourses in struggle. Meaning making emerges from the struggle of competing discourses, but those discourses are often not on an equal playing field. Discursive struggle, in other words, is rarely a discursive democracy. The term *centripetal* refers to moving toward centralization or the center, whereas the term *centrifugal* refers to the opposite dynamic of moving away from the center toward the margins. In the context of the social world, these terms hold implications for power in that what is marginalized is easily forgotten or silenced relative to what is centered. The center is easily legitimated as normative, typical, and natural, and thus it functions as a baseline against which all else is somehow positioned as a deviation. By contrast, the centrifugal margins are positioned as nonnormative, off-center, unnatural, and somehow deviant. The centripetal thus occupies a position of privilege relative to the centrifugal, and herein rests its power.

Power is a term with multiple meanings, however, and the use I am making of the concept departs from the typical view advanced in the interpersonal and family communication literature. In his classic review of the power research in the social scientific literature, Berger (1994) differentiated two basic approaches to the conceptualization of power: individual-level and relationship-level. Individual-level approaches tend to focus on motivations for power and typically examine individual dispositional differences such as Machiavellianism, authoritarianism, and so forth. By contrast, relationship-level approaches view power as the result of interactions between relational partners rather than individual desires to wield influence over others. In general, relationship approaches argue that a party's ability to wield influence over another depends on the relationship between the parties; Party A has power over Party B to the extent that Party B depends on A for his or her rewards and accepts A's dominance bids. But what, exactly, is power in individual- and relationship-level approaches? In general, both approaches conceptualize power as a person's ability to produce effects in others—whether those effects are viewed as behavioral, cognitive, or affective changes.

By contrast, the conceptualization of power in this chapter draws from a different intellectual tradition completely, described by Deetz (2001) as a dialogic perspective heavily influenced by Foucault's (1977, 1980, 1988) conception of power. From this perspective,

> The "power" of interest is not that which one possesses or acquires. . . . Such power is an outcome of more fundamental power relations. Power resides in the discursive practices and formations themselves. For example, the discourse that produces a "worker" both empowers and disempowers the group of individuals produced through this representation. In particular historical discourses, "workers" and "managers" are produced out of the open "elements" of organizational life and simultaneously provided with solidarity and interests as well as conflicts, material and symbolic resources, and self-understandings. Power thus resides in the demarcation and the systems of discourse that produce and sustain such groupings. Unions and managers mutually sustain the other in their conflicts. It is not the relative power of each that is of interest but how the distinction is reproduced. (Deetz, p. 35)

In other words, power resides in the systems of meaning—the discourses—through which social reality as we know it is constructed. Thus, power is conceptualized as the discursive capacity to define social reality. Power resides neither in individuals (neither their internal motivational states nor their capacity to influence based on the other's dependency relations) nor in social groups, but in discourses. Centripetal discourses, by definition, are more powerful than centrifugal discourses because their systems of meaning are centered or legitimated as social reality. To be sure, the interests of social groups or individuals are differentially served dependent on which discourses are centered, but such power is derived from dominant discourses.

From the perspective of power, the interesting question is how some discourses are centered while others are marginalized in the dialogic struggle of competing discourses. Although Bakhtin pointed to power in his terminology (centripetal-centrifugal), it is fair to say that his treatment of power is underdeveloped. Apart from terminology, the corpus of Bakhtin's work has an undercurrent of suspicion with respect to monologue—the dominance of a single discourse. Yet, dialogism theory is bereft of a politics in that it does not treat as a core intellectual problem the matter of how communication moves between more or less monologic tendencies. The suspicion toward monologue is addressed in Bakhtin's (1981d, 1984b) discussions of single-voiced, or authoritative, discourse.

Single-Voiced Monologue

In *Problems of Dostoevsky's Poetics*, Bakhtin (1984b) made an important distinction between single-voiced discourse and double-voiced discourse. Single-voiced discourse, as the term suggests, refers to the dominance of a single perspective or worldview: monologue. Monologue is an authoritative discourse so dominant that other, competing discourses are silenced. Authoritative discourse "demands our unconditional allegiance" (Bakhtin, 1981d, p. 343). Bakhtin described authoritative discourse as "organically connected with a past that is felt to be hierarchically higher. It is, so to speak, the word of the fathers" (p. 342). The monologue of authoritative discourse is fused with tradition and authority that affords it a taken-for-granted status. It is "not surrounded by an agitated and cacophonous dialogic life" (p. 344), but rather functions with hard-edged finality as truth. Monologue is similar to what Deetz (1992) has called *discursive closure*, what Baxter and Montgomery (1996) called *denial*, and what Baxter (1988) called *selection*. By whatever label, authoritative discourse functions to "subvert, obscure, and deny" (Baxter & Montgomery, p. 61) alternative discourses. That's why it's called single-voiced by Bakhtin.

Single-voiced monologue can be identified in some of the RDT-based research. For example, Miller-Day's (2004) ethnographic study of grandmothers, mothers, and daughters revealed a clear pattern of single-voicedness in half of her sample with respect to the negotiation of the discourses of autonomy and connection. Autonomy was sacrificed by these women, and their relationships were dominated by a level of connectedness that proved problematic for them. Miller-Day described this enmeshment as follows:

> The enmeshed relationships . . . were characterized by an extreme emotional closeness, an emotional fusion—like two candles melting together. Loyalty was demanded, high involvement and participation were expected, and separateness was generally not tolerated. In these relationships there was a general lack of boundaries or extremely permeable boundaries, in which togetherness dominated and joint activities were mandated. (p. 108)

These enmeshed familial systems stood in contrast to the connected relationships, where a more healthy interplay between the discourses of autonomy and connection was found.

In one of the few studies to examine enacted talk between relational partners, Sabourin and Stamp (1995) found support for single-voiced monologue among abusive couples compared to nonabusive couples.

Abusive couples privileged the discourse of autonomy, in contrast to the greater balance between autonomy and connection that characterized nonabusive pairs. Further, abusive couples talked in vague, rigidified ways that suggested a stagnation or calcification of the relationship's status quo, in contrast to the interactional flexibility that characterized nonabusive pairs. This clearly implicates the utterance chain at the intersection of the past and the present, as discussed in Chapter 4.

In extinguishing all but one dominant discourse, parties run risks of inflexibility, if not rigidity. Meaning can become calcified or resistant to change. Although Bakhtin (1981d) argued that there is dialogic potential in all interaction, he was suspicious of single-voiced efforts to finalize meaning. To Bakhtin, the meaning-making process should be approached for its indeterminate, fluid, and unfinalizable potential, and single-voiced discourse should be guarded against.

The Move From Monologue to Dialogue

Unlike single-voiced discourse, in which alternative discursive possibilities are silenced, double-voiced discourse implicates such alternatives either indirectly or directly (Bakhtin, 1984b). In its idealized form, double-voiced discourse is dialogic in the interplay of equally valued discourses. However, often the discursive playing field is unequal, as discussed above, with one discourse centered while alternatives are heard yet still given secondary emphasis. For example, using both interviews and taped interactions of mother-daughter pairs, Penington (2004) found that African American mother-daughter dyads privileged connection more so than the European American dyads; by contrast, European American dyads privileged autonomy more so than the African American dyads. This privileging appeared to take the form of weighting one discourse more so than the alternative discourse, rather than a complete silencing of the alternative discourse.

As a number of critical discourse analysis scholars have argued (e.g., Fairclough, 2003), the power-laced process of struggle between and among competing discourses is a complex one. Let me turn, then, to a discussion of several different ways in which discursive interplay can be enacted.

❖ THE INTERPLAY OF DISCOURSES

Throughout this book, I have referred to meaning making as a process wrought from the intertextual interplay of competing discourses. But *about to happen*

what is meant by the term *interplay?* Single-voiced discourse orients only to the referential object at hand, whereas double-voiced interplay involves a co-orientation to the referential object and to alternative discourses. In double-voiced utterances, competing discourses come into contact; they "enter into a semantic bond" (Bakhtin, 1984b, p. 189) in which the meaning of each is somehow impacted. The systems of meaning do not "exist side by side without intersecting" (Bakhtin, p. 189). Interpenetration is requisite to dialogue, because competing discourses must of necessity come into semantic contact with one another. With the litmus test of interpenetration in mind, let me turn to various praxis processes identified in existing RDT-informed research (Baxter, 1988; Baxter & Montgomery, 1996). As we shall see, some of these patterns are less dialogic than others with respect to this litmus test.

a test for acidity or alkalinity using litmus

Diachronic Separation

Two of the praxis processes identified by Baxter and Montgomery (1996) are diachronic in nature. That is, over time they are characterized by a shift in which discourse is centered and which discourse is marginalized. In the absence of longitudinal data that inform us about changes over time, it is impossible to differentiate these two diachronic practices from single-voiced monologue, because at any given point in time, one discourse is dominant. To date, RDT-informed research has relied (too heavily) on partner retrospective reports of how their relationships have progressed through time, rather than collecting longitudinal interaction data between relating partners. Nonetheless, these retrospective studies are useful in giving us some preliminary insights.

Both diachronic practices are characterized by an ebb and flow across time. *Spiraling inversion* (Baxter & Montgomery, 1996; also referred to as *cyclic alternation* by Baxter, 1988) is characterized by a back and forth pattern over time in the dominance of first one discourse and then another for a given topical or activity domain. The second diachronic process, *segmentation,* manifests a similar ebb and flow over time, but the basis of inversion is not time, per se, but rather a topical or activity domain. One domain centers one discourse; another domain privileges a competing discourse. On the assumption that two domains cannot be enacted simultaneously, the shift in domains from one time to another produces a shift in which discourse is centered.

Common to both of these diachronic practices is a separation of competing discourses, rather than their interpenetration (Baxter, 1988). Thus, both are limited in their dialogic potential. The retrospective RDT-based research suggests that relationship parties nonetheless rely extensively on these two diachronic practices. Spiraling inversion, for example, is a common process by which discourses of autonomy and connection are purportedly enacted among heterosexual romantic pairs (Baxter, 1990), marital couples (Baxter & Simon, 1993; Hoppe-Nagao & Ting-Toomey, 2002), and divorced pairs (Masheter, 1994). At one point in time, parties privilege their autonomy or independence, but at another point in time, the competing discourse of connection is privileged. Segmentation has been identified as a frequently enacted praxis process for the discursive struggle of openness and closedness among married pairs (Baxter, Braithwaite, Golish, & Olson, 2002; Hoppe-Nagao & Ting-Toomey, 2002), heterosexual romantic pairs (Baxter, 1990), lesbian couples (Suter & Daas, 2007), and stepfamily members (e.g., Braithwaite & Baxter, 2006; Baxter, Braithwaite, Bryant, & Wagner, 2004). Some topical domains are sites of negotiated openness, while others are negotiated as sites of closedness. For example, some children in stepfamilies are hesitant to discuss stepfamily life with the nonresidential parent, although they discuss other issues with the nonresidential parent. Discourses of loyalty (experiencing a sense of loyalty to that new family unit), rationality (not wanting to reveal information that might trap the child in the middle between parents), and community (not wishing to say something that might hurt the nonresidential parent) appear to be implicated in making this segmentation intelligible. Segmentation has also been identified with respect to the discursive struggle between autonomy and connection among married pairs (Hoppe-Nagao & Ting-Toomey, 2002), divorced pairs (Masheter, 1994), stepfamily members (e.g., Baxter, Braithwaite et al., 2004), and long-distance dating pairs (Sahlstein, 2006). Some activity domains are sites in which the discourse of partner autonomy is honored, while other activity domains are sites where the competing discourse of connection is privileged.

Existing research provides limited insight into how spiraling inversion and segmentation are negotiated between relating partners, and this should become a research priority for future RDT-informed research. Relational parties may simply fall into these diachronic practices of separation through a series of ad hoc enactments. That is, parties may end up privileging one discourse at a given moment when communicating on a given topic or enacting a given activity while privileging a competing discourse at another time or on another topic/activity in what appears to be a rather serendipitous manner. The exigencies of the moment may affect which discourse is privileged. *ice, unexcepted*

Schrodt and colleagues (Schrodt, Baxter, McBride, Braithwaite, & Fine, 2006) nicely illustrated this event-driven dynamic in their study of competing discourses that surrounded the construction of the meaning of the divorce decree for divorced couples. As I discussed in Chapter 3, the *divorce decree as guide* framed the divorce decree as an informal rubric to be followed with flexibility in child visitations and financial obligations depending of the immediate circumstances facing family members. By contrast, the *divorce decree as legal document* framed the decree as a binding document whose stipulations surrounding child visitation and financial obligations were to be followed absolutely. Many divorced pairs moved back and forth between these two systems of meaning for the divorce decree, depending on their frustrations at the moment. When one party appeared to be taking advantage of the spirit of the decree, an exigency was in place, from the perspective of the ex-partner, to legitimate a shift from the decree-as-guide discourse to the decree-as-legal document. When parties were frustrated with the lack of flexibility that accompanied the decree-as-legal document, this exigency provided a catalyst for shifting to the decree-as-guide discourse. Over time, ex-partners apparently shift back and forth between these two meaning systems in what may appear to be a rather erratic manner from the perspective of an outsider.   *unpredictable*

By contrast, partners may be more systematic in negotiating a process of spiraling inversion or segmentation. Illustrative of this prospective approach is Sahlstein's (2006) work on planning in long-distance dating pairs. The researcher found that many long-distance couples planned their time apart and their time together to enact discourses of autonomy and connection. For example, time apart was framed as autonomy time, good for doing one's own thing, meeting work obligations, and so forth; by contrast, pairs planned the details of how to celebrate connection in their time together. Autonomy-oriented activity was regarded as a violation of together time in this negotiated understanding.

What diachronic spiraling inversion and segmentation lack is interplay between competing discourses at a given point in time. Time and topical/activity domain are separation mechanisms that isolate competing discourses from one another. In the absence of dialogic virtuosity (Pearce & Pearce, 2000), such communication praxis processes at best can accomplish a state of equilibrium or balance rather than interplay. It is the potential for interplay that opens up the possibility for newly emergent meanings which can alter the struggling systems of meaning in unforeseeable ways.

If these diachronic processes achieve parity over time—a balance of sorts in the homage that is paid to each discourse—then one might argue we have a condition of power equality among the competing discourses. A given discourse holds dominance at a particular interactional moment but over time all discourses shift from center to margin and back again. We have limited insight into these power dynamics, but the discussion of normative evaluation in Chapter 4 would be a fruitful site to interrogate this matter. One discourse might be centered as the ideal, with exceptions legitimated only under specific conditions marked by the presence of a given topic or activity. For example, in their study of the competing discourses of motherhood surrounding a pregnant woman's decision to consume alcohol, first discussed in Chapter 3, Baxter and her colleagues (Baxter, Hirokawa et al., 2004) found that motherhood understood from the discourse of individualism was the dominant, idealized discourse, while the competing discourse of responsible motherhood was allowable only in a narrow set of circumstances, specifically, when the pregnant woman explicitly sought advice about drinking, when the relationship between women was sisterlike, or when the pregnant woman was perceived to be drinking in excess. Even then, participants in the Baxter, Hirokawa et al. study reported that they would broach the topic of drinking cautiously, framing the matter as one of choice for the woman, thereby reinforcing a meaning of motherhood from the discourse of individualism. What the Baxter, Hirokawa et al. study failed to address is the communicative process by which these contingency conditions became legitimated as the exceptions to the normative expectation that it was a social taboo to infringe on the individual rights of a woman by discussing her decision to drink alcohol.

Does diachronicity inevitably preclude interpenetration? As I discussed in the last chapter, time is implicated most directly in two sites of the utterance chain: where a relationship's past comes into contact with its present and where the present engages anticipated future responses. But these discursive sites are synchronic in nature; that is, at a given point in time, utterances are laced with carry-over meanings from the past and anticipated meaningful responses from the future. These discursive traces of the past and anticipated future hold much dialogic potential. Thus, for example, a weekend spent together could develop new meaning for a long-distance pair after a lengthy period of separation. This emergence of new meaning for togetherness clearly demonstrates interpenetration with the past's period of separation. However, this interpenetration takes place synchronically, not diachronically. That is, the meanings of separation and connection take place once they are reunited. But such interpenetration is far from inevitable. A long-distance pair that alternates periods of separation with periods of togetherness, without changing their underlying systems of meaning for time apart and time together is experiencing the separation of spiraling inversion. The significance of synchrony in this example draws attention to the greater dialogic potential that exists when discourses co-occur at the same point in time in the enactment of the utterance. Let me turn, then, to a discussion of synchronic praxis.

Synchronic Interplay

In contrast to the diachronic processes of spiraling inversion and segmentation are a number of synchronic processes which by definition implicate the co-occurrence of multiple discourses at a given point in time. In essence, synchronic interplay focuses attention on the four sites of the utterance chain, as developed in Chapters 3 and 4. Certainly, one could productively categorize synchronic praxis by these four discursive sites: traces of distal already-spokens in enacted utterances; traces of proximal already-spokens in enacted utterances; the anticipation of proximal not-yet-spokens in enacted utterances; and the anticipation of distal not-yet-spokens in enacted utterances. However, in this chapter I want to overlay a different conceptual lens to the utterance chain by discussing four underlying features of the utterance that cut across the four discursive sites. These four features are conceptualized as dimensions: *antagonistic-nonantagonistic struggle; direct-indirect struggle; serious-playful struggle;* and *polemical-transformative struggle.* These dimensions are distilled from Bakhtin's (1984b) discussion of double voicedness (pp. 181–266), which he illustrated through examples from the novels of Dostoevsky but which I seek to generalize to interpersonal communication. These four features will require future researchers to attend to the details of talk in ways that have been largely glossed over in existing research.

Antagonistic-Nonantagonistic Struggle

Baxter and Montgomery (1996) distinguished antagonistic from nonantagonistic contradictions, and I continue to find this a productive conceptual contrast. Bakhtin (1984b) noted a similar distinction in his discussion of semantic positions (p. 184). A semantic position is a worldview, a system of meaning, a discourse. Sometimes two speakers align with different semantic positions; this is an *antagonistic struggle.* For example, if one party privileges the discourse of autonomy and the partner privileges a discourse of connection (e.g., Sahlstein & Dun, 2008), the struggle of these discourses might lead to what some might be tempted to call a conflict. I prefer to steer clear of this term, however, because most communication scholars conceptualize conflict as a person-against-person struggle, whereas a dialogic perspective views this as an instance of discourse-against-discourse. From a dialogic perspective, the clash is between different systems of meaning, not between two persons with competing goals. From a dialogic perspective, antagonistic struggle is what Pearce and Littlejohn (1997) call *moral conflict,* that is, conflict in which "people deeply enmeshed in incommensurate social worlds come to clash" (pp. 49–50).

By contrast, a nonantagonistic struggle is one in which multiple discourses can be identified within each speaker's utterances. As Bakhtin (1984b, p. 184) noted, "Dialogic relationships can permeate inside the utterance, even inside the individual word, as long as two voices [discourses] collide within it." For example, the utterance "I guess you could say we're dating—I like him and everything and we see each other pretty often—but we're not really 'dating'—I see other people, too." The *but* in this utterance marks a struggle between two different meanings of dating. The first clause makes sense within a discourse of romanticism, whereas the second makes sense within a discourse of individualism (Chornet Roses, 2006).

Of course, these two forms of struggle are not mutually exclusive. One could identify dialogic utterances embedded inside of moral conflicts. Further, the distinction between antagonistic and nonantagonistic conflict is not as neat and tidy as this discussion makes it appear. Conflict is based on a discrepancy in beliefs, even if the level of the discrepancy is "You are blocking my goal" bumping up against "No, I'm not." Antagonistic conflict erupts when systems of meaning are at stake, although this is admittedly a vague threshold.

A tidy distinction between antagonistic and nonantagonistic struggle is complicated, as well, by what Bakhtin (1981d) described as the personification of discourse. Through their language use, speakers sometimes couple discourse "with the image of a particular kind of speaker" rather than reference discourse in some "depersonalized" way (pp. 400–401). Such personification is evident, for example, when a speaker parodies a particular individual or stereotypical social group member in order to ridicule the discourse with which he or she is associated. When discourses are personified in language use, they take on the appearance of an antagonistic struggle, although this may be nothing more than a linguistic device through which criticism of a discourse is accomplished.

I have emphasized nonantagonistic struggles in Chapters 3 and 4, largely because of the methodological overreliance on interview data with individual relationship parties in which participants construct the meanings of their relationships by talking about them. At least in the interview context, nonantagonistic struggles appear to be pervasive in the talk of relationship parties. Less studied are antagonistic struggles

(Erbert, 2000). Many scholars new to RDT are attracted to interpersonal conflict under the mistaken belief that all instances of dialogic struggle are interpersonal conflicts. Clearly, this is not so.

Antagonistic and nonantagonistic struggles can be identified at each of the four discursive sites of the utterance chain discussed in Chapters 3 and 4. When relationship parties are aligned with different cultural discourses, we have antagonistic struggle at the site of the distal already-spoken. When each party's talk invokes coexisting discourses that compete in the culture (e.g., individualism and community; see Chapter 3), we have instances of nonantagonistic struggle at the site of the distal already-spoken.

Imagine a family discussion in which some family members want to go to the same vacation spot as in prior years because it is a family tradition. Other family members want to go to someplace new because the children have outgrown the old vacation spot. The family members are aligning themselves, respectively, with a past discourse of family identity and an alternative discourse about the family in the present. This illustrates an antagonistic struggle at the site of the proximal already-spoken, where the meaning of the family in the past clashes with a different meaning of the family in the present. Alternatively, imagine a family discussion in which all of the family members express ambivalence about the old vacation spot—they express attraction to the spot for sentimental reasons of family tradition, yet they discuss the value of the family changing with its growing children. This alternative discussion illustrates a nonantagonistic struggle of the relational past and present.

When a boyfriend says to his college girlfriend, "I know you won't be happy with this decision, but I've accepted the job offer to relocate in a different state," we have an example of an anticipated antagonistic struggle at the site of the proximal not-yet-spoken. The boyfriend anticipates that his girlfriend won't approve of the job offer, and he recognizes that disagreement explicitly in how he frames his utterance to her. Now imagine this alternative utterance said by the boyfriend as he anticipates his girlfriend's reaction: "I know we talked and are on the same page about the pros and cons of the job offer. It will keep us apart for a semester until you graduate, but it's a perfect first job for me. I think I'm going to accept it anyway, so don't be upset." This utterance, also located at the site of the not-yet-spoken, suggests that the two are in agreement in their ambivalence about the job—whose meaning implicates a discourse of connection and a discourse of autonomy. (This second utterance also functions as a site of the distal already-spoken; lurking in its meaning making are cultural discourses of individualism and community. It also illustrates the proximal already-spoken by mentioning a prior conversation between the two parties.)

Let's shift to the last site of the utterance chain: the distal not-yet-spoken, where parties anticipate the reactions of third parties of a particular or generalized nature. The boyfriend described in the prior paragraph thinks that his parents will urge him to accept the job offer, because they have worked so hard to put him through school. His girlfriend thinks that his dad might react that way, but she suspects that his mother will want him to do whatever keeps them together as a couple because the mother wants them to get married and settle down. The two are in an antagonistic struggle about what his parents will regard as the preferred decision that should be made about the job offer. Now imagine an alternative interaction, in which both parties are in agreement that his parents hold differing views about whether he should accept the job offer in a different city—the father's anticipated opinion is grounded in a discourse of autonomy and achievement, and the mother's anticipated opinion is grounded in a discourse of connection. This scenario illustrates a nonantagonistic struggle between them at the distal not-yet-spoken site of the utterance chain: They agree in their view that others' reactions will be fragmented. The scenario also brings us back full circle by implicating cultural discourses of achievement and connection.

It is easy to imagine a conversation between the boyfriend and girlfriend that moves back and forth between sites of the utterance chain, and thus shifts in and out of an antagonistic or nonantagonistic quality.

Synchronic interplay can vary not only with respect to the antagonistic or nonantagonistic quality of the interaction between relationship parties. A second dimension by which to characterize talk in the moment is its directness or indirectness.

Direct-Indirect Struggle

Bakhtin (1984b, p. 196) made the distinction between open and hidden speech, which I shall refer to as a continuum of directness-indirectness. Indirectness allows for ambiguity of meaning, which potentially can function in at least three discursive ways with respect to the interpenetration of discourses.

First, ambiguity can function as a way for parties to elide, or avoid, the direct interplay between competing discourses. Baxter (1988) referred to this as *disqualification,* a form of praxical *neutralization.* As Eisenberg (1984) stated, it allows for "multiple interpretations to exist among people who contend that they are attending to the same message" (p. 231). So long as parties have semantic wiggle room and don't have to confront the different systems of meaning which they attribute to a communicative utterance, each party presumes that his or her interpretation is the centered one. Chornet Roses (2006) nicely illustrated the ambiguity that surrounds use of the term *dating* among some U.S. college students. Use of the term *dating* implicated distal already-spokens in the competing cultural discourses of romance/commitment and individualism, proximal not-yet-spokens in the anticipation of how a dating partner would interpret the use of the term (would they interpret it to mean a level of seriousness or commitment that exceeds one's own meaning of the term?), and distal not-yet-spokens in the anticipation of what others would think of one's intimacy habits (e.g., whether others would think negatively of someone if they switched dating partners too often in a series of uncommitted one-night stands). His focus-group participants readily agreed that *dating* was a highly ambiguous term. The semantic openness of the term potentially allowed dating partners to celebrate the discourse of romance/commitment *and* the discourse of individualism. When his participants said they were *dating* someone, it meant that they were attracted to the person, voluntarily spent time together in ways that were fun and pleasurable, probably experienced sexual gratification, and were committed to one another at the moment—elements compatible with both the discourse of romance/ commitment and the discourse of individualism. Ambiguity then, provided a "safety net" for dating partners (Chornet Roses, 2006, p. 129). To the partner who thinks of dating as a way to achieve individualistic gratifications without long-term commitment, the discourse of individualism is centered; to the partner who thinks of dating as a stepping stone toward long-term partnership, the discourse of romance/ commitment is centered.

The second way in which ambiguity can function discursively is to produce marginalization of alternative discourses by responding to them only indirectly. When a competing discourse is addressed directly, it suggests a legitimation of it that is denied when dismissively polemic speech is employed indirectly. Bakhtin (1984b) devoted most of his discussion to polemical hidden speech, which he characterized as "the word with a sideward glance at [a] hostile word" (p. 196), and which he regarded as prevalent in everyday talk. Speech with a sideward glance fails to put alternative discourses on a direct equal footing with the centripetal discourse. Those alternative discourses are given an ambiguous verbal nod for purposes of indirect refutation. As Bakhtin noted, "Here belong, in everyday speech, all words that 'make digs at others' and all 'barbed' words" (p. 196). Imagine a parent who says to her child, "I know your closest friends want to go away for the weekend, but you're simply too young to do this without adult supervision. You're not going." This utterance directly names the persons who favor going away and directly refutes it. Now consider this indirect polemic which also refutes the child's desire to go away with friends for the weekend: "My parents wouldn't let me go away with friends until I was 17, and so you're not going." The friends' view is dismissed with a sideward glance in which they are never implicated directly.

Third, ambiguous speech can also function indirectly to temper the authoritativeness of a dominant discourse. Whenever an otherwise authoritative discourse is characterized by "self-deprecating . . . speech that repudiates itself in advance, speech with a thousand reservations, concessions, loopholes and the like," it "cringes in the presence or the anticipation of someone else's word, reply, objection" (Bakhtin, 1984b, p. 196). Indirect hedges such as "sometimes" (as opposed to "always"), "some people" (as opposed to "everyone"), or "a little bit" (as opposed to "a great deal") indirectly admit that the centered discourse is not without criticism of its presumed all-encompassing totality. It is somewhat similar to what Baxter (1988) referred to as *neutralization-moderation*. Such verbal modesty is indirect and fails to give detailed voice to these antitotalizing criticisms, which are, again, given a verbal nod without granting them full and equal discursive footing.

By contrast, direct unambiguous speech that implicates competing discourses gives us an interplay in which at least two distinct discourses are given voice. Centrifugal discourses may not yet be on an equal discursive playing field with the centripetal discourse, but at least they are not elided or reduced to mere discursive tokens too easily dismissed with verbal nods. *Omitted*

Stylistically, utterances can differ not only with respect to their directness-indirectness but additionally, the extent to which they are serious or playful. This serious-playful dimension also holds potential for dismissing competing discourses.

Parody: produce a humorously exaggerated imitation of...

Serious-Playful Struggle

The serious-playful dimension draws attention to the tone of an utterance. Bakhtin (1981d; 1984b) focused especially on the role of playfulness in communication, because he claimed that it is a sophisticated verbal resource through which competing discourses can be challenged. Bakhtin (1981d) discussed in particular the communicative resources of the *rogue,* the *fool,* and the *clown* as playful devices through which a competing discourse can be challenged. The playful rogue parodies a competing discourse by attributing it to a specific person or group who is then mocked. Discourse is coupled "with the image of a

i.e., ridiculed

particular kind of speaker ... not as an expression in some depersonalized language" (1981d; pp. 400–401). In *Problems of Dostoevsky's
Poetics* (1984b), Bakhtin discussed the role of parody in accomplishing
a radical skepticism toward the ridiculed system of meaning. For
example, imagine someone who privileges the discourse of romance
enacting a critical parody of the discourse of rationality. Our speaker
might say, in a tone indicating that it is to be understood as parody,
"How do I love thee? Let me count the ways. . . . your car, your job,
your income, your vacation days, your home, your retirement pack-
age. . . ." If executed successfully, the hearer will understand the deep
ridicule directed at a rational, pragmatic approach to love. Clearly, parody is an indirect communicative act of playfulness. This discursive
struggle is located at the site of the distal already-spoken, with two
opposing cultural discourses of love at stake—a romantic ideology and
a pragmatic ideology. In addition, it is located at the site of the proximal not-yet-spoken in the anticipation that the parody will be understood as mockery.

Assuming the stance of the fool is also a playful way of indirectly
challenging a competing discourse (Bakhtin, 1981d). The stance of the
fool involves a "deliberate stupidity" (p. 403) toward a given discourse,
a misunderstanding of it that "has the effect of 'making strange'" (p. 402)
its coherence. The taken-for-granted assumptions of the discourse are
unmasked by this feigned incomprehension, thereby functioning as a
kind of discursive estrangement. The child who adopts the stance of the
fool in his utterance claim that he doesn't understand a directive of his
parents effectively challenges the discourse of parental authority, albeit
indirectly and playfully. By aligning himself with an alternative view of
parenting in the present, he is challenging the parental authority system
that has historically organized the parent-child relationship in this
family. The example is located at the site of the proximal already-spoken
in its struggle between the relationship identity in place in the past and
a potential redefinition of the relationship in the present.

The third discursive form of playfulness that Bakhtin (1981d) discussed is the clown who merges the rogue and the fool: "He is a rogue
who dons the mask of the fool in order to motivate distortions and
shufflings of languages and labels" (p. 405). Whereas the rogue enacts
parody and the fool enacts misunderstanding, the stance of the clown
involves a playfully "malicious distortion" (p. 405) of a given system of
meaning, creating the possibility for laughter at the absurdity of the
targeted discourse. When a child enacts a distorted and exaggerated
impersonation of her parents' style of reprimand which brings everyone
to laughter, she is playfully challenging the discourse of parental
authority in the family. The child is opening the possibility of a different

sharp disapproval

parenting style for the present in challenging the parenting style that has organized her parent-child relationship in the past; the discursive struggle is thus located at the site of the proximal already-spoken of past and present relational identities.

Bakhtin (1981d; 1984b) discussed the playfulness of the rogue, fool, and clown exclusively in the context of novels. But these discursive forms hold rich potential for understanding how playful interaction between relational partners and family members can function to contest systems of meaning. Baxter (1992a) observed that play does serious work in relationships, although perhaps in nonobvious ways. For example, relationship parties can sometimes defuse the tensions of interpersonal conflict by framing their complaints as playful teasing.

Polemical–Transformative Struggle

i.e., express critical opinion

With the fourth, and last, dimension of synchronic interplay the possibility exists to move from a zero-sum logic, in which competing discourses are jockeying for center-margin positioning, to a profound realignment of discourses in which new meanings are created. The other three dimensions—antagonistic-nonantagonistic, direct-indirect, serious-playful—are largely features of communication practices that are, in one way or another, polemic (Bakhtin, 1984b, p. 195). That is, the utterance is a site where centripetal and centrifugal discourses strike "polemic blow[s]" (p. 195) that are hostile and aggressive toward one another. In polemical utterances, discourses are in play in a competitive, opposing manner.

i.e., mild

Polemical interplay is its most benign when discourses enact what Baxter and Montgomery (1996) called *balance*. While the alternative discourses are still framed in a zero-sum competition, balance is a discursive truce of sorts enacted through compromise. In discursive compromise, neither discourse is embraced fully, but both are partially affirmed. For example, consider a marital couple nonantagonistically discussing how to spend their Christmas holiday; they are torn between wanting to spend it alone as a couple, a decision embedded in a discourse of individualism, or whether to spend it with her parents, a decision embedded in a discourse of community. This discursive struggle is located at two sites: the distal already-spoken (with the cultural discourses of individualism and community) and the distal not-yet-spoken (the anticipation of what her parents expect). The couple discusses the pros and cons, appreciating that neither decision is without disadvantage, and they jointly decide to spend Christmas Eve with her parents and Christmas Day by themselves. This discursive compromise still positions the competing discourses as a zero-sum exercise; from the couple's perspective, they can't have it both ways. The decision they reach compromises both discourses, partially satisfying both and partially denying both.

An example of balance, or compromise, in the RDT-informed research is the study by Kline, Stafford, & Miklosovic (1996) on women's surname choices upon marriage. Women who used combinations of the wife's surname with the husband's surname made sense of this decision as a compromise between their loyalty to their own family legacy and to their professional identity, on the one hand, and the traditional expectation of marriage, on the other hand. Discourses of individualism and community framed this decision and its meaning.

Transformation marks idealized dialogue in which one discourse "no longer oppressively dominates the other [discourses] . . . it loses its composure and confidence, becomes agitated, internally undecided and two-faced" (Bakhtin, 1984b, p. 198). In this idealized discursive moment of dialogue, discourses lose their zero-sum relation of opposition and become open to the possibility for newly emergent meanings. In dialogism theory, discursive transformation is evaluated as superior to all forms of polemic enactment, because it realizes the dialogic potentiality for creativity—emergent new meanings.

Baxter and Montgomery (1996) referred to these transformational possibilities as *integration* and *recalibration*. Drawing more closely on Bakhtin's (1981d, 1993) language, Baxter and Braithwaite (2008b) referred to them as *hybrids* and *aesthetic moments*, respectively, and I will adopt these terms here. Both involve a mixing of discourses in a way that moves beyond a zero-sum dynamic. Hybridization—the formation of discursive hybrids—is a process of mixing two or more distinct discourses to create a new meaning. Baxter and Braithwaite provided this description of a hybrid discursive construction: "Think of hybrids as salad dressing made by mixing oil and vinegar. The discourses (oil and vinegar) are distinct, yet they combine to form a new meaning—salad dressing" (p. 354). The discourses are distinct, yet they are no longer framed as oppositional. Instead their interplay constructs something new—discursive salad dressing. The other form of transformation—the aesthetic moment (Bakhtin, 1990b, p. 67)—involves the interpenetration of discourses in such a way that each meaning system is profoundly reconstructed. Baxter and Braithwaite described this kind of transformation in this way: "Think of aesthetic moments as akin to what chemists call 'reactions.' For example, two molecules of hydrogen combine with one molecule of oxygen to produce an entirely new entity—water" (p. 355). Unlike salad dressing—in which the oil and vinegar sustain their own integrities as they mix, the constituent elements of water are profoundly altered in their reaction.

Much of the RDT-centered work on rituals examines discursive transformations, and I discuss rituals below in the next section of this chapter devoted to communication genres. However, let me illustrate some nonritualized enactments of discursive transformation. Miller-Day's (2004) detailed study of grandmother-mother-daughter relationships nicely illustrates the enactment of hybrids for her connected relationships, in contrast to her enmeshed relationships. As discussed earlier, these female relationships were organized into two types—enmeshed and connected. Whereas daughter autonomy was framed as oppositional to connection in enmeshed relationships, connected relationships were able to embrace the autonomy that comes from a daughter who grows up. According to Miller-Day, "Differentiation [autonomy] in nonenmeshed relationships did not appear to be interpreted as a threat. . . . In fact, most women in the connected maternal relationships expressed pride in the unique qualities of their grandmothers/mothers/daughters" (p. 120). Autonomy (differentiation) and connection were discrete systems of meaning; in her nonenmeshed maternal relationships, however, (grand)mothers and (grand)daughters were able to transform them from competitive to noncompetitive.

Baxter and DeGooyer (2001) examined whether relationship parties could recall experiencing aesthetic moments in their interactions with familial and nonfamilial significant others. Their participants reported that indeed they had experienced such events, characterized by a sense of fleeting consummation or wholeness from seemingly disparate fragments. Participants felt as if these events were moments of aesthetic beauty—pieces of interactional art, if you will. A variety of experiences were reported, of which *conversational flow* was one type, and which other researchers have similarly identified as such (e.g., Tannen, 1984). Baxter and DeGooyer described this aesthetic moment this way:

> This category refers to a sense of emotional connection with another achieved by somehow being "in sync." Participant accounts described these interaction events as effortless, easy, and flowing. The parties reported experiencing a sense of seamlessness, as if they were completing each other's thoughts. . . . The focus is on the moment and the way the parties are able to craft jointly an enjoyable, effortless exchange. Often, participants made a point of telling us that they could not recall the details of the conversation—the topics of discussion, who said what. Rather, the event's meaning was derived from the way in which the conversation was enacted. (p. 9)

Conversational flow is a fleeting experience in which parties feel as if they are able to reframe basic differences of Self and Other into a sense of seamless oneness. This interactional flow illustrates the essence of an aesthetic moment: opposing discourses (here, embodied in the disparate worldviews of Self and Other) are temporarily reconstituted along new lines of meaning in which the old systems of meaning are dissolved.

The aesthetic moment is an interactional event that sits in the affective realm, rather than the rational realm. Much of the research in interpersonal and family communication is framed in a logic of rationality (Cronen, 1998). This logic frames interpersonal communication as a means-end operation in which the researcher's goal is that of determining the goals or ends that an individual seeks to accomplish and the communicative means by which those goals are obtained. The strategies and tactics tradition of research exemplifies this rationality bias (e.g., Daly & Wiemann, 1994). A number of scholars have suggested that more attention should instead be paid to the place of emotion in interpersonal communication (e.g.,Vangelisti, 1993). Aesthetic interactions are emotion-laden interactions characterized by deep pleasure, stimulation, and joy as a result of interactional beauty (Williams, 1983). Although communicators can achieve the joy of accomplishment in achieving their communicative goals, the joy of the aesthetic moment is not organized around goal achievement but rather the fleeting wholeness that is constructed from disparate parts. Writing at about the same time as Bakhtin (1990b), Dewey (1934) noted the value of complementing a focus on rationality with a focus on aesthetics.

To Bakhtin (1990b), aesthetic moments are peak experiences (Goodall & Kellett, 2004) in which parties are able to transform a disparate system of meaning into a new meaning of the moment, a new meaning that dissolves discursive struggles into a felt wholeness of some sort. As I discussed in Chapter 2, Bakhtin focused on the different worldviews of Self and Other, but here, I broaden the aesthetic moment to include any discursive struggle that is temporarily transformed. It is important to distinguish the aesthetic moment from a traditional Hegelian dialectic that moves from thesis to antithesis to synthesis. Whereas synthesis is a permanent resolution of oppositions, Bakhtin's aesthetic moment is a fleeting interactional moment.

Both hybrids and aesthetic moments share the spotlight of idealized dialogue, according to Bakhtin (1981d; 1984b). In dialogism theory, as well as RDT, they are preferred communication praxis enactments because they realize fully the dialogic potential to construct new systems of meaning wrought from the struggle of competing discourses.

To this point in the chapter, I have discussed communication characteristics of the utterance chain based on the simplistic assumption that the utterance, while intertextual, is nonetheless the only unit of analysis by which to understand competing discourses in play. In fact, utterances are embedded in larger social packages known as genres, to which I turn next.

❖ COMMUNICATION GENRES OF DISCURSIVE STRUGGLE

For purposes of our discussion, communication genres can be understood as "historically and culturally specific, prepatterned and complex solutions to recurrent communicative problems" (Gunthner & Knoblauch, 1995, p. 8). Typical everyday genres in contemporary mainstream American communication include such phenomena as *small talk* (in response to the communicative problem of passing time in a pleasant but not overly intimate manner), *making plans* (in response to the communicative problem of coordinating future action between persons), and *catching up* (in response to the communicative problem of establishing continuity with someone not seen in a while), among others (Goldsmith & Baxter, 1996). Although researchers have studied genres from several analytical perspectives (for useful discussions, see Goldsmith & Baxter, 1996, and Mayes, 2005), Bakhtin (1986b) suggested the value of examining genres with a dialogic eye, attending to the ways in which they are "filled with dialogic overtones" (p. 92). In particular, Bakhtin observed that communication genres may vary in their dialogic potential. White (2003) elaborated on this point, suggesting that ways of speaking can be "broadly divided into those which entertain or open up the space for dialogic alternatives and . . . those which suppress or close down the space for such alternation" (p. 259). Genres that feature what White calls "heteroglossic engagement" (p. 261) are *dialogically expansive*, whereas genres that have more limited heteroglossic engagement are *dialogically contractive*.

Throughout his career, Bakhtin repeatedly returned to two genres of communication that he identified, in White's (2003) terms, as dialogically expansive: the novel and the carnival. I will adapt these to interpersonal communication below in discussing narrative stories and the carnivalesque, respectively. To these two I add a third genre that has emerged in the RDT-based research as dialogically expansive: relationship rituals. Certainly, this discussion of three dialogically expansive genres does not exhaust the domain. The consideration of genres with respect to their heteroglossic engagement is a significant issue for future RDT-based scholars to pursue. But this discussion will give us a starting point.

Narrative Stories

As a literary scholar, Bakhtin (1981a; 1981c; 1981d; 1984b) argued that the novel is a profoundly dialogic genre, especially when authored by the novelist he most admired—Dostoevsky. In shifting from literary genres to interpersonal talk, I shift scholarly gaze from the novel to narrative stories. To Bakhtin's way of thinking, the artistry of Dostoevsky was in realizing the novel's potential to move beyond a single monolithic authorial viewpoint to capture a multiplicity of clashing viewpoints, often embodied in characters who embody "specific world views, each characterized by its own objects, meanings and values" (Bakhtin, 1981d, p. 292).

Any narrative story—whether in the form of a novel or a tale told aloud—holds dialogic potential because of its capacity to place several viewpoints in play simultaneously. And the narrator doesn't have to have Dostoevsky's skill as a novelist to tell dialogically expansive stories; ordinary people do this with some poignancy. In 1992, I wrote that my understanding of interpersonal communication was

> soundly shaken the first time I conducted an in-depth narrative interview study about people's experiences in their personal relationships. I was struck by the contradictions, contingencies, nonrationalities, and multiple realities to which people gave voice in their narrative sense making of their relational lives. (Baxter, 1992b, p. 330)

Because of the potential for the narrative story to be dialogically expansive, researchers would be well served by listening to them for the interplay of competing discourses at any of the four sites of the utterance chain that I discussed in the prior two chapters. Unfortunately, only limited research has adopted a dialogic eye in narrative inquiry (e.g., De Fina, 2003; Maybin, 1996; Menard-Warnick, 2005). My own program of research with several colleagues over the years, discussed at several points throughout the chapters of this book, has relied on the narrative accounts that participants enact in the context of in-depth interviews. Although these elicited narratives provide a fruitful ground to examine discursive struggles, they are removed from everyday storytelling. The research program of Bochner and his colleagues (e.g., Bochner, 2002; Bochner & Ellis, 1992; Bochner, Ellis, & Tillmann-Healy, 1997, 1998) has focused on researcher-told autoethnographic narratives as a way to illuminate the human communicative experience. Contradiction features centrally in their understanding of everyday narratives:

> Our project reconfigures dialectic as a narrative activity permeated by contradiction. Narrative is both a means of coping with contradiction and a way of communicating to others the concrete details associated with the experiencing of contradictions. . . . A narrative approach to dialectical research on personal relationships is intended to show how people breach canonical conventions and expectations; how they cope with exceptional, difficult, and transformative crises in their relationships; how they invent new ways of speaking when old ways fail them; how they make the absurd sensible and the disastrous manageable; and how they turn the calamities of fate into the gifts of humanity. (Bochner et al., 1998, p. 53)

A useful exemplar of a dialogically-focused study of narratives is Menard-Warnick's (2007) analysis of an extended personal narrative from a life history interview with a female Mexican immigrant. This narrative constructed for the hearer the identity of her Mexican family of origin and her identity as a "good daughter" (p. 293) within that family. In telling the story of the reactions of family and community members to her younger sister's unmarried pregnancy in her home village in Mexico, the narrator wove together multiple discourses with competing gender ideologies. Her father's voice represented the discourse of sexual morality, a worldview in which a woman must be a virgin when she marries. The sister was viewed critically by the father for her violation of this discursive mandate. The narrator positioned herself as a good daughter in her own refusal to emigrate with her boyfriend before marriage, but she framed this less as a matter of loyalty to the discourse of sexual morality and more as a matter of consideration for the father's feelings, an action that is intelligible in the discourse of family unity. The family unity discourse functioned to provide an alternative system of meaning by which to understand the narrator's decision to remain a virgin, thereby challenging indirectly the authoritative voice of the sexual morality discourse. A third discourse organized the narrative, that of educational advancement. The good daughter's sister was eventually portrayed as succeeding in life by getting ahead educationally, earning respect as the owner of a small business in their hometown. This success functioned to further neutralize the discourse of sexual morality, as the "bad" daughter still made good after all.

Many narrative scholars who focus on the structural features of stories emphasize the importance of their being complete (e.g., Koenig Kellas & Manusov, 2003) or fully formed (e.g., Labov &Waletsky, 1967);

that is, social conventions exist for effective storytelling and narrators risk judgments of narrative incoherence in failing to adhere to those conventions. However, in privileging narrative coherence or completeness, researchers may pay less attention to the contradictions and fragmentations that characterize narrative stories, or worse, view them as features of incompleteness or incoherence. From a dialogic perspective, it is precisely these discursive ruptures that merit serious scholarly attention in their own right, even as they challenge the canon of a neat and tidy story with a beginning, middle, and end. A dialogic approach to narrative thus bears close resemblance to recent work on postmodern narratives which emphasize stories as fragmented, nonlinear, and disrupted (e.g., Frank, 1995).

To this point, I have emphasized the dialogic expansiveness of narrative stories based on careful study of their content. In addition, the process of storytelling (as opposed to the story's content) brings a second kind of dialogic expansiveness to bear. Stories are told to others, a feature that implicates their addressivity, a notion discussed in Chapter 4. Listeners are rarely just that, and often join the narrator as a coteller in what is a jointly constructed telling of a story (e.g., Koenig Kellas, 2005; Koenig Kellas & Trees, 2006; Veroff, Sutherland, Chadiha, & Ortega, 1993). Listeners also function as the anticipated not-yet-spoken, and narrators, anticipating their listeners' reactions, adapt accordingly as they undertake the telling of the story.

I will return to narrative stories in the next chapter where I discuss the methodological value of studying all dialogically expansive genres, including narrative stories.

The Carnivalesque

A second genre that received attention from Bakhtin (1984b, 1984c) is the medieval carnival, and more generally, social events characterized by a carnivalesque spirit. The carnivalesque spirit embraces the playful tone described earlier in this chapter. Carnivalesque events are those in which social life "is drawn out of its usual rut, it is to some extent 'life turned inside out, the reverse side of the world'" (1984b, p. 122). The ordinary rules, roles, and expectations that organize day-to-day life are suspended, especially hierarchical structure and "all forms of reverence, piety, and etiquette connected with it" (1984b, p. 123). Carnival "combines the sacred with the profane, the lofty with the low, the great with the insignificant, the wise with the stupid" (1984b, p. 123). The carnivalesque spirit features a mock decrowning of all that is normally accepted as appropriate, as participants enact "eccentricity, the violation of the usual and the generally accepted, life drawn out of its usual rut" (1984b, p. 126). The carnivalesque is characterized by satire, parody and laughter directed toward centripetal discourses, creating openings for alternative discourses to be heard and celebrated. Opposing discourses are in outrageous conversation, "all annihilating and all-renewing" (1984b, p. 124). The carnivalesque spirit is one of ambivalence which "absolutizes nothing, but rather proclaims the joyful relativity of everything" (1984b, p. 125). Although some critics argue that Bakhtin's carnivalesque is a mere venting device that temporarily relieves social frustrations with social hierarchy before a return to life as usual, Bakhtin believed that the carnivalesque spirit holds dialogic potential for profound social change. It is, thus, a genre that is dialogically expansive in its hybridization of discourses. Competing discourses are copresent but their opposition is temporarily suspended in the playful quality of their interplay.

Very little work has been done on the carnivalesque with respect to communication in personal relationships. It is most certainly an understudied phenomenon that merits serious attention from scholars. Clark's (2005) ethnographic study of Halloween in some American families is a useful exemplar of a carnivalesque communication event. Clark found that the celebration of Halloween by children and their parents was steeped in the carnivalesque spirit. The event was characterized by power reversals in which normal parental expectations and rules (e.g., "don't talk to strangers," "don't eat candy," "don't play outside at night") were upended. Children and their parents suspended such constraints as etiquette, decency, and hierarchy. Children were the empowered parties, with threats of tricking adults in the absence of treats. Children jettisoned their normal roles as dependent beings, transforming themselves through costumes into frightful entities who provoked mock fear in themselves and from the adult community. Adults participated in provoking fear in children through their decorations and organized feats such as haunted houses, but it was refracted through a carnivalesque spirit of laughter and fun. Fear and fun, the imagery of death (e.g., ghosts and ghouls) in play with life (the youthful vitality of children)—these were the symbolic currencies of the Halloween event. Clark argued that Halloween suspends the constraints that organize childhood, providing children with a glimpse of the broader horizons that await them in adult life and alternative ways to negotiate the parent-child relationship.

What are other candidates for the carnivalesque in everyday interpersonal life? I suspect that families may have inversion events of one kind or another, in which children act as parents for the moment, assuming temporary positions of authority to parents who perform in child-dependent ways. When children satirize, parody, or tease their parents, similar carnivalesque work may be underway, as well. Family vacations may bracket life as usual, allowing family members to escape from their everyday ruts, opening up discursive space for episodes of crazy time in which centripetal discourses of one kind or another may be challenged in a mocking way.

Research on adult play in romantic and marital relationships and in friendship relationships suggests that it may feature the carnivalesque. Baxter (1992a), for example, found that some forms of adult play allow parties to deal with sensitive issues in ways that allow the parties to distance their personal identities and egos from the event. Such playfulness may enact the serious work of creating openings for alternative perspectives to be heard by the parties.

Carnivalesque enactments are a specific form of ritual, the third dialogically expansive genre to which I turn next.

Relationship Rituals

RDT-informed research has identified the transformative work that characterizes the enactment of meaningful rituals in personal and familial relationships. For our purposes, a ritual can be understood as "a voluntary, recurring, patterned communication event whose jointly enacted performance by family members [or relationship partners more generally] pays homage to what they regard as sacred, thereby producing and reproducing a family's [relationship's] identity and its web of social relations" (Baxter & Braithwaite, 2006a, pp. 262–263). When a ritual is successfully performed, it is transformative in the dialogical sense, enacting either a hybrid construction or perhaps even an aesthetic moment. Roberts (1988) analyzed rituals in this way, which builds the case for rituals as communicative hybrids:

> Rituals can hold both sides of a contradiction at the same time. We all live with the ultimate paradoxes of life/death, connection/distance, ideal/real, good/evil. Ritual can incorporate both sides of contradictions so that they can be managed simultaneously. For instance, a wedding ceremony has within it both loss and mourning and joy and celebration. (p. 16)

Roberts's claim envisions rituals as combinations of opposing discourses, but his description suggests that the combination is on the order of the metaphorical salad dressing characteristic of the hybrid: the discourses, while combined in a collaborative way, still sustain their discrete meanings. By contrast, when rituals function to realize aesthetic moments, the integrity of the competing discourses dissolves into a fleeting wholeness—the metaphorical chemical reaction I described earlier in the chapter.

Both hybrids and aesthetic moments can be identified from existing RDT-based research on rituals. An example of a hybrid ritual is Bryant's (2006) study of stepfamilies formed after the death of a spouse/parent. She found that some stepfamilies, which she labeled *integrated* families, honored through rituals both the new stepfamily relationships as well as the relationships with the deceased spouse/parent. For example, the ritual of the stepparent and stepchild visiting the grave of the deceased parent in honor of that person's day of birth was a way to celebrate the closeness of the stepparent-stepchild bond as well as to honor the memory of the deceased parent-child bond.

Stepfamily rituals are empty or hollow when either the old family identity or the new family identity is silenced. Baxter and her colleagues (Baxter, Braithwaite et al., 2009) found support for this claim in the ritual of the remarriage ceremony in stepfamilies. Although the remarrying adults found joy in their remarriage ceremony, stepchildren often reported that the event was empty because it paid insufficient homage to the memory of their family of origin. By contrast, the remarriage ceremony was a meaningful event to those stepchildren who felt that both their old family of origin and the new family were receiving honor in some way. For example, a stepchild reported how meaningful it was for all of the stepchildren to receive rings at the wedding ceremony of her parent and stepparent; the children were honored rather than positioned as baggage left over from a failed marriage, and the newly formed stepfamily was honored in its symbolic inclusion of all family members in the ring ceremony.

The meaningfulness of these stepfamily rituals hinges on whether two competing discourses are reframed to overcome their relation of opposition to construct a both/and celebration of both. However, each discourse retains its integrity as a meaning system, and successful rituals are those in which both intact discourses are honored. This hybrid celebration is different from the ritualized aesthetic moment.

A candidate for a ritualized aesthetic moment is the marriage renewal event among long-time married couples (Baxter & Braithwaite, 2002; Braithwaite & Baxter, 1995). Based on in-depth interviews with spouses who had renewed their wedding vows, Baxter and Braithwaite identified several competing discourses at play in the ritual: marriage as a private relationship versus marriage as a public institution, marriage as a stable institution versus marriage as a dynamic system, marriage as a convention versus marriage as a unique creation of two, and marriage as a celebration of individualism versus marriage as a celebration of community. However, the participant accounts of their ceremony were closer to a chemical reaction than a salad dressing. That is, the renewal vows were regarded as meaningful because of the sense of consummation or wholeness that was experienced. For example, one participant spoke of the renewal event as "more like celebrating the whole family, the whole experience. Families are coming together in love, and [the renewal] acknowledges that in the affirmation [of the marital vows]" (Braithwaite & Baxter, p. 185). To this woman, there was a seamlessness between the marriage dyad and the larger extended family—in the ceremony, they were synergistically merged in a larger celebration of family.

Additional dialectically oriented research on rituals supports the claim that rituals are dialogically expansive in their capacity to sustain multiple competing discourses; however, these studies lack sufficient detail to determine whether the rituals are hybrid enactments or aesthetic moments. For example, Bruess & Pearson (2002) found in their study of adult friendships and marital relationships that

> rituals provide members with mechanisms to cope simultaneously with a variety of dialectical oppositions. . . . Participants in this study frequently commended the ability of their rituals to simultaneously provide a sense of familiarity via their predictability and a sense of excitement in their often spontaneous adaptability. Comments also reveal that rituals function to manage other common oppositional forces, such as needs for both openness and closedness. (p. 324)

On its face, this description implies a hybrid construction in which the integrity of both competing discursive systems is sustained in a given ritual enactment, but readers are given insufficient detail to determine whether this is the case. Other dialectically oriented studies of ritual similarly lack the rich detail necessary to sort out hybrid rituals from aesthetic moments, although they support in general the dialogic expansiveness of the ritual genre (e.g., Suter, Bergen, Daas, & Durham, 2006; Toller, 2005). Clearly, future research needs to attend systematically to the two ways in which discursive transformations can be constructed in rituals: the hybrid and the aesthetic moment. Although both forms support the ritual genre as dialogically expansive, they accomplish this expansiveness in different ways.

❖ CONCLUSION

In this chapter, I have attended to the processes and forms of dialogic struggle, in contrast to the prior two chapters in which I focused on the discourses that were in competition. This chapter has given serious attention to power—the unequal discursive playing field marked by centripetal and centrifugal positioning of discourses. Many utterances and genres perform a reproductive function in that they perpetuate the dominance of centripetal discourses. All utterances, however, hold dialogic potential to shift the power relations among competing discourses. Further, some utterances and genres—those that are dialogically expansive—hold the greatest potential to produce new systems of meaning, not simply reshuffle the center-margin positions of existing discourses. In the end, the dialogic project is most interested in those occasions when new meanings are wrought from existing systems of meaning—occasions of transformation through hybrids or aesthetic moments.

Taken as a set, Chapters 3, 4, and 5 provide a conceptual grid with which to think about discursive struggle, and I will discuss the methodological implications of this grid in the next chapter.

❖ ENDNOTE

1. Although I continue to use the term *praxis*, it is important to note for the interested reader that this chapter's development of the concept modifies the Baxter and Montgomery (1996) eight-fold typology of praxis enactments in several ways. RDT 2.0 eliminates two of those praxis enactments because they represent general attitudes toward discursive struggle rather than communicative enactments. *Disorientation* was identified by Baxter and Montgomery as a fatalistic attitude in which discursive struggles are regarded negatively; relationship parties feel trapped and unable to cope with their contradictory relationship. By contrast, *reaffirmation* was identified by Baxter and Montgomery as an attitudinal acceptance, perhaps even celebration, of the inevitability of discursive struggle. Although both of these attitudes are important with respect to the potential for relationship parties to function dialogically, they are not communicative in and of themselves, and I eliminate them from further discussion. Further, the three major points developed in this chapter depart in some important ways from Baxter and Montgomery's treatment of praxis. RDT 2.0 centers power, which was not developed in the 1996 articulation of the theory. Additionally, this chapter emphasizes synchronic interpenetration of discourses more so than diachronic praxis. Last, RDT 2.0 emphasizes that different genres of communication vary in their dialogic potential, a point undeveloped in 1996.

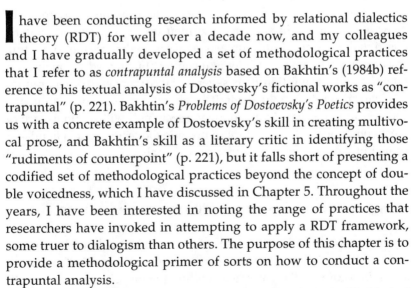

6

Doing Contrapuntal
Analysis

❖ ❖ ❖

I have been conducting research informed by relational dialectics
theory (RDT) for well over a decade now, and my colleagues
and I have gradually developed a set of methodological practices
that I refer to as *contrapuntal analysis* based on Bakhtin's (1984b) reference to his textual analysis of Dostoevsky's fictional works as "contrapuntal" (p. 221). Bakhtin's *Problems of Dostoevsky's Poetics* provides
us with a concrete example of Dostoevsky's skill in creating multivocal prose, and Bakhtin's skill as a literary critic in identifying those
"rudiments of counterpoint" (p. 221), but it falls short of presenting a
codified set of methodological practices beyond the concept of double voicedness, which I have discussed in Chapter 5. Throughout the
years, I have been interested in noting the range of practices that
researchers have invoked in attempting to apply a RDT framework,
some truer to dialogism than others. The purpose of this chapter is to
provide a methodological primer of sorts on how to conduct a contrapuntal analysis.

At its most general level, contrapuntal analysis is a specific kind of
discourse analysis. As Taylor (2001) has indicated, discourse analysis is

"best understood as a field of research rather than a single practice" (p. 5). She advanced a loose definition as a cover term for the family of approaches that individually and collectively are labeled *discourse analysis:* "Discourse analysis is the close study of language in use" (p. 5). What distinguishes one form of discourse analysis from another are the particular analytic concepts involved in studying language in use:

> Analytic concepts are given by the theoretical tradition, the research questions, and so on. The discourse analyst searches for patterns in language in use, building on and referring back to the assumptions she or he is making about the nature of language, interaction and society and the interrelationships between them. It is this theoretical underpinning rather than any sorting process which distinguishes discourse analyses. (Taylor, p. 39)

The view that discourse analysis is a family of methodological practices that vary by the analytic perspective of the researcher is a common one among discourse analysis scholars (e.g., Phillips & Hardy, 2002; Van Dijk, 1985; Wood & Kroeger, 2000). The key to contrapuntal analysis is marked by the term *contrapuntal,* which is a musical term that refers to the playing of contrasting or counterpoint melodies in conjunction with one another. A contrapuntal analysis focuses on the interplay of contrasting discourses (i.e., systems of meaning, points of view, world views) in spoken or written texts. The general analytic question that guides contrapuntal analysis is, "What are the competing discourses in the text and how is meaning constructed through their interplay?" This question flags several key components of contrapuntal analysis, each of which merits elaboration: text, competing discourses, and interplay. In the following sections, I will attend to each of these components in an attempt to provide the reader with a hands-on primer on how to execute a contrapuntal analysis.

❖ SELECTING TEXTS IN CONTRAPUNTAL ANALYSIS

It is impossible to address the issue of text selection without drawing on the Bakhtinian notion of the utterance chain elaborated in Chapters 3 and 4. In Bakhtin's dialogism, a text is an utterance chain in which both proximal and distal discourses interpenetrate—what I have called intertextuality elsewhere in the book. A researcher using contrapuntal analysis interprets communicative texts in order to understand them as utterance chains.

Although dialogism presupposes that all communication texts hold dialogic potential, I have learned over the years that the transparency of the struggle between competing discourses varies from text to text. As noted in Chapter 5, on a continuum from fully monologic to fully dialogic (Bakhtin, 1984b), some texts are dialogically contractive (Martin & White, 2005; White, 2003); that is, the text is characterized by a narrow range of discourses, perhaps only a single monologic perspective. Other texts, by contrast, are dialogically expansive (Martin & White; White), in which it is easier to hear multiple competing discourses at play. Both kinds of texts are worthy of analysis, but for different purposes. Dialogically contractive texts are worthy of attention from a critical lens, focusing the scholar's energies around identifying the discursive practices by which some discourses are marginalized and dismissed. Dialogically expansive texts, in which multiple voices are at play (although not necessarily on an equal discursive playing field), are fruitfully analyzed in order to examine how meaning emerges from the interpenetration of various discourses.

My general advice to a beginning dialogic scholar who seeks to understand relationship communication from an RDT perspective is to select communication texts in which competing discourses are likely to be etched in bold relief. But how does one know which those are? One possible starting point is to select communication enactments that exemplify dialogically rich genres of communication. As discussed in Chapter 5, narrative stories, carnivalesque events, and relationship rituals are, on theoretical grounds, potentially fruitful discursive sites in which to identify contrapuntal intertextuality.

Alternatively, the RDT-informed scholar might be attracted to communicative enactments that are commonly purported to be problematic or are sites of rupture, challenge, or change, because the animation of competing discourses is likely to be particularly salient. For example, colleagues and I have conducted several studies on stepfamily communication using RDT as a theoretical framework (e.g., Baxter, Braithwaite, Bryant, & Wagner, 2004; Braithwaite & Baxter, 2006), because a common finding in prior stepfamily research was that this is a very problematic family form for stepparents, stepchildren, and the remarried couple, replete with hints of antagonistic struggles among divergent systems of meaning. More recently, colleagues and I have begun a series of investigations into voluntary kin—those persons we think of as "family" even though they aren't related by blood or law (e.g., Baxter, Braithwaite, & Bach, 2009; Braithwaite et al., (in press). Existing research suggested to us the liminal status of these relationships, and we thought it might be a

dialogically expansive site because of its very liminality at the boundaries of what is regarded as family. A number of other RDT-informed
researchers have also been attracted to particular relationships in part
because they have been identified in existing research as somehow
problematic or challenging in some way, and I have reviewed much
of this research in prior chapters.

In addition, relationship transitions are likely candidates for high-
lighting dialogic struggles in bold relief. In Chapter 4, I discussed the
concept of the turning point (Bolton, 1961) as a moment of change in a
relationship, and I flag it here as a fruitful method by which to identify
these significant points of transition in any relationship's history.
Turning points are moments of change—both qualitative and quantitative and both positive and negative. At a minimum, they afford
researchers an opportunity to concentrate on a particular site in the
utterance chain: the proximal already-spoken in which the communicative past of a relationship is put in play with the communicative present.
Researchers can benefit, as well, from identifying a particular kind of
transition as a site for gathering communication texts; for example, the
transition from marital status to divorced status (e.g., Graham, 2003).

When in doubt about whether a given relational site is dialogically
expansive, colleagues and I have often found it productive to ask participants what, if anything, they find challenging about the communicative conduct of their relationships. When competing discourses are
salient in the meaning-making process, parties often talk of this with
ambivalence, referring to feeling caught in a catch-22, feeling trapped
between the proverbial rock and a hard place, feeling "damned if they
do, damned if they don't," and so forth. However, for parties who have
constructed meaning hybrids or aesthetic moments, such markers of
ambivalence will be absent. Thus, this strategy's usefulness is probably
limited to nonantagonistic struggles in which discourses are still in
competition with one another.

Although the generic analytic question that guides contrapuntal
analysis inquires about the interplay of competing discourses in texts,
researchers may have more focused research questions in mind. For
example, if a researcher is particularly interested in understanding
relationship communication as an instance of cultural communication,
the focus will probably narrow to the sites of the utterance chain where
cultural discourses appear to be most salient: the distal already-spoken
and the distal not-yet-spoken. I have more to say about how one identifies cultural discourses in the next section of the chapter, for they are
often implicit rather than explicit in language use. For now, I simply
note that a researcher interested in understanding relationships as

deeply cultured communication processes needs expertise in the communication codes of the specific culture, whether that expertise is derived from immersion in the research literature on that culture's communication codes or from ethnographic participant observation as part of the researcher's own study (e.g., Fitch, 1998).

Relationship parties always speak culture in the privacy of the conversations between them, but they also speak culture when they communicate at the borders of private and public life—those communication episodes in which relationships are enacted in so-called public settings. When relationship parties present themselves publicly to outsiders, when parties talk about their relationship to third parties, when others talk about relationships in their midst through gossip and similar communicative enactments—these are occasions when cultural codes are implicated in order to render the relationship intelligible to fellow members of the culture. Border work—communicative enactments in which relationships go public in a variety of ways—is thus fruitful in understanding cultural discourses of relating.

It is this argument, in fact, that has led my colleagues and me to conduct interviews with relationship parties across several studies reviewed elsewhere in this book. However, our understanding of the interview departs from the standard conception of this method as a neutral data-gathering device in which the interviewee transmits information to the interviewer who subsequently analyzes its content as a referential record of what happens in a relationship. Our understanding of the interview is closer to that articulated by Mishler (1986); that is, an interview is itself a speech event with at least two participants engaged in the joint enterprise of meaning making—the interviewer and the interviewee. In this alternative understanding of the interview, participants are engaged in border work in which they are publicly constructing their relationship to a stranger—the interviewer. In this approach to interviewing, a participant's language use is viewed as identity work, an occasion in which the identity of the relationship is constructed and presented to the interviewer in order to render it intelligible. The stories that interviewees tell, the accounts they give of their successes and failures—these draw on cultural discourses in order to render them intelligible to cultural outsiders, most immediately the interviewer.

A researcher interested in a dialogic understanding of how a relationship's systems of meaning change over time would probably emphasize a different site of the utterance chain: the proximal already-spoken. As discussed in Chapter 4, this site focuses analytic attention on how relationship identity changes from the past to the present across a relationship's history. Obviously, an interest in this discursive site would benefit from longitudinal methods that allow the researcher to gather communication texts from at least two points in time. In the absence of communication texts from different points in time, the researcher can rely on retrospective constructions provided by the relationship partici- pants themselves, often in an interviewing venue but not necessarily. Participants can talk about their relationships to others in naturally occurring talk, for example, storytelling. As noted in the prior para- graph, however, the focus is less on viewing the participant words as a referential record of the objective relational past and more on viewing the language use as a way to understand how the participant himself or herself does relational identity work in rendering intelligible to outsiders (the interviewer) how the relational past is in play with the relational present. However, an interest in the proximal already-spoken is best served by interactional data between relationship parties.

A researcher interested in the parties' self-identity work in the moment would probably approach the process of identifying texts with a focus on yet a different site in the utterance chain: the proximal not- yet-spoken. As discussed in Chapter 4, this site focuses analytic atten- tion on how it is that parties anticipate one another's responses when they speak and thus navigate the dance of their similarities and differ- ences. A researcher interested in this site of the utterance chain could benefit most from gathering naturally occurring conversations enacted between the parties.

In short, researchers might choose to emphasize one or another of the sites of the utterance chain over others, depending on the particu- lar focus of the research question. Depending on which facets of the utterance chain hold interest to the researcher, he or she will be attracted to different kinds of texts for subsequent analysis, drawing upon an array of data-gathering methods including ethnographic par- ticipant observation, in-depth interviewing, and observing naturally occurring talk between partners. To date, the bulk of the RDT-informed research has relied heavily on texts in the form of interview transcripts. Although these texts inform us about pieces of the utterance chain, future researchers need to draw upon a wider range of communication enactments in order to shed a more comprehensive view of the totality of the utterance chain that constitutes the relationship. There is, then, a practical reason why Chapter 3 is so lengthy relative to Chapter 4; interviews position us to understand the distal already-spoken cultural discourses that render relationships publicly intelligible (at least to the outsider-interviewer). The other sites of the utterance chain have not received the research attention they deserve, in part because of the data gathering bias toward interviewing.

RDT-informed researchers need to justify why they gathered texts of a particular kind. Certain kinds of communication enactments make it easier or harder to understand various facets of the utterance chain, and the researcher bears the methodological obligation to make wise decisions with respect to the kind of text(s) gathered for purposes of contrapuntal analysis.

Once a researcher has a corpus of texts—interview transcripts, field notes, conversational transcriptions—the nitty-gritty process of analysis begins. This first section has glossed over that process by simply emphasizing the sites of the utterance chain as a theoretical framework to guide analysis. The next section turns to the details of how a researcher can identify competing discourses.

❖ IDENTIFYING COMPETING DISCOURSES

Once a researcher has a corpus of texts ready for analysis, the issue is how to go about identifying its competing discourses, if in fact more than one discourse is present. In this section, I will first elaborate in more detail on how one identifies a discourse, and then I will turn to the matter of how one determines whether multiple discourses are in contrapuntal relation to one another.

Identifying Discourses in Texts

As noted repeatedly throughout the book, a discourse is a system of meaning. Although relational communication can construct meanings about anything, the systems of meanings, or discourses, that I'm particularly interested in are two-fold: discourses that are implicated in individual identity (Who am I in this relationship? Who are you?) and discourses implicated in relationship identity (Who are "we"? What is our relationship?).

Discourses—systems of meaning—can be sociocultural or interpersonal in nature. Sociocultural discourses—those emphasized in the distal already-spoken and the distal not-yet-spoken—are invoked whenever relationship parties talk, individually or jointly; parties talk culture whenever they open their mouths. Interpersonal discourses are those systems of meaning that are crafted jointly between relationship parties and reflect their unique history together. These interpersonal discourses have been referred to as a relational culture (Wood, 1982), a miniculture crafted between the relationship parties and probably unique to their relationship. Interpersonal discourses are emphasized in the proximal already-spoken and the proximal not-yet-spoken. Although those who approach interpersonal communication from a psychological perspective might be tempted to add a third kind of discourse—intrapersonal and idiosyncratic to the individual's biography—I am not conceptualizing this kind of discourse as distinct from interpersonal discourses, given the dialogic view, first introduced in Chapter 2 and then elaborated in Chapter 4, that the individual Self is a social construction that emerges from the interaction of at least two parties; that is, since the individual is an interpersonal phenomenon, the Self is an interpersonal discourse for our purposes.

How does a researcher go about identifying the discourses at play in a given text? In general, the contrapuntal analyst relies on interpretive methods common to other qualitative analyses of texts. In particular, a thematic analysis is conducted. A thematic analysis is "a method for identifying, analyzing and reporting patterns (themes) within data" (Braun & Clarke, 2006, p. 79). For our purposes, a semantic theme can be regarded as a discourse. Because the steps involved in conducting a thematic analysis are fairly common across all interpretive methods, they will be only briefly discussed here. For greater detail in executing interpretive analysis in general, the interested reader can go to any number of excellent methods books (e.g., Dey, 1993; Erlandson, Harris, Skipper, & Allen, 1993; Lincoln & Guba, 1985; Lindlof & Taylor, 2002; Strauss & Corbin, 1998).

But before I discuss in a general way the steps of a thematic analysis, the distinction between manifest and latent themes must be addressed. Whereas manifest themes sit on the surface of talk—what is said—latent themes rest below the surface, functioning as the underlying meaning that often sits implicit in words. Discourses, in other words, can be both said and unsaid, a concept first discussed in Chapter 2.

A thematic analysis needs to attend to discourses at both manifest and latent levels. The identification of manifest themes is fairly straightforward because it is explicitly marked in the content of talk. Sometimes a discourse is explicitly introduced into talk through a phenomenon referred to as *reported speech* (Voloshinov, 1986) or *active double-voicedness* (Bakhtin, 1984b). Research on reported speech interestingly has a long history independent of Bakhtin's focus on competing discourses (e.g., Buttny, 1997; Holt, 1996, 2000; Tannen, 2004). Various features have been noted about reported speech (Sternberg, 1982). A basic distinction is often made between direct and indirect reported speech (Coulmas, 1986; Li, 1986). Think of direct reported speech as quotation and indirect reported speech as paraphrase. Direct reported speech names the source of the reported speech (e.g., a specific person or group of persons) and reproduces the source's words and the stylistic and other performative aspects of how the words were originally uttered (Bauman, 1986). For example, consider this utterance by a husband to his spouse: "Your mother called today and said to me in a snide way, 'How many diapers have you changed today?' It made me feel like a deadbeat dad the way she said it." This husband quotes the mother and invokes a discourse of fatherhood in which fathers and mothers are expected to share in the mundane tasks of childcare, in order to critique the mother, and perhaps the underlying discourse, as well. By contrast, indirect speech indicates the source of the reported speech and communicates the propositional content but without direct quotation. Consider the same husband who utters this statement to his wife: "Your mother called today and quizzed me about whether I'm changing diapers along with you. I don't think she feels I'm doing my share in taking care of the baby." This statement paraphrases what the mother said but does not quote it. Introduced through the indirect reported speech is the same discourse of fatherhood in which father participation in the mundane tasks of baby care is expected. Reported speech, whether direct or indirect, functions to personify a discourse by attributing it to another speaker or to a collective group of persons.

Although the identification of manifest discourses is a relatively straightforward undertaking, it is more complicated to identify discourses from unsaid, taken-for-granted presuppositions. As I conduct contrapuntal analyses, I always ask myself, "What does a listener need to know in order to render this textual segment intelligible? What sociocultural and interpersonal discourses need to be invoked to understand what this textual segment means?" It helps if the researcher has supplementary information about these discourses so that he or she can identify them, as appropriate. Thus, someone skilled at contrapuntal analysis must rely on more than the immediate textual data at hand, using a variety of methods to understand both the culture and the relational history in which a given textual utterance is embedded. Although a researcher may enter the analysis searching for these predefined discourses, executing a more deductively based analysis, I prefer to conduct contrapuntal analysis in a more inductive way, identifying discourses in an emergent way from the data. Supplementary knowledge of possible sociocultural and interpersonal discourses is used as a sensitizing tool only. That is, this knowledge is available to assist in interpreting textual data, but the researcher is first and foremost open to the possibilities of the data (Erlandson et al., 1993).

Martin and White's (2005) articulation of appraisal theory is instructive with respect to how one might locate unsaid ideological discourses in textual utterances. Appraisal theory is an extension of the systemic functional linguistic (SFL) framework of M. A. K. Halliday and his colleagues (see, for example, Halliday, 2004). Basically, it is a pragmatic linguistic analysis of how meaning is constructed in utterances with particular attention to "how writers/speakers approve and disapprove, enthuse and abhor, applaud and criticize, and with how they position their readers/listeners to do likewise" (Martin & White, p. 1). Of particular relevance to the identification of unsaid discourses is their discussion of judgment; that is, the discursive resources that speakers/writers deploy when evaluating or judging something. Judgments reflect the value-laden dimension of discourses—what is regarded as typical, good, bad, appropriate, inappropriate, etc. Thus, when a judgment is made in talk, it is grounded in an often unstated discursive system of meaning.

For example, by invoking lexical terms which indicate that something is either typical or out of the ordinary, a discourse of normality is presupposed as an unsaid backdrop. When a family member describes her family by saying, "We're a pretty normal family; we argue and make up, hate and love each other at the same time," this participant is telling us her view of what a typical, or normal family is like; she is invoking a particular discourse of family normalcy in judging her own as normal. Speakers also invoke a discourse of normality or typicality when they use lexical terms such as *naturally, obviously, of course* (Martin & White, 2005). Such lexical markers indicate in an unstated way what is taken for granted as a dominant discourse.

Similarly, judgments of propriety often invoke unstated discourses of the accepted to render them intelligible. For example, when one relationship partner says to the other, "Why didn't you call first?" the meaning of this utterance relies on an unstated discourse of propriety in which calling first is the expected, appropriate action. As a second example, consider the situation in which a relationship party advances a justification or an accounting of his or her action to another (either the relationship partner or an interviewer). Because we tend to justify our inappropriate actions rather than our appropriate actions, this kind of justificatory textual data is useful for its insights into discourses of propriety and normality.

In general, it is always helpful to imagine a given textual utterance as part of a larger conversation—in this way, a researcher is ongoingly reminded of the utterance chain of which a textual segment is a part. From a dialogic perspective, a given textual segment always refers to, or responds to, what has been said before and anticipates possible responses from actual or imagined listeners. As Voloshinov (1986) indicated,

[Communication] inevitably orients itself with respect to previous performances in the same sphere. . . . Thus [it] engages, as it were, in ideological colloquy of a large scale: it responds to something, affirms something, anticipates possible responses and objections, seeks support, and so on. (p. 139)

Bakhtin (1984b) suggested that it was useful to "unfold" (p. 214) an utterance by imagining the larger conversation of which it is a part, asking, "What prior utterances might this utterance be a response to?" and "What subsequent responses are invited by this utterance?" This process of unfolding draws attention to the already-spoken and the not-yet-spoken.

The analytical strategy of unfolding a given utterance is very helpful when the competition among discourses is not contained within a single speaker's utterance but rather diffused across the speaker's utterances (nonantagonistic struggle), or when the struggle is an antagonistic one and thus identified only through the clash of utterances by different speakers. As I note below, there is no predetermined length of talk that counts as a unit of analysis in contrapuntal analysis; rather, a given datum is that segment of text necessary to answer the analytic question. Discursive struggle may be identified within a single utterance; it may be apparent when a given utterance is followed up later in the conversation by a subsequent utterance by the same speaker; it may be evident in an adjacency pair of utterances exchanged between two speakers; it may be evident in a given utterance by one speaker and a later utterance by the partner which can be heard as responsive to the first utterance. My general point here is that there is no hard and fast rule that dictates the length of a single datum. It all depends on the particular text being analyzed.

With this discussion of the said and the unsaid in hand, the researcher can begin the formal analysis of the textual data in order to identify its themes. The six-step process of thematic analysis outlined by Braun and Clarke (2006) is common to most qualitative/interpretive analyses and is fruitful in the identification of discourses.

Step 1: Becoming familiar with the data set

Familiarity begins with an appropriate transcription of the spoken words one seeks to analyze, a process I recommend the researcher undertake himself or herself, at least in part. Unlike other kinds of discourse analyses such as conversation analysis, which require attention to minute details of how talk is uttered using some variation of the elaborate Jeffersonian system (Atkinson & Heritage, 1984), thematic analysis does not require the same level of detail. As Braun and Clarke (2006) note, "At a minimum, it requires a rigorous and thorough 'orthographic' transcript—a 'verbatim' account of all verbal (and sometimes nonverbal—e.g., coughs) utterances" (p. 88). Although transcription is a resource-intensive undertaking, there is no better way to become immersed in the data set. Once appropriate transcriptions have been generated, the researcher should then read the complete set of transcripts from beginning to end in order to gain a holistic sense of it.

Step 2: Generating initial coding categories

These are the coding categories which combine at a later stage to form themes (discourses). Let's think back to Chapter 1 in which I defined what a discourse is, using the pedestrian example of a discourse of appleness to illustrate what a system of meaning might look like. A coding category called *tartness* might consist of such textual segments as "Tart apples make really good pies" and "Tart apples are good for making caramel apples." At subsequent stages of category combination, this category might combine with a category called *sweet taste* into a larger thematic category called *apple tastes*. And so on.

The process of generating initial codes is an iterative one. The researcher starts with the first text and develops an initial code category from a textual segment that permits an answer to the general analytic question: "What is being said or implied about individual or relationship identity (or apples for that matter)?" Textual segments can vary in length, ranging from a phrase to a larger utterance chunk, as I noted above. The researcher continues interpreting the text until a second textual segment has been identified that sheds insight into individual or relationship identity construction (or apples), and this is assigned to a code category, either the same one as already identified or a new coding category. The researcher proceeds in a back-and-forth manner, coding textual segments into coding categories, revising the list of coding categories as the process unfolds until no new coding categories emerge. This is known as the point of saturation (Strauss & Corbin, 1998).

Step 3: Generating themes (discourses)

Codes developed in step 2 cohere into larger systems of meaning, which Braun and Clarke (2006) refer to as *themes*. Themes may be discourses or subcategories within a discourse domain, depending on the complexity of the discourse system. This coding stage is a re-organization task in which the researcher seeks to identify the larger patterns by clustering the lower-level codes. As in step 2, this process of reaggregation is an iterative one. It is quite likely that a semantic hierarchy will emerge at the end of this stage, in which some identified themes emerge as subthemes of higher-order themes identified in later iterations of the reaggregation process. Like step 2, this process continues until the point of saturation. Stage 3 coding may run through several cycles, with the combining of coding categories continuing until the researcher concludes that it is not possible or fruitful to continue the exercise. At the final round of stage 3, the researcher will have identified discourses.

It is important to mention that a given textual segment could become a coding category within more than one theme/discourse. For instance, recall from Chapter 3 that discourses of autonomy, connection, expression, and closedness often interpenetrate. Thus a given category developed at stage 2 or even stage 3 might do double duty by contributing to two or more related discourses. Imagine this textual segment uttered by an interviewee about her relationship with her fiancé: "Even though we're now engaged, I still don't tell him everything. I still have a life separate from him, and the same with him." The "even though" and "I still" phrases in the first independent clause of the initial sentence invoke a discourse in which engaged parties are expected to be totally open with one another; the speaker is departing from that discourse in this sentence's second independent clause and is providing the interviewer with a justification for that deviation in the second sentence. A discursive struggle of normative evaluation (how an engaged couple ought to act versus how this relationship functions in everyday life) is evident in this segment. The discourse of engaged couple status implicates a discourse of connection, and deviation from the relational script expected of engaged couples is justified by invoking a discourse of individualism. However, because expression and nonexpression are discussed as the basis of conventionality (and deviation), this textual segment also holds relevance to a discursive struggle of expression.

How code categories end up being classified for membership in given themes/discourses depends on the holistic analysis of the complete data set and thus cannot be productively settled by considering a single, isolated textual segment. My general point is that a given textual segment can, indeed, do double duty. Because the analytic enterprise is a qualitative, interpretive one, rather than a quantitative exercise of counting, we need not be concerned about giving undue weighting to a given textual segment by double counting its salience in the meaning-making process.

Step 4: Reviewing themes (discourses)

This is a checking stage in which the researcher asks himself or herself whether the identified themes are valid. Key to this step is checking the identified themes/discourses against additional data in the original data set or newly gathered texts to determine whether identified themes/discourses are replicated.

Step 5: Defining and naming themes (discourses)

During this step, the themes/discourses are finalized and conceptually defined. Additionally, the researcher is well advised to undertake additional validity checks, such as those described in Lincoln and Guba (1985), for example, researcher triangulation and member checking.

Step 6: Locating exemplars

Exemplars are identified from the data that capture the essence of a given theme/discourse. Exemplars illuminate concretely the discourses identified in steps 1–5 above.

At the completion of a thematic analysis, the researcher should have identified the discourses at play in the texts. But are the discourses competing? I turn next to this issue. In focusing on the competition of discourses, contrapuntal analysis departs from an ordinary thematic analysis, and we need to supplement the analytic process accordingly.

Identifying Whether Discourses Compete

Contrapuntal analysis presumes the native's point of view; that is, it is important to support the claim that the researcher's identification of competing discourses rings true to participants themselves. Contrapuntal analysis uses the term *native* in two ways. First, it is used to mean the participants in one's study, in which case the researcher is looking for evidence in the participants' talk that identified discourses are positioned in counterpoint relation. Second, it is used to mean a typical member of the culture in which the participants are embedded. Contrapuntal analysis opens up the term *native* in this second way to enrich the understanding of cultural discourses that may animate the distal already-spoken and the distal not-yet-spoken.

In addition, this second meaning of *native* is important in the identification of transformations in the interplay of discourse. As discussed in Chapter 4, transformative struggle involves a reframing of the contrapuntal relation between discourses so that they are no longer competing. In order to identify such reframings, the researcher may find it helpful to argue that discourses are framed as competing by typical members of a cultural system. For example, the long-time married couples in the Baxter and Braithwaite (2002) study of the renewal of marriage vows did not position marriage-as-a-stable-institution and marriage-as-dynamic as competing; rather, these two discourses were reframed as integral to one another. However, the authors identified in their review of literature evidence to support the claim that in the mainstream American culture, these two discursive positions are not framed as compatible but competing visions of what marriage is. This discrepancy between the attributed view of the cultural native and the natives of the study is suggestive of a possible transformation of the meaning of marriage by those who enacted the renewal vow ceremony.

The remainder of this section is focused on how natives in the first sense of the term mark discourses as competing in their talk. Contrapuntal analysis at this step benefits greatly from the work on engagement in appraisal theory (Martin & White, 2005). Engagement refers to "all those locutions which provide the means for the authorial voice to position itself with respect to, and hence to 'engage' with, the other voices and alternative positions constructed as being in play in the current communicative context" (Martin & White, p. 94). According to appraisal theory, a speaker's talk can be examined for the ways in which the speaker's position is aligned or disaligned with respect to various value positions (discourses) at play. Research on engagement by appraisal theorists has identified several discourse markers by which alignment/disalignment is accomplished in speaker talk. Not all of these markers, however, are relevant to the intertextuality of competing discourses, the focus of contrapuntal analysis. Thus, I draw only selectively from the engagement work.

However, before I turn to a discussion of these discourse markers, three caveats are needed. First, RDT is interested in joint actions between speakers, in addition to utterances by individual speakers, the latter of which is the sole focus of appraisal theory (Martin & White, 2005). As I have noted, especially in Chapter 5, utterances embedded in different communication events (interviews, conversations between relating parties, and other genres of communication) implicate different links in the utterance chain. All utterances can be viewed as sites of discursive struggle in the utterance chain but in different ways.

Second, appraisal theorists are interested in understanding the discursive positions of a given speaker as an analytic end in and of itself. RDT, by contrast, is not interested in understanding a given speaker's position, per se, but instead is interested in how discourses are positioned as competing. To be sure, a given speaker can align himself or herself with a given discourse, and then, by agreeing or disagreeing with an alternative discursive position, thereby establish the relationship between the two discourses, more or less akin to the transitivity principle: A speaker associates with Discourse *B* and disassociates from Discourse *C*, thereby establishing by inference a relationship of disalignment between Discourses *B* and *C*. For example, a speaker says to his partner in the midst of shopping for an automobile, "I know it's not very green of me, but I really want an SUV because it would be a status thing for me." The speaker aligns with a discourse of consumption in which it is appropriate to purchase a vehicle based on its status, and distances from the discourse of "going green." The construction of the sentence through the connective *but* positions the discourse of *green* in a contrapuntal relation with a discourse in which an SUV is an appropriate choice. Whereas appraisal theorists would find the sentence interesting because it informs us about the view of the particular speaker, RDT finds the sentence interesting at this stage of analysis because of its marking of discourses in counterpoint.

Third, appraisal theory presumes that a speaker either aligns with, or disaligns from, discourses, and a third possibility seems just as likely: A speaker (or jointly acting speakers) can identify multiple competing discourses without necessarily aligning or disaligning with any of them. A speaker (or joint action between speakers) can establish a relationship of alignment/disalignment between discourses without necessarily claiming an association with either discourse. For example, the same speaker from the prior example might have voiced this statement in the shopping trip for a new vehicle: "We can either go green and get a smaller hybrid, or we can go for one of those SUVs that would be the envy of the neighbors." In this statement, the speaker neither aligns with nor distances from two discourses; we don't know whether the speaker wants to go green or not. However, the either-or construction of the statement positions two discourses in competition with one another.

Three kinds of discourse markers in the engagement research are important in identifying discourses positioned in counterpoint relation to one another: negating, countering, and entertaining. Other lexical markers might function in talk to mark the competition of discursive positions, and this awaits future researchers as a fruitful area to pursue. In the meantime, these three engagement devices identified by Martin and White (2005) afford a useful beginning point for contrapuntal analysis. As discussed in Chapter 5, most dialogic struggle is polemic—short of transformation, the struggle of discourses is adversarial in nature. Further, the discourses are not likely to be struggling on an equal playing field; one discourse is likely to be more dominant than its alternatives. The three markers discussed below capture the polemic nature of centripetal-centrifugal struggle.

Negating

Negating is a kind of disclaiming. Disclaimings serve to reject or supplant a discourse, or to claim it as irrelevant (Martin & White, 2005, p. 117). Negating is the acknowledgement of an alternative, competing discourse for purposes of rejecting it (Martin & White, p. 118).

i.e., rejection

Negating is readily apparent in antagonistic struggles in which the parties align with different discourses. For example, imagine a conversation between two relationship partners, who are aligned with discourses of autonomy and connection, respectively. When one speaker says to the other "You want to smother me by denying me time to spend on my own thing" and the reply is "You are so selfish and place our relationship second to your friends," it is probably reasonable to infer that both parties see discourses of autonomy and connection in counterpoint, with the first speaker negating the discourse of connection while the second speaker negates the discourse of autonomy.

Negating can also occur in the absence of a copresent adversary whose discursive alignment is different from a speaker's. For example, consider a daughter who answers an interviewer question about her relationship with her mother with this response: "We see each other maybe once a month. I don't believe that spending 24/7 together is necessary at my age." No prior talk in the interview made mention of parents and children spending "24/7 together," so the introduction of this meaning kernel—likely part of a larger discourse of interdependence between parents and children—allowed for its negation ("I don't believe"). From this excerpt, we don't know who to attribute the "24/7" meaning kernel to. Regardless, speakers can fold an alternative discourse into their talk for purposes of negating it even in the absence of another co-present speaker who has aligned with that discursive position.

Negating can also be accomplished through direct or indirect reported speech. As discussed above, a discursive position can be linked directly or indirectly to a given source and then refuted.

Countering

counter

Another kind of disclaiming is countering, by which some discursive position replaces or supplants an alternative discursive position that would normally have been expected in its place (Martin & White,

2005, p. 120). Consider the statement, "We're friends even though we broke up." The claim of friendship counters the discursive position that ex's can't be friends. A number of conjunctions and connectives accomplish countering, including *although, however, but, yet, nonetheless,* and so forth (Martin & White, p. 120).

Adjuncts, including such words as *even, only, just,* and *still* also carry what Martin and White regard as a "counterexpectational aspect to their meaning" (p. 121). For example, consider this statement by a speaker: "We even go to dinner every week," which counters the implicit expectation that they should not be expected to engage in that practice.

Countering can also be accomplished through selected comment adjuncts/adverbials (Martin & White, p. 121). For example, in the statement, "Surprisingly, we still exchange Christmas gifts after the divorce," *Surprisingly* functions to counter the implicit expectation by some unstated Other that the exchange of gifts between divorced persons is not typical or appropriate.

Entertaining

Also known as epistemic modality (Coates, 1983) or evidentiality (Chafe & Nichols, 1986), entertaining functions to indicate that a given discursive position is but one possibility among alternative discursive positions. As Martin and White (2005) have indicated, entertaining acknowledges the following:"that the value position being advanced is contingent and hence but one of a number of potential dialogistic alternatives. . . . It acts to acknowledge a heteroglossic backdrop for the proposition by presenting it as potentially at odds with some dialogic alternative" (p. 106). In short, competing dialogic alternatives are entertained in talk.

The discourse markers by which entertaining is accomplished include a wide range of lexical options (Martin & White, 2005). Modal auxiliaries (e.g., *may, might, must, could*) and modal attributes (e.g., *it's possible that, it's likely that*) indicate that a given discursive position is but one possibility among several, thereby marking the presence of other competing discourses. Martin and White also include evidence/appearance postulations (e.g., *it seems, it appears, apparently*) as a form of entertaining. For example, the declaration that something *seems* a certain way is a more tempered statement than the assertion that something *is* that way, thereby marking the possibility of at least one alternative discursive position. Implicit in entertaining are competing discourses in which a given discursive position is posited as but one of several alternative positions that could be taken; its perspective is not claimed as absolute or the only possibility.

i.e., language use

Lexical choices such as *on the one hand* paired with *on the other hand* also mark the presence of multiple discourses, thereby denying universalizing claims in favor of only one discourse. Constructions that place discourses in an either-or relation also mark the presence of at least two competing discourses. For example, consider, "I feel that I can either support my friend or support my girlfriend in this situation." The either-or construction points to two different viewpoints and their zero-sum relation. These lexical practices mark the fact that multiple discourses are being entertained in talk.

Once the researcher has identified the competing discourses of a text, it is necessary to turn to the third component of contrapuntal analysis: the identification of the interplay of competing discourses.

❖ IDENTIFYING THE INTERPLAY OF COMPETING DISCOURSES

As I observed in Chapter 5, too much of existing RDT-informed research stops the research process after identifying competing discourses, failing to attend to the all important issue of how those discourses textually play off with and against one another. Analytically, the task at this stage of contrapuntal analysis is that of determining whether the text enacts monologue, diachronic separation, or synchronic interplay (see Chapter 5 where these concepts are developed at length). As I observed in Chapter 5, too much of the research that does address the interplay of discourses functions at a general level, glossing over the details of talk. My argument in Chapter 5 is that we lose much insight into the interplay of discourses by ignoring the discursive details of centripetal-centrifugal struggle. It is particularly challenging to identify monologue and synchronic interplay without attending to these details. Thus, this section of the chapter draws attention in a preliminary way to how struggle is constituted at the microlevel in texts. I place emphasis on the centripetal-centrifugal relation between discourses, because this concept holds the greatest potential for understanding how dominant and marginalized discourses interpenetrate.

It is useful to begin this section by reminding the reader of the distinction noted in the prior chapter between dialogically expansive and dialogically contractive talk (Martin & White, 2005; White, 2003). Bakhtin (1984b) conceptualized a continuum of dialogicity in utterances, whose endpoints are bounded by monologue and idealized dialogue. The interactions of everyday life are probably located somewhere between total monologues and idealized dialogue. They sit in the prosaic of centripetal-centrifugal struggle. When talk moves toward the monologue endpoint, it is dialogically contractive, and when talk moves toward the idealized dialogue endpoint, it is dialogically expansive. But how can a researcher identify where talk is located along this continuum?

Dialogically Contractive Discursive Practices

In Chapter 5 and in prior sections of this chapter, I have already identified a number of discursive practices that can function polemically to challenge competing discourses, thereby establishing or sustaining the dominance of a centripetal discourse, perhaps to the point of total exclusion of alternative voices, that is, monologue. In particular, the prior chapter discussed Bakhtin's (1981d) concepts of the rogue (parody), the fool (enacted ignorance for purposes of unmasking implicit assumptions), and the clown (malicious distortion of a discursive position for purposes of laughing at its absurdity). All three of these discursive forms can be deployed to challenge alternative discourses for purposes of marginalizing, and even silencing, them. Future RDT-informed scholars need to attend to the micropractices in talk by which each of these discourse forms is enacted in relational communication. In the prior section of this current chapter, I drew upon the research in engagement (Martin & White, 2005) to suggest more microscopic discursive forms that can function to challenge alternative discourses, in particular, the polemic actions of negating and countering.

Several critical scholars have identified a number of discursive practices by which some discourses are challenged and other discourses are privileged. The discussion below is not intended as exhaustive but rather illustrative of the multitude of ways in which centripetal-centrifugal struggle can be enacted contractively. In the end, I favor an inductive analytic process in which the contrapuntal analyst interrogates the particular texts at hand for purposes of identifying the in situ practices of dialogic contraction. However, the researcher should be aware of the practices described below to assist in the interpretive process.

In his classic work in organizational communication, Deetz (1992) has identified a number of practices of discursive closure that can be productively imported into the study of relational communication. I will elaborate on six of these in particular. First, Deetz identified disqualification, a discursive move in which alternative discourses are denied a hearing because the embodied persons or groups aligned with those positions are presented as lacking expertise or the right of expression. For example, when a parent says to her child, "I'm sorry, but you lost the privilege of critiquing the dinner because you didn't meet your kitchen responsibilities," she is disqualifying the child's right to expression, thereby allowing the parent-determined menu choices to stand unchallenged. Disqualification might invoke the rogue and clown mentioned above, for both of these discursive efforts can function to undermine the perceived competence of those aligned with marginalized discourses. For example, imagine that a popular child enacts a clownlike imitation of a less popular peer, portraying the person as totally lacking in any social skills; through the exaggerated parody, the peer's basic credibility is brought into doubt in others' eyes, thereby disqualifying him or her from a future role in the social group.

Second, Deetz (1992) identified naturalization, the discursive practice of reification (Lukacs, 1971). When a discourse is positioned as a given in nature and talked of as if it is a transparent representation of the way things are, it is reified. For example, imagine an interview in which a wife comments to the interviewer that "My husband has cheated on me several times; that's just the way men are." This wife is positioning male infidelity as a natural phenomenon, one that is "fixed and eternal" (Deetz, p. 190) and thus dominant. Naturalization might be discursively marked through lexical choices such as *naturally* or *of course,* as discussed above. Naturalization centers a discourse, thereby constructing its immunity to alternative systems of meaning.

Third, Deetz (1992) has identified neutralization. Neutralization is talk in which value-laden discursive positions are treated as if they were value free or objective. I would prefer an alternative label such as *camouflage* to capture the discursive force of this practice. Camouflage can be enacted in any number of ways. The discursive practice of proclaiming (Martin & White, 2005) seems particularly powerful in camouflaging value-laden claims under the mask of objectivity. According to Martin and White, speakers can use reported speech from presumed authorities to argue that the weight of evidence and expert opinion objectively supports a given discursive position. For example, imagine a teenager who says to her parent "My teacher says that the job of teenagers is to be independent of their parents—it's part of growing up and becoming an adult. So you can't tell me what to do anymore." This teenager is invoking a powerful discourse from developmental psychology in which children are expected to grow into adulthood through independence from their parents. The teenager is using indirect reported speech, paraphrasing her teacher as an expert source of what objective knowledge presumably demonstrates. When a discourse is constructed as the objective truth, it gains a privileged position relative to alternative, presumably nonobjective, discourses.

Fourth, Deetz (1992) has identified the discursive practice of topical avoidance. Under the mantle of propriety, certain alterative discursive positions are constructed as off limits for discussion. For example, a number of scholars of domestic abuse have long argued that cultural discourses of privacy and patriarchy have functioned to silence disclosure of abuse perpetrated by men against women and adults against children (e.g., Foley, 2006). When a discourse is constructed as off limits, criticism of it is muted, if not silenced completely. Topic avoidance might be evident, for example, in a pattern of interruption or topic shifting whenever the taboo topic is broached in conversation.

Fifth, the subjectification of experience is a powerful discursive practice by which competing discourses can be silenced (Deetz, 1992). In arguing that a given value position is simply a matter of individual opinion or experience, as opposed to being a social formation, speakers can close down challenges from competing discursive positions. Imagine an antagonistic struggle in which a party says to his partner, "This is just the way I feel about it. You can't tell me how to feel—you're not me." This statement is a powerful one that functions to close down the integrity of all alternative viewpoints with the single exception of the standpoint of the speaker.

Last, pacification is a powerful discursive practice by which competing discourses can be silenced (Deetz, 1992). In positioning differences as either trivial or futile to resolve, competing discourses are pacified and thereby discursively stripped of their force. When a relationship party says to his partner, "We just have different backgrounds, and that isn't going to change. So let's set aside our differences and focus on our similarities," the discursive force of the statement is to close down discussion of those differences, thereby privileging a discourse of relationships in which similarity is valued as the primary currency of closeness (Baxter, Foley, & Thatcher, 2008).

Competing discourses can also be pacified by a discursive plea to a higher order discursive position such as consensus (Fairclough, 2003). A family meeting in which a parent pronounces "It's important for us all to reach agreement on this and speak with one voice" functions discursively to trump an alternative discursive position, in which differences are valued, with a discourse of consensus.

Competing discourses can also be pacified through co-optation (Fairclough, 2003). For example, imagine two spouses who are disagreeing about how to spend the upcoming weekend. The husband has indicated that he needs to work, but his wife argues that he needs to join the rest of the family in traveling to a family reunion. A discourse of economic well being is competing with a discourse of family allegiance in this antagonistic struggle between the husband and the wife. Then the husband asserts, "Your dad and granddad always tell stories of how the family has gotten ahead for generations because its bread winners worked their tails off! I'll call your dad and mom, even your grandparents if you like, and explain. They'll understand that I'm putting my family first by working this weekend." The force of the husband's utterance is to co-opt the discourse of family allegiance, arguing that working hard is an ultimate form of family devotion and commitment.

The centripetal-centrifugal struggle of competing discourses often is polemic, and I have argued in this section that researchers need to attend to the finer details of talk in order to do analytic justice to monologue and synchronic interplay in particular. But the interplay of discourses can also move toward idealized dialogue in dialogically expansive ways. What are the discursive practices of dialogic expansion?

Dialogically Expansive Discursive Practices

The issue of speaker alignment with a given discourse is an analytically important one in arguing that a given discourse practice functions contractively or expansively. When speakers align with marginalized discursive positions for purposes of dislodging the dominance of centripetal discourses, the function of such discursive work is to open up the conversation to those alternative voices. Thus, several of the practices identified in the prior section can ironically produce dialogic expansion when they are targeted at dominant discourses. However, these same practices can function to contract struggle when speakers are aligned with dominant discourses; in this circumstance, they function to sustain the existing imbalance of power between discourses.

In the section *Identifying Competing Discourses*, I identified some discursive practices that appear more expansive than contractive. In particular, through entertainings such as *sometimes, a little bit*, and so forth, a given discursive position is marked as one possibility among several alternative positions. In addition, through such lexical choices as *on the one hand/on the other hand*, talk can function to voice multiple discursive positions in ways that open up meaning rather than functioning to contract meaning. These lexical choices do not position one discourse as more central than a competing discourse; both are given voice on a more or less equal discursive playing field.

Martin and White (2005) have identified a use of reported speech that can function in dialogically expansive ways, which they label *attributing*. As discussed above, reported speech can function to silence competing discourses when it is introduced for ridicule or as expert evidence to support the centripetal dominance of a given discursive position. However, in attributing, it can also function to bring alternative discursive positions into the utterance. In particular, when speakers directly or indirectly acknowledge the voices of others in their talk, this can add a discursive place setting at the conversational table and thereby open up subsequent utterances in unimagined ways. Consider a conversation between relationship partners in which they are trying to make an important life decision about whether to move away from her family in order to accept a job offer. One party says, "I don't know what I think. My mom's advice is that we ought to take the job offer and move even though they'll see us less often. My sister says this would just crush my dad because he's so close to me. When I talked to dad about it, he said 'I want what's best for you guys.'" This utterance invokes the discursive positions of three family members; the mother's and sister's voices are introduced into the utterance chain through indirect reported speech, whereas the father's voice is introduced through direct reported speech. The function of this attributing is to put several discursive positions into play in the conversation between the relationship parties. The speaker goes out of her way not to align with any of these discursive positions ("I don't know what I think"). By acknowledging these discursive positions, the pair can use them as resources to expand the semantic possibilities of their joint meaning making.

This section on dialogic expansion is noticeably short. Future RDT-informed research needs to address the micropractices of talk in order to identify ways in which communication moves toward the idealized dialogue endpoint of Bakhtin's (1984b) continuum. As Chapter 5 made evident, existing work on dialogic expansion largely sits at the level of genre study, with narratives, the carnivalesque, and rituals identified for their dialogically expansive potential. Scholars need to supplement this genre work with attention to the micropractices of enacted talk. Earlier in the book, I reviewed the growing work in dialogue that takes a more prescriptive approach, that is, work designed to intervene in communication systems for purposes of encouraging the practice of more dialogically expansive communication. Future researchers could productively turn to this body of prescriptive work for possible insights into the ways relationship parties might move toward idealized dialogue in naturally occurring interactions. Researchers could, for example, determine whether naturally occurring wonderings in partner talk, that is, partner meta-talk about their current interaction patterns, function to elicit new discursive viewpoints in subsequent interactions.

In order to help the reader gain a more concrete understanding of contrapuntal analysis, I turn next to a very brief sample analysis that allows me to illustrate at least some of the analytic points developed in this chapter.

❖   **A SAMPLE CONTRAPUNTAL ANALYSIS:
A "DEAR BIRTH MOTHER" LETTER**

The Text

Although domestic adoption in the U. S. appears to be on the increase (Galvin, 2006), it is still evaluated negatively against the cultural ideal of the nuclear family comprised of parents and their biological offspring (e.g., Baxter, Henauw et al., 2009). Adoption is often a stigmatized relationship in the U.S. (e.g., Wegar, 2000). Adoption is commonly understood as a last resort way to parent, often linked to infertility. It is framed as a time of abandonment and loss for the birth parents and for the child who is adopted. Birth parents, especially mothers, are stereotyped as bad parents, perhaps selfish and unable to provide good homes. Against this cultural backdrop, Norwood and Baxter (2009) chose to study "Dear Birth Mother" letters (Jones, 2005), online letters that prospective adoptive parents write to birth mothers in an attempt to persuade them to select the couple as the adoptive parents of the unborn baby. Their research question was that of identifying the meaning of adoption discursively constructed in a sample of these letters.

These texts represent a genre of persuasion in which the persuader seeks a very personal commitment from the target (adoption of the birth mother's baby) without having a history with her. The birth mother is known only as a member of a social group (pregnant women who are considering placing their children up for adoption). In the absence of a prior relationship with the target, there is no proximal already-spoken link in the utterance chain; the persuader has no recourse but to fall back on distal already-spokens—cultural discourses that can be intelligible to the birth mother through common membership in the U.S. society. Because the persuader is seeking a favorable evaluation by the addressee, she or he is attending, as well, to the proximal not-yet-spoken reaction of the birth mother; but the persuader has no knowledge of the particular birth mother and thus must rely on anticipated responses that reflect distal not-yet-spoken cultural ideals. However, as discussed above, those cultural discourses (distal already-spoken and distal not-yet-spoken) do not construct adoption in a favorable light; against the centripetal discourse of the nuclear family, adoption is a deviant family form. "Dear Birth Mother" letters are thus positioned as a problematic communication event—problematic to the prospective adoptive parents in the anonymity of the addressee and problematic, as well, because adoption is stigmatized.

Fitch (2003) has argued that persuasion is cultural communication in that persuaders draw upon cultural premises. However, from a dialogic perspective, culture is far from a unitary and coherent system of premises; instead, it is characterized by a struggle of competing discourses. What, then, are the competing discourses that struggle in "Dear Birth Mother" letters, and how is the meaning of adoption constructed through their interplay?

Initial Coding for Lower-Level Categories

Here is an excerpt from one such letter that was posted on one of several online adoption sites (http://www.parentprofiles.com). In the interests of space, ellipses are used to eliminate contiguous statements that do not contribute to the analysis. I have marked textual segments in brackets and have numbered them K–1, K–2, etc. for ease of referencing them in the analysis that follows. A segment is a kernel of text that sheds insight into the analytical question, "What is adoption?"

Dear [Friend], [K-1]

Thank you so much for learning about us! [We haven't met yet, but we have something in common, we are both mothers who love your child]. [K-2] [You love your child so deeply that you are willing [to share him or her][K-4] with another family,][K-3] and [we yearn to love your child and welcome him or her into our home and family for eternity.][K-5] We truly feel that [adoption is a gift]. [K-6] [We know that this is a very big decision. We understand that this isn't a decision that you have come to lightly][K-7] and [want to assure you that neither have we. We have felt the peace and comfort that the Spirit brings with confirmation that our little family is supposed to grow through adoption][K-8] and [not through traditional means][K-9].... (Husband's name) and I knew from the beginning of our relationship that we wanted children in our family. [We knew right away that adoption of our children was right for us][K-5].... [We have embraced adoption with much excitement and joy in our hearts][K-5] and [feel very strongly that this is God's will for us]. [K-8] [We look forward to sharing our lives and providing a secure home for the children we will be blessed with][K-4].... [We *would embrace an open adoption to give a child the chance to know where he or she comes from. We would want you to be comfortable in this new relationship, and would be willing to explore all options with you]*[K–4]*.... [We have the highest respect for you in choosing to adopt].* [K–10] *[We can't imagine what you must be going through in choosing adoptive parents].*[K–7] *...*

[All our love], [K–1]

(first names of prospective adoptive family)

The K–1 through K–8 code markers in this letter represent the following lower-level coding categories: K–1: emotional bond with birth mother; K–2: commonality between birth mother and prospective adoptive parents in love for child; K–3: birth mother's love for her child; K–4: sharing in open adoption; K–5: adoption as preferred choice not last resort for prospective parents; K–6: adoption as a gift; K–7: difficult decision process for birth mother; K–8: fate for prospective parents; K–9: adoption as nontraditional; K–10: respect for birth mother's decisions. In turn, these lower-level coding categories cohere in higher-order themes.

Identification of Themes

This letter (and the others in the study's sample) can be read as a rejoinder to the already circulating cultural discourse that privileges the traditional nuclear family of parents and their biological children. Although the writers of this letter never explicitly name the stigmatization of adoption embedded in the centripetal discourse of the nuclear family, they do refer to it indirectly through two themes that can be identified. It is most blatantly referenced in line 9 where adoption is contrasted with "traditional means" of parenting [K–9]. Thus the first theme I identify is captured in a single code category: *Adoption as a nontraditional form of parenting*. However, the writers give a discursive nod in recognizing that not everyone shares this view; in line 11 we are told that adoption "was right for us," a form of *entertaining* that marks the writers' position as only one possible discursive position with the implicit suggestion that it might not be right for others. Additionally, at several points in the text, we are given meaning kernels about how difficult the decision-making process is for the birth mother [K–7]. If adoption were accepted as natural and normal, it probably would not garner repeated recognition by the writers as something that is difficult. Thus, the second theme in the data, linked to a single code category, is *adoption as a difficult decision-making process for the birth mother*. Taken together, these two themes function as a sideward glance to the centripetal power of the dominant cultural discourse in which the nuclear family is privileged.

In contrast to the dominant cultural discourse in which adoption is framed as a loss for the birth mother and for the child, the K–4 code category suggests a reframing of adoption as a sharing of the adopted child in an expanded sense of family in which the birth mother is constructed with an ongoing presence—as much or as little as she feels comfortable with so as not to infringe on her individual autonomy. Although adoption is constructed as nontraditional, it is constructed as an alternative of choice in which a new family form is crafted—the open adoption in which the birth mother and the adoptive parents share in the joy of witnessing a child's development. Sharing is flagged explicitly in the K–4 code category, but other categories support this nontraditional conception of family. Commonality in loving the child is identified in K–2; and the references to the emotional bonding the prospective parents feel for the birth mother also creates the possibility for sharing (K–1). These three code categories collectively are coherent in forming a theme of *adoption as a shared, open family*.

Several code categories construct an identity for the birth mother as positive, a clear refutation of the culturally dominant discursive positioning of the birth mother as a negative persona. K–2 establishes commonality between the prospective adoptive mother and the birth mother, uniting them in love for the unborn child. K–3 explicitly declares that the birth mother loves her child. The K–7 kernels that emphasize the difficulty of the decision process for the birth mother construct her as a responsible mother who is taking the process seriously. K–10 explicitly indicates that the birth mother has earned the respect of the prospective adoptive parents for her decision making. Last, K–1 kernels suggest emotional affection for the birth mother, something that wouldn't make sense if she were a bad mother. Taken together, these code categories cohere around a theme of *the birth mother as a responsible parent* who loves her child and who merits respect and affection.

Several code categories indirectly refute the dominant cultural discourse in which adoption is stigmatized as last-resort parenting. K–5 meaning kernels suggest that the prospective parents are excited and joyous about adoption. The K–6 category frames adoption as a gift from the birth parent. K–8 meaning kernels suggest, through use of religious referents, that the prospective parents are destined to adopt. These three code categories construct a theme of *adoption as a chosen form, not a last resort, for prospective adoptive parents*.

The thematic analysis produced five themes relevant to adoption. They are subcategories within a discourse of adoption understood as a legitimate alternative family form, the shared, open-adoption family.

The Interplay

The prospective adoptive parents work diligently to displace the dominant cultural discourse of the nuclear family, and its stigmatization of adoption, by centering instead an alternative discourse of adoption. This text is thus dialogically expansive. This excerpt can be understood as an example of interplay in the form of indirect negation, or hidden polemic. The interplay is one of displacement. The unarticulated centripetal discourse that privileges the nuclear family is moved to the periphery, and the writers' language functions to position the alternative discourse at the center. It is indirect interplay, because the propositions entailed in the nuclear family discourse (adoption as loss, the birth mother as a bad parent, and adoption as a last-resort means of parenting for prospective parents) are never stated directly.

The interplay of the text also illustrates how a given discourse can contain possible disjunctures in which tensions emerge internally within a system of meaning. The construction of adoption as a process of sharing implicates ongoing interdependence of some sort between the birth mother, the child, and his or her adoptive parents. However, an open adoption could possibly constrain the birth mother's autonomy. In lines 16–17, the prospective parents display sensitivity to this issue, assuring the birth mother that she will not be made uncomfortable by such sharing. This expressed sensitivity is intelligible to us because of the discursive struggle between connection and autonomy that circulates in the culture at large.

This short contrapuntal analysis of a single "Dear Birth Mother" letter addresses the three steps of the contrapuntal process: selection of the text, identification of competing discourses, and the meaning that is constructed from the interplay of discourses. Of course, a complete study would examine multiple texts until the point of saturation, and it would present validity evidence to argue for the reasonableness of the interpretation that is advanced.

❖ CONCLUSION

In this chapter, I have articulated a three-part process by which contrapuntal analysis can be undertaken. I understand that methods other than contrapuntal analysis have been employed by researchers in conducting much of the research discussed in prior chapters of this book, and my intent is not to belittle those efforts. Such a move would be dialogically contractive, and the irony of such a move does not escape me! Instead, my motivation for writing this chapter is to be dialogically expansive. I wanted to add to the scholarly conversation among RDT-informed researchers by giving coherent voice to one methodological option by which to examine dialogic relational communication. It is the method-ological option I favor, but it is certainly not the only viable way in which dialogic communication can be studied.

I end this book by bringing it back full circle to how it began. In the opening sentence of Chapter 1, I claimed that a theory is like a living organism, never finalized and ever changing. The first decade and a half since the publication of RDT 1.0 in 1996 has witnessed its positive reception among scholars of interpersonal and family communication. This book articulates RDT 2.0, attempting to provide researchers with new conceptual and methodological tools to allow the theory to grow into the future.

References

Afifi, T. D. (2003). "Feeling caught" in stepfamilies: Managing boundary turbulence through appropriate communication rules. *Journal of Social and Personal Relationships, 20*, 729–756.

Afifi, T. D., & Keith, S. (2004). A risk and resiliency model of ambiguous loss in post-divorce stepfamilies. *Journal of Family Communication, 4*, 65–98.

Afifi, T. D., McManus, T., Hutchinson, S., & Baker, B. (2007). Inappropriate parental divorce disclosures, the factors that prompt them, and their impact on parents' and adolescents' well-being. *Communication Monographs, 74*, 78–102.

Afifi, W. A., & Burgoon, J. K. (1998). "We never talk about that": A comparison of cross-sex friendships and dating relationships on uncertainty and topic avoidance. *Personal Relationships, 5*, 255–272.

Afifi, W. A., & Guerrero, L. K. (1998). Some things are better left unsaid, II: Topic avoidance in friendships. *Communication Quarterly, 46*, 231–249.

Afifi, W. A., & Guerrero, L. K. (2000). Motivations underlying topic avoidance in close relationships. In S. Petronio (Ed.), *Balancing the secrets of private disclosures* (pp. 165–179). Mahwah, NJ: Erlbaum.

Afifi, W. A., & Weiner, J. L. (2004). Toward a theory of motivated information management. *Communication Theory, 14*, 167–190.

AhYun, K. (2002). Similarity and attraction. In M. Allen, R. W. Preiss, B. M. Gayle, & N. A. Burrell (Eds.), *Interpersonal communication research: Advances through meta-analysis* (pp. 145–168). Mahwah, NJ: Lawrence Erlbaum.

Aleman, M. W. (2001). Complaining among the elderly: Examining multiple dialectical oppositions to independence in a retirement community. *Western Journal of Communication, 65*, 89–112.

Aleman, M. W. (2003). "You should get yourself a boyfriend" but "Let's not get serious": Communicating a code of romance in a retirement community. *Qualitative Research Reports in Communication, 4*, 31–37.

Aleman, M. W. (2005). Embracing and resisting romantic fantasies as the rhetorical vision on a SeniorNet discussion board. *Journal of Communication, 55*, 5–21.

Allen, G. (2000). *Intertextuality*. New York: Routledge.

Altman, I., & Taylor, D. (1973). *Social penetration: The development of interpersonal relationships*. New York: Holt, Rinehart & Winston.

Anderson, R., Baxter, L. A., & Cissna, K. N. (Eds.). (2004). *Dialogue: Theorizing difference in communication studies*. Thousand Oaks, CA: Sage.

Arneson, P. (Ed.). (2007). *Perspectives on philosophy of communication*. West Lafayette, IN: Purdue University Press.

Atkinson, J. M., & Heritage, J. (1984). *Structures of social action: Studies in conversation analysis*. Cambridge, UK: Cambridge University Press.

Babrow, A. S. (2001). Uncertainty, value, communication, and problematic integration. *Journal of Communication, 51*, 553–573.

Bachen, C. M., & Ellouz, E. (1996). Imagining romance: Young people's cultural models of romance and love. *Critical Studies in Mass Communication, 13*, 279–308.

Bakhtin, M. M. (1981a). Epic and novel. In M. Holquist (Ed.), *The dialogic imagination: Four essays by M. M. Bakhtin* (C. Emerson & M. Holquist, Trans. pp. 3–40). Austin, TX: University of Texas Press. (Original work published in 1975)

Bakhtin, M. M. (1981b). Forms of time and of the chronotope in the novel. In M. Holquist (Ed.), *The dialogic imagination: Four essays by M. M. Bakhtin* (C. Emerson & M. Holquist, Trans., pp. 84–258). Austin, TX: University of Texas Press. (Original work published in 1975)

Bakhtin, M. M. (1981c). From the prehistory of novelistic discourse. In M. Holquist (Ed.), *The dialogic imagination: Four essays by M. M. Bakhtin* (C. Emerson & M. Holquist, Trans. pp. 41–83). Austin, TX: University of Texas Press. (Original work published in 1975)

Bakhtin, M. M. (1981d). Discourse in the novel. In M. Holquist (Ed.), *The dialogic imagination: Four essays by M. M. Bakhtin* (C. Emerson & M. Holquist, Trans. pp. 259–422). Austin, TX: University of Texas Press. (Original work published in 1975)

Bakhtin, M. M. (1984a). Appendix II: Toward a reworking of the Dostoevsky book. In C. Emerson (Ed. & Trans.), *Problems of Dostoevsky's poetics* (pp. 283–304). Minneapolis, MN: University of Minnesota Press. (Original work published in 1963)

Bakhtin, M. M. (1984b). *Problems of Dostoevsky's poetics* (C. Emerson, Ed. & Trans.). Minneapolis, MN: University of Minnesota Press. (Original work published in 1929)

Bakhtin, M. M. (1984c). *Rabelais and his world* (H. Iswoksky, Trans.). Bloomington, IN: Indiana University Press. (Original work published in 1965)

Bakhtin, M. M. (1986a). From notes made in 1970–71. In C. Emerson & M. Holquist (Eds.), *Speech genres & other late essays* (V. W. McGee, Trans. pp. 132–158). Austin, TX: University of Texas Press. (Original work published in 1979)

Bakhtin, M. M. (1986b). The problem of speech genres. In C. Emerson & M. Holquist (Eds.), *Speech genres & other late essays* (V. W. McGee, Trans. pp. 60–102). Austin, TX: University of Texas Press. (Original work published in 1979)

Bakhtin, M. M. (1986c). The problem of the text in linguistics, philology, and the human sciences: An experiment in philosophical analysis. In C. Emerson & M. Holquist (Eds.), *Speech genres & other late essays* (V. W. McGee, Trans. pp. 103–131). Austin, TX: University of Texas Press. (Original work published in 1979)

Bakhtin, M. M. (1990a). Art and answerability. In M. Holquist (Ed.), *Art and answerability: Early essays by M. M. Bakhtin* (V. Liapunov, Trans. pp. 1–3). Austin, TX: University of Texas Press. (Original work published in 1919)

Bakhtin, M. M. (1990b). Author and hero in aesthetic activity. In M. Holquist (Ed.), *Art and answerability: Early essays by M. M. Bakhtin* (V. Liapunov, Trans. pp. 4–256). Austin, TX: University of Texas Press. (Original work published in 1979)

Bakhtin, M. M. (1993). *Toward a philosophy of the act* (V. Liapunov, Ed., & M. Holquist, Trans.). Austin, TX: University of Texas Press. (Original work published in 1986)

Barge, J. K., & Little, M. (2002). Dialogical wisdom, communicative practice, and organizational life. *Communication Theory, 12*, 375–397.

Bathurst, R. (2004). Dialogue and communication: Exploring the centrifugal force metaphor. *Communication Journal of New Zealand, 5*, 1–19.

Bauman, R. (1986). *Story, performance, and event: Contextual studies of oral narrative*. Cambridge, UK: Cambridge University Press.

Baxter, L. A. (1988). A dialectical perspective on communication strategies in relationship development. In S. Duck (Ed.), *Handbook of personal relationships* (pp. 257–274). London: Wiley.

Baxter, L. A. (1990). Dialectical contradictions in relationship development. *Journal of Social and Personal Relationships, 7*, 69–88.

Baxter, L. A. (1992a). Forms and functions of intimate play in personal relationships. *Human Communication Research, 18*, 336–363.

Baxter, L. A. (1992b). Interpersonal communication as dialogue: A response to the "Social Approaches Forum." *Communication Theory, 2*, 330–337.

Baxter, L. A. (1993). The social side of personal relationships: A dialectical perspective. In S. Duck (Ed.), *Social context and relationships* (pp. 139–165). Newbury Park, CA: Sage.

Baxter, L. A. (1998). Locating the social in interpersonal communication. In J. S. Trent (Ed.), *Communication: Views from the helm for the 21st century* (pp. 60–64). Boston: Allyn & Bacon.

Baxter, L. A. (2004). Distinguished scholar article: Relationships as dialogues. *Personal Relationships, 11*, 1–22.

Baxter, L. A. (2007). Problematizing the problem in communication: A dialogic perspective. *Communication Monographs, 74*, 119–125.

Baxter, L. A., & Akkoor, C. (2008). Aesthetic love and romantic love in close relationships: A case study in East Indian arranged marriages. In R. C. Arnett & K. G. Roberts (Eds.), *Communication ethics: Between cosmopolitanism and provinciality* (pp. 23–46). New York: Peter Lang.

Baxter, L. A., & Babbie, E. (2004). *The basics of communication research.* Thousand Oaks, CA: Sage.

Baxter, L. A., & Braithwaite, D. O. (2002). Performing marriage: The marriage renewal as cultural performance. *Southern Communication Journal, 67,* 94–109.

Baxter, L. A., & Braithwaite, D. O. (2006a). Family rituals. In L. Turner & R. West (Eds.), *The family communication sourcebook* (pp. 259–280). Thousand Oaks, CA: Sage.

Baxter, L. A., & Braithwaite, D. O. (2006b). Introduction. In D. O. Braithwaite & L. A. Baxter (Eds.), *Engaging theories in family communication* (pp. 1–16). Thousand Oaks, CA: Sage.

Baxter, L. A., & Braithwaite, D. O. (2006c). Social dialectics: The contradictions of relating. In B. Whaley & W. Samter (Eds.), *Contemporary communication theories and exemplars* (pp. 275–292). Mahwah, NJ: Lawrence Erlbaum.

Baxter, L. A., & Braithwaite, D. O. (Eds.). (2008a). *Engaging theories in interpersonal communication.* Thousand Oaks, CA: Sage.

Baxter, L. A., & Braithwaite, D. O. (2008b). Relational dialectics theory. In L. A. Baxter & D. O. Braithwaite (Eds.), *Engaging theories in interpersonal communication* (pp. 349–362). Thousand Oaks, CA: Sage.

Baxter, L. A., & Braithwaite, D. O. (2009). Reclaiming uncertainty: The formation of new meanings in relationships. In W. Afifi & T. Afifi (Eds.), *Handbook of uncertainty and information regulation* (pp. 26–44). New York: Routledge.

Baxter, L. A., Braithwaite, D. O., & Bach, B. (2009). *Communicative challenges of voluntary kin relationships.* Manuscript under review.

Baxter, L. A., Braithwaite, D. O., & Bryant, L. (2006). Types of communication triads perceived by young-adult stepchildren in established stepfamilies. *Communication Studies, 57,* 381–400.

Baxter, L. A., Braithwaite, D. O., Bryant, L., & Wagner, A. (2004). Stepchildren's perceptions of the contradictions in communication with stepparents. *Journal of Social and Personal Relationships, 21,* 447–467.

Baxter, L. A., Braithwaite, D. O., Golish, T. D., & Olson, L. N. (2002). Contradictions of interaction for wives of elderly husbands with adult dementia. *Journal of Applied Communication Research, 30,* 1–26.

Baxter, L. A., Braithwaite, D. O., Kellas, J. K., LeClair-Underberg, C., Lamb, E., Routsong, R., & Thatcher, M. (2009). Empty ritual: Young-adult stepchildren's perceptions of the remarriage ceremony. *Journal of Social and Personal Relationships, 26,* 1–21.

Baxter, L. A., & DeGooyer, D., Jr. (2001). Perceived aesthetic characteristics of interpersonal conversations. *Southern Communication Journal, 67,* 1–18.

Baxter, L. A., & Erbert, L. A. (1999). Perceptions of dialectical contradictions in turning points of development in heterosexual romantic relationships. *Journal of Social and Personal Relationships, 16,* 547–569.

Baxter, L. A., Foley, M., & Thatcher, M. (2008). Marginalizing difference in personal relationships: A dialogic analysis of partner talk about their difference. *Journal of Communication Studies, 1,* 33–55.

Baxter, L. A., Henauw, C., Huisman, C., Livesay, C., Norwood, K., Su, H., Wolf, B., & Young, B. (2009). Lay conceptions of "family": A replication and extension. *Journal of Family Communication, 9,* 170–189.

Baxter, L. A., Hirokawa, R., Lowe, J., Pearce, L., & Nathan, P. (2004). Dialogic voices in talk about drinking and pregnancy. *Journal of Applied Communication Research, 32,* 224–248.

Baxter, L. A., Mazanec, M., Nicholson, J., Pittman, G., Smith, K., & West, L. (1997). *Journal of Social and Personal Relationships, 14,* 655–678.

Baxter, L. A., & Montgomery, B. M. (1996). *Relating: Dialogues and dialectics.* New York: Guilford.

Baxter, L. A., & Pittman, G. (2001). Communicatively remembering turning points of relationship development. *Communication Reports, 14,* 1–18.

Baxter, L. A., & Simon, E. (1993). Relationship maintenance strategies and dialectical contradictions in personal relationships. *Journal of Social and Personal Relationships, 10,* 225–242.

Baxter, L. A., & West, L. (2003). Couple perceptions of their similarities and differences: A dialectical perspective. *Journal of Social and Personal Relationships, 20,* 491–514.

Baxter, L. A., & Widenmann, S. (1993). Revealing and not revealing the status of romantic relationships to social networks. *Journal of Social and Personal Relationships, 10,* 321–338.

Baxter, L. A., & Wilmot, W. W. (1985). Taboo topics in close relationships. *Journal of Social and Personal Relationships, 2,* 253–269.

Baxter, L. A., & Wolf, B. (in press). Turning points in relationships. In H. T. Reis & S. Sprecher (Eds.), *Encyclopedia of human relationships.* Thousand Oaks, CA: Sage.

Bellah, R. N., Madsen, R., Sullivan, W. M., Swidler, A., & Tipton, S. M. (1985). *Habits of the heart: Individualism and commitment in American life.* Berkeley, CA: University of California Press.

Berger, C. R. (1994). Power, dominance, and social interaction. In M. L. Knapp & G. R. Miller (Eds.), *Handbook of interpersonal communication* (2nd ed., pp. 450–507). Thousand Oaks, CA: Sage.

Berger, C. R. (2005). Interpersonal communication: Theoretical perspectives, future prospects. *Journal of Communication, 55,* 415–447.

Berger, C. R., & Bradac, J. J. (1982). *Language and social knowledge: Uncertainty in interpersonal relationships.* London: Edward Arnold.

Berger, C. R., & Calabrese, R. J. (1975). Some explorations in initial interaction and beyond: Toward a developmental theory of interpersonal communication. *Human Communication Research, 1,* 99–112.

Bergman, T. (2004). Personal narrative, dialogism, and the performance of "truth" on *Complaints of a Dutiful Daughter. Text & Performance Quarterly, 24,* 20–37.

Bialostosky, D. (1992). Bakhtin and rhetorical criticism: A symposium. *Rhetoric Society Quarterly, 22,* 1–3.

Billig, M., Condor, S., Edwards, D., Gane, M., Middleton, D., & Radley, A. (1988). *Ideological dilemmas: A social psychology of everyday thinking.* Newbury Park, CA: Sage.

Blumer, H. (1969). *Symbolic interactionism: Perspective and method.* Berkeley, CA: University of California Press.

Bocharov, S. (1994). Conversations with Bakhtin. *PMLA, 109,* 1009–1024.

Bochner, A. P. (1985). Perspectives on inquiry: Representation, conversation, and reflection. In M. L. Knapp & G. R. Miller (Eds.), *Handbook of interpersonal communication* (pp. 27–58). Beverly Hills, CA: Sage.

Bochner, A. P. (2002). Perspectives on inquiry III: The moral of stories. In M. L. Knapp & J. A. Daly (Eds.), *Handbook of interpersonal communication* (3rd ed., pp. 73–101). Thousand Oaks, CA: Sage.

Bochner, A. P., & Ellis, C. (1992). Personal narrative as a social approach to interpersonal communication. *Communication Theory, 2,* 165–172.

Bochner, A. P., Ellis, C., & Tillmann-Healy, L. (1997). Relationships as stories. In S. Duck (Ed.), *Handbook of personal relationships: Theory, research and interventions* (2nd ed., pp. 307–324). New York: John Wiley.

Bochner, A.P., Ellis, C., Tillmann-Healy, L. (1998). Mucking around looking for truth. In B. M. Montgomery & L. A. Baxter (Eds.), *Dialectical approaches to studying personal relationships* (pp. 41–62). Mahwah, NJ: Lawrence Erlbaum.

Bohm, D. (1996). *On dialogue* (L. Nichol, Ed.). London: Routledge.

Bolton, C. (1961). Mate selection as the development of a relationship. *Marriage and Family Living, 23,* 234–240.

Boss, P. (1977). A clarification of the concept of psychological father presence in families experiencing ambiguity of boundary. *Journal of Marriage and the Family, 39,* 141–151.

Boss, P. (1999). *Ambiguous loss.* Cambridge, MA: Harvard University Press.

Braithwaite, D. O. (2002). "Married widowhood": Maintaining couplehood when one spouse is in a nursing home. *Southern Communication Journal, 67,* 160–190.

Braithwaite, D. O., Bach, B. W., Baxter, L. A., DiVerniero, R., Hammonds, J., Nunziata, A. M., Willer, E. K., & Wolf, B. (in press). Constructing family: A typology of voluntary kin. *Journal of Social and Personal Relationships.*

Braithwaite, D. O., & Baxter, L. A. (1995). "I do" again: The relational dialectics of renewing marriage vows. *Journal of Social and Personal Relationships, 12,* 177–198.

Braithwaite, D. O., & Baxter, L. A. (2006). "You're my parent, but you're not": Dialectical tensions in stepchildren's perceptions about communication with the nonresidential parent. *Journal of Applied Communication Research, 34,* 30–48.

Braithwaite, D. O., & Baxter, L. A. (2008). Introduction. In L. A. Baxter & D. O. Braithwaite (Eds.), *Engaging theories in interpersonal communication* (pp. 1–18). Thousand Oaks, CA: Sage.

Braithwaite, D. O., Baxter, L. A., & Harper, A. M. (1998). The role of rituals in the management of the dialectical tensions of "old" and "new" in blended families. *Communication Studies, 49,* 101–120.

Braithwaite, D. O., Toller, P., Daas, K., Durham, W., & Jones, A. (2008). Centered, but not caught in the middle: Stepchildren's perceptions of the contradictions of communication of co-parents. *Journal of Applied Communication Research, 36,* 33–55.

Brashers, D. E. (2001). Communication and uncertainty management. *Journal of Communication, 51*, 477–497.

Braun, V., & Clarke, V. (2006). Using thematic analysis in psychology. *Qualitative Research in Psychology, 3*, 77–101.

Bridge, K., & Baxter, L. A. (1992). Blended relationships: Friends as work associates. *Western Journal of Communication, 56*, 200–225.

Brown, S., Stevens, L., & Maclaran, P. (1999). I can't believe it's not Bakhtin!: Literary theory, postmodern advertising, and the gender agenda. *Journal of Advertising, 28*, 11–24.

Bruess, C. J. S., & Pearson, J. C. (2002). The function of mundane ritualizing in adult friendship and marriage. *Communication Research Reports, 19*, 314–326.

Bruner, M. L. (2005). Carnivalesque protest and the humorless state. *Text & Performance Quarterly, 25*, 136–155.

Bryant, L. E. (2006). Ritual (in)activity in postbereaved stepfamilies. In L. H. Turner & R. West (Eds.), *The family communication sourcebook* (pp. 281–293). Thousand Oaks, CA: Sage.

Buber, M. (1970). *I and thou* (W. Kaufmann, Trans.). New York: Scribners.

Burr, V. (2003). *Social constructionism (2nd ed.)*. New York: Routledge.

Buttny, R. (1997). Reported speech in talking race on campus. *Human Communication Research, 23*, 477–506.

Canary, D. J., & Dainton, M. (Eds.). (2003). *Maintaining relationships through communication: Relational, contextual, and cultural variations*. Mahwah, NJ: Lawrence Erlbaum.

Caughlin, J. P., & Afifi, T. D. (2004). When is topic avoidance unsatisfying? Examining moderators of the association between avoidance and dissatisfaction. *Human Communication Research, 30*, 479–513.

Caughlin, J. P., Golish, T. D., Olson, L. N., Sargent, J. E., Cook, J. S., & Petronio, S. (2000). Intrafamily secrets in various family configurations: A communication boundary management perspective. *Communication Studies, 51*, 116–134.

Chafe, W. L., & Nichols, J. (Eds.). (1986). *Evidentiality: The linguistic coding of epistemology*. Norwood, NJ: Ablex.

Chen, T. C., Drzewiecka, J. A., & Sias, P. M. (2001). Dialectical tensions on Taiwanese international student friendships. *Qualitative Research Reports in Communication, 2*, 57–65.

Chornet Roses, D. (2006). *"I could say I am 'dating,' but that could mean lots of different things": "Dating" in the U. S. as a dialogic relational process*. Unpublished doctoral dissertation, University of Iowa, Iowa City.

Cissna, K. N., Cox, D. E., & Bochner, A. P. (1990). The dialectic of marital and parental relationships within the stepfamily. *Communication Monographs, 57*, 44–61.

Clark, C. E. (2005). Tricks of festival: Children, enculturation, and American Halloween. *Ethos, 33*, 180–205.

Clark, K. & Holquist, M. (1984). *Mikhail Bakhtin*. Cambridge, MA: Harvard University Press.

Coates, J. (1983). *The semantics of modal auxiliaries.* London: Croom Helm.

Coates, R. (1998). *Christianity in Bakhtin: God and the exiled other.* Cambridge, UK: Cambridge University Press.

Conquergood, D. (1985). Performing as a moral act: Ethical dimensions of the ethnography of performance. *Literature in Performance, 5,* 1–13.

Conville, R. L. (1991). *Relational transitions: The evolution of personal relationships.* New York: Praeger.

Conway, G. (2003). Inevitable reconstructions: Voice and ideology in two landmark U. S. Supreme Court opinions. *Rhetoric & Public Affairs, 6,* 487–507.

Coulmas, F. (1986). Reported speech: Some general issues. In F. Coulmas (Ed.), *Direct and indirect speech* (pp. 1–28). New York: Mouton de Gruyer.

Cronen, V. E. (1998). Communication theory for the twenty-first century: Cleaning up the wreckage of the psychology project. In J. S. Trent (Ed.), *Communication: Views from the helm for the 21st century* (pp. 18–38). Boston: Allyn and Bacon.

Curnutt, H. (2009). "A fan crashing the party": Exploring reality-celebrity in MTV's Real World franchise. *Television & New Media, 10,* 251–256.

Dailey, R. M., & Palomares, N. A. (2004). Strategic topic avoidance: An investigation of topic avoidance frequency, strategies used, and relational correlates. *Communication Monographs, 71,* 471–496.

Daly, J. A., & Wiemann, J. M. (Eds.). (1994). *Strategic interpersonal communication.* Hillsdale, NJ: Lawrence Erlbaum.

Deetz, S. (1992). *Democracy in an age of corporate colonization: Developments in communication and the politics of everyday life.* Albany, NY: State University of New York Press.

Deetz, S. (2001). Conceptual foundations. In F. M. Jablin & L. L. Putnam (Eds.), *The new handbook of organizational communication: Advances in theory, research, and methods* (pp. 3–46). Thousand Oaks, CA: Sage.

Deetz, S., & Simpson, J. (2004). Critical organizational dialogue: Open formation and the demand of "otherness." In R. Anderson, L. A. Baxter, & K. N. Cissna (Eds.), *Dialogue: Theorizing difference in communication studies* (pp. 141–158). Thousand Oaks, CA: Sage.

De Fina, A. (2003). *Identity in narrative: A study of immigrant discourse.* Philadelphia: John Benjamins.

Derlega, V. J., & Grzelak, J. (1979). Appropriateness of self-disclosure. In G. J. Chelune (Ed.), *Self-disclosure: Origins, patterns, and implications of openness in interpersonal relationships* (pp. 151–176). San Francisco: Jossey-Bass.

Derlega, V. J., Metts, S., Petronio, S., & Margulis, S. T. (1993). *Self-disclosure.* Newbury Park, CA: Sage.

Derlega, V. J., Winstead, B. A., & Folk-Barron, L. (2000). Reasons for and against disclosing HIV-Seropositive test results to an intimate partner: A functional perspective. In S. Petronio (Ed.), *Balancing the secrets of private disclosures* (pp. 53–70). Mahwah, NJ: Lawrence Erlbaum.

De Tocqueville, A. (1969). *Democracy in America* (J. P. Mayer, Ed., G. Lawrence, Trans.). New York: Doubleday, Anchor Books. (Original work published in 1835)

Deutsch, M. (1973). *The resolution of conflict: Constructive and destructive processes.* New Haven, CT: Yale University Press.

Dewey, J. (1934). *Art as experience.* New York: Perigree Books.

Dey, I. (1993). *Qualitative data analysis: A user-friendly guide for social scientists.* New York: Routledge.

Diamondstone, J. V. (1997). Contexted relations and authoritative texts: Seventh-grade students (1987) and legal professionals (1954) argue Brown v. Board of Education. *Written Communication, 14,* 189–220.

Dickson, F. C., Hughes, P. C., & Walker, K. L. (2005). An exploratory investigation into dating among later-life women. *Western Journal of Communication, 69,* 67–82.

Dindia, K. (2003). Definitions and perspectives on relational maintenance communication. In D. J. Canary & M. Dainton (Eds.), *Maintaining relationships through communication: Relational, contextual, and cultural variations* (pp. 1–30). Mahwah, NJ: Lawrence Erlbaum.

Dindia, K., & Canary, D. J. (1993). Definitions and theoretical perspectives on maintaining relationships. *Journal of Social and Personal Relationships, 10,* 163–173.

Drew, P. (2005). Conversation analysis. In K. L. Fitch & R. E. Sanders (Eds.), *Handbook of language and social interaction* (pp. 71–102). Mahwah, NJ: Lawrence Erlbaum.

Druick, Z. (2009). Dialogic absurdity: TV news parody as a critique of genre. *Television & New Media, 10,* 294–308.

Duck, S. (1994). *Meaningful relationships: Talking, sense, and relating.* Thousand Oaks, CA: Sage.

Duck, S. (2002). Hypertext in the key of G: Three types of "history" as influences on conversational structure and flow. *Communication Theory, 12,* 41–62.

Eisenberg, E. M. (1984). Ambiguity as strategy in organizational communication. *Communication Monographs, 51,* 227–242.

Ellinot, L., & Gerard, G. (1998). *Dialogue: Rediscover the transforming power of conversation.* New York: John Wiley.

Emerson, C. (1997). *The first hundred years of Mikhail Bakhtin.* Princeton, NJ: Princeton University Press.

Erbert, L. A. (2000). Conflict and dialectics: Perceptions of dialectical contradictions in marital conflict. *Journal of Social and Personal Relationships, 17,* 638–659.

Erbert, L. A., & Aleman, M. W. (2008). Taking the grand out of grandparent: Dialectical tensions in grandparent perceptions of surrogate parenting. *Journal of Social and Personal Relationships, 25,* 671–695.

Erlandson, D. A., Harris, E. L., Skipper, B. L., & Allen, S. D. (1993). *Doing naturalistic inquiry: A guide to methods.* Newbury Park, CA: Sage.

Fairclough, N. (2003). *Analysing discourse: Textual analysis for social research.* London: Routledge.

Farmer, F. (Ed.). (1998). *Landmark essays on Bakhtin, rhetoric, and writing.* Mahwah, NJ: Hermagoras.

Feeney, J. A. (1999). Issues of closeness and distance in dating relationships: Effects of sex and attachment style. *Journal of Social and Personal Relationships, 16,* 571–590.

Feeney, J. A., & Noller, P. (1991). Attachment style and verbal descriptions of romantic partners. *Journal of Social and Personal Relationships, 8,* 187–215.

Felmlee, D. H. (1998). "Be careful what you wish for . . .": A quantitative and qualitative investigation of "fatal attraction." *Personal Relationships, 5,* 235–253.

Fenske, M. (2004). The aesthetic of the unfinished: Ethics and performance. *Text & Performance Quarterly, 24,* 1–19.

Fiske, J. (1986). Television: Polysemy and popularity. *Critical Studies in Mass Communication, 3,* 391–408.

Fitch, K. L. (1998). *Speaking relationally: Culture, communication, and interpersonal connection.* New York: Guilford Press.

Fitch, K. L. (2003). Cultural persuadables. *Communication Theory, 1,* 100–123.

Foley, M. K. (2006). Locating "difficulty": A multi-site model of intimate terrorism. In D. C. Kirkpatrick, S. Duck, & M. K. Foley (Eds.), *Relating difficulty: The processes of constructing and managing difficult interaction* (pp. 43–60). Mahwah, NJ: Lawrence Erlbaum.

Ford, L. A., Ray, E. B., & Ellis, B. H. (1999). Translating scholarship on intrafamilial sexual abuse: The utility of a dialectical perspective for adult survivors. *Journal of Applied Communication Research, 27,* 139–157.

Foster, E. (2005). Desiring dialectical discourse: A feminist ponders the transition to motherhood. *Women's Studies in Communication, 28,* 57–83.

Foucault, M. (1977). *Discipline and punish: The birth of the prison* (A. Sheridan, Trans.). New York: Pantheon.

Foucault, M. (1980). *The history of sexuality* (R. Hurley, Trans.). New York: Pantheon.

Foucault, M. (1988). Technologies of the self. In L. Martin, H. Gutman, & P. Hutton (Eds.), *Technologies of the self* (pp. 16–49). Amherst, MA: University of Massachusetts Press.

Frank, A. W. (1995). *The wounded storyteller: Body, illness, and ethics.* Chicago: University of Chicago Press.

Freeden, M. (2003). *Ideology: A very short introduction.* Oxford, UK: Oxford University Press.

Friedman, M. (2001). Martin Buber and Mikhail Bakhtin: The dialogue of voices and the word that is spoken. *Religion & Literature, 33,* 25–36.

From, U. (2006). Everytalk talk and the conversational patterns of the soap opera. *Nordicom Review, 27,* 227–242.

Gal, S. (2005). Language ideologies compared: Metaphors of public/private. *Journal of Linguistic Anthropology, 15,* 23–37.

Galvin, K. M. (2006). Diversity's impact on defining the family: Discourse-dependence and identity. In L. H. Turner & R. West (Eds.), *The family communication sourcebook* (pp. 3–20). Thousand Oaks, CA: Sage.

Garvey, T. G. (2000). The value of opacity: A Baktinian analysis of Habermas's discourse ethics. *Philosophy and Rhetoric, 44,* 370–390.

Geertz, C. (1973). *The interpretation of cultures: Selected essays by Clifford Geertz*. New York: Basic Books, Inc.

Geertz, C. (1983). *Local knowledge: Further essays in interpretive anthropology*. New York: Basic Books.

Geist, P., & Dreyer, J. (1993). The demise of dialogue: A critique of medical encounter ideology. *Western Journal of Communication, 57*, 233–246.

Gergen, K. J. (1999). *An invitation to social constructionism*. Thousand Oaks, CA: Sage.

Goldsmith, D., & Baxter, L. A. (1996). Constituting relationships in talk: A taxonomy of speech events in social and personal relationships. *Human Communication Research, 23*, 87–114.

Golish, T. D. (2000). Is openness always better? Exploring the role of topic avoidance, satisfaction, and parenting styles of stepparents. *Communication Quarterly, 48*, 137–158.

Golish, T. D., & Caughlin, J. P. (2002). "I'd rather not talk about it": Adolescents' and young adults' use of topic avoidance in stepfamilies. *Journal of Applied Communication Research, 30*, 78–106.

Golish, T. D., & Powell, K. A. (2003). "Ambiguous loss": Managing the dialectics of grief associated with premature birth. *Journal of Social and Personal Relationships, 20*, 309–334.

Goodall, H. L., Jr., & Kellett, P. M. (2004). Dialectical tensions and dialogic moments as pathways to peak experiences. In R. Anderson, L. A. Baxter, & K. N. Cissna (Eds.), *Dialogue: Theorizing difference in communication studies* (pp. 159–174). Thousand Oaks, CA: Sage.

Gottman, J. M. (1999). *The marriage clinic: A scientifically based marital therapy*. New York: Norton.

Graham, E. E. (1997). Turning points and commitment in post-divorce relationships. *Communication Monographs, 64*, 350–368.

Graham, E. E. (2003). Dialectic contradictions in postmarital relationships. *Journal of Family Communication, 3*, 193–214.

Grano, D. (2007). Wise ignorance and Socratic interiority: Recovering a dialogic rhetoric. *Rhetoric Society Quarterly, 37*, 1–18.

Greene, J. O. (2008). Action assembly theory: Forces of creation. In L. A. Baxter & D. O. Braithwaite (Eds.), *Engaging theories in interpersonal communication* (pp. 23–35). Thousand Oaks, CA: Sage.

Guerrero, L. K., & Afifi, W. A. (1995a). What parents don't know: Topic avoidance in parent-child relationships. In T. J. Socha & G. H. Stamp (Eds.), *Parents, children, and communication: Frontiers of theory and research* (pp. 219–245). Hillsdale, NJ: Lawrence Erlbaum.

Guerrero, L. K., & Afifi, W. A. (1995b). Some things are better left unsaid: Topic avoidance in family relationships. *Communication Quarterly, 43*, 276–296.

Gunthner, S., & Knoblauch, H. (1995). Culturally patterned speaking practices— The analysis of communicative genres. *Pragmatics, 5*, 1–32.

Habermas, J. (1975). *Legitimation crisis*. Boston: Beacon Press.

Halasek, K. (1992). Feminism and Bakhtin: Dialogic reading in the academy. *Rhetoric Society Quarterly, 22*, 63–73.

Hall, S. (1992). The question of cultural identity. In S. Hall, D. Held, & T. McGrew (Eds.), *Modernity and its futures* (pp. 273–316). Cambridge, England: Polity Press.

Halliday, M. A. K. (2004). *An introduction to functional grammar* (3rd ed.). London: Edward Arnold.

Hariman, R. (2008). Political parody and public culture. *Quarterly Journal of Speech, 94,* 247–272.

Hatfield, E., & Rapson, R. (1996). *Love and sex: Cross-cultural perspectives.* Boston: Allyn and Bacon.

Hauser, G. (1998). Vernacular dialogue and the rhetoricality of public opinion. *Communication Monographs, 65,* 83–107.

Hawes, L. C. (1998). Becoming-other-wise: Conversational performance and the politics of experience. *Text and Performance Quarterly, 18,* 273–299.

Hays, S. (1996). *The cultural contradictions of motherhood.* New Haven, CT: Yale University Press.

Hermans, H. J. M. (1996a). Opposites in a dialogical self: Constructs as characters. *Journal of Constructivist Psychology, 9,* 1–26.

Hermans, H. J. M. (1996b). Voicing the self: From information processing to dialogical interchange. *Psychological Bulletin, 119,* 31–50.

Hermans, H. J. M. (2001). The dialogical self: Toward a theory of personal and cultural positioning. *Culture & Psychology, 7,* 243–281.

Hermans, H. J. M. (2002). The dialogical self as a society of mind: Introduction. *Theory & Psychology, 12,* 147–160.

Hermans, H. J. M. (2004). Introduction: The dialogical self in a global and digital age. *Identity: An International Journal of Theory and Research, 4,* 297–320.

Hermans, H. J. M., & Demaggio, G. (2007). Self, identity, and globalization in times of uncertainty: A dialogical analysis. *Review of General Psychology, 11,* 31–61.

Hermans, H. J. M., & Kempen, H. J. G. (1993). *The dialogical self: Meaning as movement.* San Diego, CA: Academic Press.

Hess, J. A. (2000). Maintaining nonvoluntary relationships with disliked partners: An investigation into the use of distancing behaviors. *Human Communication Research, 26,* 458–488.

Hess, J. A. (2002). Distance regulation in personal relationships: The development of a conceptual model and a test of representational validity. *Journal of Social and Personal Relationships, 19,* 663–683.

Hewes, D. E., & Planalp, S. (1987). The individual's place in communication science. In C. R. Berger & S. H. Chaffee (Eds.), *Handbook of communication science* (pp. 146–183). Newbury Park, CA: Sage.

Hirschkop, K. (1999). *Mikhail Bakhtin: An aesthetic for democracy.* New York: Oxford University Press.

Hirschkop, K. (2001). Bakhtin's linguistic turn. *Dialogism, 5/6,* 21–34.

Hofstede, G. (1980). *Culture's consequences: International differences in work-related values.* Beverly Hills, CA: Sage.

Holland, D. C., & Eisenhart, M. A. (1990). *Educated in romance: Women, achievement, and college culture.* Chicago: University of Chicago Press.

Holland, D. C., & Skinner, D. (1987). Prestige and intimacy: The cultural models behind Americans' talk about gender types. In D. C. Holland & N. Quinn (Eds.), *Cultural models in language and thought* (pp. 78–111). Cambridge, UK: Cambridge University Press.

Holt, E. (1996). Reporting on talk: The use of direct reported speech in conversation. *Research on Language and Social Interaction, 29,* 219–246.

Holt, E. (2000). Reporting and reacting: Concurrent responses to reported speech. *Research on Language and Social Interaction, 33,* 425–454.

Holt, R. (2003). Bakhtin's dimensions of language and the analysis of conversation. *Communication Quarterly, 51,* 225–245.

Holquist, M. (2002). *Dialogism* (2nd ed.). New York: Routledge.

Honeycutt, J. M., & Cantrill, J. G. (2001). *Cognition, communication, and romantic relationships.* Mahwah, NJ: Lawrence Erlbaum.

Hoppe-Nagao, A., & Ting-Toomey, S. (2002). Relational dialectics and management strategies in marital couples. *Southern Communication Journal, 67,* 142–159.

Hoy, M. (1994). Joyful mayhem: Bakhtin, football songs, and the carnivalesque. *Text & Performance Quarterly, 14,* 289–305.

Huston, T. L., Surra, C. A., Fitzgerald, N. M., & Cate, R. M. (1981). From courtship to marriage: Mate selection as an interpersonal process. In S. Duck (Ed.), *Personal relationships 2: Developing personal relationships* (pp. 53–88). London: Academic Press.

Isaacs, W. (1999). *Dialogue and the art of thinking together.* New York: Doubleday.

Janack, J. A. (2006). The rhetoric of "The Body": Jesse Ventura and Bakhtin's carnival. *Communication Studies, 57,* 197–214.

Jasinski, J. (1997). Heteroglossia, polyphony, and *The Federalist Papers*. *Rhetoric Society Quarterly, 27,* 23–46.

Johnson, A. J., Wittenberg, E., Villagran, M. M., Mazur, M., & Villagran, P. (2003). Relational progression as a dialectic: Examining turning points in communication among friends. *Communication Monographs, 70,* 230–249.

Jones, S. H. (2005). (M)othering loss: Telling adoption stories, telling performativity. *Text and Performance Quarterly, 25,* 113–135.

Kline, S. L., Stafford, L., & Miklosovic, J. C. (1996). Women's surnames: Decisions, interpretations and associations with relational qualities. *Journal of Social and Personal Relationships, 13,* 593–617.

Kluckholm, F., & Strodtbeck, F. (1961). *Variations in value orientations.* New York: Row, Peterson.

Knee, C. R. (1998). Implicit theories of relationships: Assessment and prediction of romantic relationship initiation, coping, and longevity. *Journal of Personality and Social Psychology, 74,* 360–370.

Koczanowicz, L. (2000). Freedom and communication: The concept of human self in Mead and Bakhtin. *Dialogism, 4,* 54–66.

Koenig Kellas, J. (2005). Family ties: Communicating identity through jointly told stories. *Communication Monographs, 72,* 365–389.

Koenig Kellas, J., & Manusov, V. (2003). What's in a story? The relationship between narrative completeness and tellers' adjustment to relationship dissolution. *Journal of Social and Personal Relationships, 20,* 285–307.

Koenig Kellas, J., & Trees, A. R. (2006). Finding meaning in difficult family experiences: Sense-making and interaction processes during joint family storytelling. *Journal of Family Communication, 6,* 49–76.

Kvigne, K., & Kirkevold, M. (2003). Living with bodily strangeness: Women's experiences of their changing and unpredictable body following a stroke. *Qualitative Health Research, 13,* 1291–1310.

Labov, W., & Waletsky, J. (1967). Narrative analysis: Oral versions of personal experience. In J. Helm (Ed.), *Essays on the verbal and visual arts: Proceedings of the 1966 annual spring meeting of the American Ethnological Society* (pp. 12–44). Seattle, WA: University of Washington Press.

Lannamann, J. W. (1992). Deconstructing the person and changing the subject of interpersonal studies. *Communication Theory, 2,* 139–147.

Lannamann, J. W. (1995). The politics of voice in interpersonal communication research. In W. Leeds-Hurwitz (Ed.), *Social approaches to communication* (pp. 114–134). New York: Guilford.

Li, C. N. (1986). Direct and indirect speech: A functional study. In F. Coulmas (Ed.), *Direct and indirect speech* (pp. 29–45). New York: Mouton de Gruyter.

Lincoln, Y. S., & Guba, E. G. (1985). *Naturalistic inquiry.* Beverly Hills, CA: Sage.

Lindlof, T. R., & Taylor, B. C. (2002). *Qualitative communication research methods (2nd ed.).* Thousand Oaks, CA: Sage.

Lukacs, G. (1971). *History and class consciousness* (R. Livingston, Trans.). Cambridge, MA: MIT Press.

Macpherson, C. B. (1962). *The political theory of possessive individualism.* London: Oxford University Press.

Mandelbaum, J. (2008). Conversation analysis theory: A descriptive approach to interpersonal communication. In L. A. Baxter & D. O. Braithwaite (Eds.), *Engaging theories in interpersonal communication* (pp. 175–188). Thousand Oaks, CA: Sage.

Martin, J. R., & White, P. R. R. (2005). *The language of evaluation: Appraisal in English.* New York: Palgrave Macmillan.

Martin, P., & Renegar, V. (2007). "The man for his time": *The Big Lebowski* as carnivalesque social critique. *Communication Studies, 58,* 299–313.

Masheter, C. (1994). Dialogues between ex-spouses: Evidence of dialectic relationship. In R. Conville (Ed.), *Uses of structure in communication studies* (pp. 83–101). Westport, CT: Praeger.

Maybin, J. (1996). Story voices: The use of reported speech in 10–12 year-olds' spontaneous narratives. *Current Issues in Language and Society, 3,* 36–48.

Mayes, P. (2005). Linking micro and macro social structure through genre analysis. *Research on Language and Social Interaction, 38,* 331–370.

Mead, G. H. (1934). *Mind, self and society* (C. W. Morris, Ed.). Chicago: University of Chicago Press.

Medved, C. E., & Graham, E. E. (2006). Communicating contradictions: (Re)producing dialectical tensions through work, family, and balance: Socialization messages. In L. H. Turner & R. West (Eds.), *The family communication sourcebook* (pp. 353–372). Thousand Oaks, CA: Sage.

Meltzer, B. N., Petras, J. W., & Reynolds, L. T. (1975). *Symbolic interactionism: Genesis, varieties and criticism.* Boston: Routledge & Kegan Paul.

Menard-Warnick, J. (2005). Transgression narratives, dialogic voicing and cultural change. *Journal of Sociolinguistics, 9,* 534–557.

Menard-Warnick, J. (2007). "My little sister had a disaster, she had a baby": Gendered performance, relational identities, and dialogic voicing. *Narrative Inquiry, 17,* 279–297.

Miller, G. R., & Steinberg, M. (1975). *Between people.* Chicago: Science Research Associates.

Miller, K. (2005). *Communication theories: Perspectives, processes, and contexts* (2nd ed.). New York: McGraw Hill.

Miller-Day, M. (2004). *Communication among grandmothers, mothers, and adult daughters.* Mahwah, NJ: Lawrence Erlbaum.

Mishler, E. G. (1986). *Research interviewing: Context and narrative.* Cambridge, MA: Harvard University Press.

Mongeau, P. A., & Miller Henningsen, M. L. (2008). Relationship stage theories: Charting the course of interpersonal communication. In L. A. Baxter & D. O. Braithwaite (Eds.), *Engaging theories in interpersonal communication* (pp. 363–376). Thousand Oaks, CA: Sage.

Montgomery, B. M., & Baxter, L. A. (Eds.). (1998). *Dialectical approaches to studying personal relationships.* Hillsdale, NJ: Lawrence Erlbaum.

Morse, K. A., & Neuberg, S. L. (2004). How do holidays influence relationship processes and outcomes? Examining the instigation and catalytic effects of Valentine's Day. *Personal Relationships, 11,* 509–527.

Morson, G. S., & Emerson, C. (1990). *Mikhail Bakhtin: Creation of a prosaics.* Stanford, CA: Stanford University Press.

Murphy, J. M. (2001). Mikhail Bakhtin and the rhetorical tradition. *Quarterly Journal of Speech, 87,* 259–277.

Murphy, R. F. (1971). *The dialectics of social life: Alarms and excursions in anthropological theory.* New York: Columbia University Press.

Murray, J. W. (1999). Bakhtinian answerability and Levinasian responsibility: Forging a fuller dialogical communicative ethics. *Southern Communication Journal, 65,* 133–150.

Newcomb, H. M. (1984). On the dialogic aspects of mass communication. *Critical Studies in Mass Communication, 1,* 34–50.

Norwood, K., & Baxter, L. A. (2009). *"Dear Birth Mother": Addressivity and the Meaning-Making of Adoption in Online Ads from Prospective Adoptive Parents.* Unpublished manuscript, University of Iowa, Iowa City.

Olbrys, S. G. (2006). Disciplining the carnivalesque: Chris Farley's exotic dance. *Communication and Critical/Cultural Studies, 3,* 240–259.

Pawlowski, D. R. (1998). Dialectical tensions in marital partners' accounts of their relationships. *Communication Quarterly, 46,* 396–416.

Pawlowski, D. R. (2006). Dialectical tensions in families experiencing acute health issues: Stroke survivors' perceptions. In L. H. Turner & R. West (Eds.), *The family communication sourcebook* (pp. 469–490). Thousand Oaks, CA: Sage.

Pearce, W. B. (1995). A sailing guide for social constructionists. In W. Leeds-Hurwitz (Ed.), *Social approaches to communication* (pp. 88-113). New York: Guilford Press.

Pearce, W. B., & Littlejohn, S. W. (1997). *Moral conflict: When social worlds collide.* Thousand Oaks, CA: Sage.

Pearce, W. B., & Pearce, K. A. (2000). Combining passions and abilities: Toward dialogic virtuosity. *Southern Communication Journal, 65,* 161–175.

Penington, B. A. (2004). The communicative management of connection and autonomy in African American and European American mother-daughter relationships. *Journal of Family Communication, 4,* 3–34.

Petronio, S. (1991). Communication boundary management: A theoretical model of managing disclosure of private information between marital couples. *Communication Theory, 1,* 311–335.

Petronio, S. (2002). *Boundaries of privacy: Dialectics of disclosure.* Albany, NY: SUNY Press.

Phillips, N., & Hardy, C. (2002). *Discourse analysis: Investigating processes of social construction.* Thousand Oaks, CA: Sage.

Philips, S. U. (1983). *The invisible culture: Communication in classroom and community on the Warm Springs Indian reservation.* New York: Longman.

Pitcher, K. (2006). The staging of agency in *Girls Gone Wild. Critical Studies in Mass Communication, 23,* 200–218.

Pitts, M. J., Fowler, C., Kaplan, M. S., Nussbaum, J., & Becker, J. C. (2009). Dialectical tensions underpinning family farm succession planning. *Journal of Applied Communication Research, 37,* 59–79.

Planalp, S. (1993). Friends' and acquaintances' conversations, II: Coded differences. *Journal of Social and Personal Relationships, 10,* 339–354.

Planalp, S., & Benson, A. (1992). Friends' and acquaintances' conversations, I: Perceived differences. *Journal of Social and Personal Relationships, 9,* 483–506.

Pomerantz, A., & Mandelbaum, J. (2005). Conversation analytic approaches to the relevance and uses of relationship categories in interaction. In K. L. Fitch & R. E. Sanders (Eds.), *Handbook of language and social interaction* (pp. 149–174). Mahwah, NJ: Lawrence Erlbaum.

Powell, K. A., & Afifi, T. D. (2005). Uncertainty management and adoptees' ambiguous loss of their birth parents. *Journal of Social and Personal Relationships, 22,* 129–151.

Prentice, C. (2009). Relational dialectics among in-laws. *Journal of Family Communication, 9,* 67–89.

Quinn, N., & Holland, E. (1987). Culture and cognition. In D. Holland & N. Quinn (Eds.), *Cultural models in language and thought* (pp. 3–40). Cambridge, MA: Cambridge University Press.

Rawlins, W. K. (1983a). Negotiating close friendship: The dialectic of conjunctive freedoms. *Human Communication Research, 9,* 255–266.

Rawlins, W. K. (1983b). Openness as problematic in ongoing friendships: Two conversational dilemmas. *Communication Monographs, 50,* 1–13.

Rawlins, W. K. (1989). A dialectical analysis of the tensions, functions, and strategic challenges of communication in young adult friendships. *Communication Yearbook, 12,* 157–189.

Rawlins, W. K. (1992). *Friendship matters: Communication, dialectics, and the life course.* New York: Aldine de Gruyter.

Roberts, J. (1988). Setting the frame: Definitions, functions, and typology of rituals. In E. Imber-Black, J. Roberts, & R. A. Whiting (Eds.), *Rituals in families and family therapy* (pp. 3–46). New York: Norton.

Rogers, L. E. (2006). Relational communication theory: An interactional family theory. In D. O. Braithwaite & L. A. Baxter (Eds.), *Engaging theories in family communication* (pp. 115–129). Thousand Oaks, CA: Sage.

Rogers, R. (1998). A dialogics of rhythm: Dance and the performance of cultural conflict. *Howard Journal of Communication, 9,* 5–27.

Rollins, D., Waterman, D., & Esmay, D. (1985). Married widowhood. *Activities, Adaptation, and Aging, 7,* 67–71.

Roloff, M. E., & Ifert, D. (1998). Antecedents and consequences of explicit agreements to declare a topic taboo in dating relationships. *Personal Relationships, 5,* 191–205.

Roloff, M. E., & Ifert, D. (2000). Conflict management through avoidance: Withholding complaints, suppressing arguments, and declaring topics taboo. In S. Petronio (Ed.), *Balancing the secrets of private disclosures* (pp. 151–165). Mahwah, NJ: Lawrence Erlbaum.

Roloff, M. E., & Johnson, K. L. (2002). Serial arguing over the relational life course: Antecedents and consequences. In A. L. Vangelisti & H. T. Reis (Eds.), *Stability and change in relationships* (pp. 107–128). New York: Cambridge University Press.

Roloff, M. E., & Soule, K. P. (2002). Interpersonal conflict: A review. In M. L. Knapp & J. A. Daly (Eds.), *Handbook of interpersonal communication* (3rd ed., pp. 475–528). Thousand Oaks, CA: Sage.

Rosenberg, A. (1988). *Philosophy of social science.* Boulder, CO: Westview Press.

Rosenfeld, L. B. (1979). Self-disclosure avoidance: Why I am afraid to tell you who I am. *Communication Monographs, 46,* 63–74.

Rosenfeld, L. B., & Kendrick, W. L. (1984). Choosing to be open: Subjective reasons for self-disclosing. *Western Journal of Speech Communication, 48,* 326–343.

Sabourin, T. C. (2006). Theories and metatheories to explain family communication: An overview. In L. H. Turner & R. West (Eds.), *The family communication sourcebook* (pp. 43–60). Thousand Oaks, CA: Sage.

Sabourin, T. C., & Stamp, G. H. (1995). Communication and the experience of dialectical tensions in family life: An examination of abusive and nonabusive families. *Communication Monographs, 62,* 213–242.

Sacks, H., Schegloff, E., & Jefferson, G. (1974). A simplest systematics for the organization of turn-taking for conversation. *Language, 50,* 696–735.

Sahlstein, E. M. (2004). Relating at a distance: Negotiating being together and being apart in long-distance relationships. *Journal of Social and Personal Relationships, 5,* 689–710.

Sahlstein, E. M. (2006). Making plans: Praxis strategies for negotiating uncertainty-certainty in long-distance relationships. *Western Journal of Communication, 70,* 147–165.

Sahlstein, E. M., & Baxter, L. A. (2001). Improvising commitment in close relationships: A relational dialectics perspective. In J. H. Harvey & A. Wenzel (Eds.), *Close romantic relationships: Maintenance and enhancement* (pp. 115–132). Mahwah, NJ: Lawrence Erlbaum.

Sahlstein, E., & Dun, T. (2008). "I wanted time to myself and he wanted to be together all the time": Constructing breakups as managing autonomy-connection. *Qualitative Research Reports in Communication, 9,* 37–45.

Sampson, E. E. (1993). *Celebrating the other: A dialogic account of human nature.* Boulder, CO: Westview Press.

Sarch, A. (1997). Those dirty ads! *Critical Studies in Mass Communication, 14,* 31–48.

Sargent, J. (2002). Topic avoidance: Is this the way to a more satisfying relationship? *Communication Research Reports, 19,* 175–182.

Saussure, F. (1983). *Course in general linguistics* (C. Bally & A. Sechehaye, Eds., & R. Harris, Trans.). London: Duckworth. (Original work published in 1916)

Schneider, D. M. (1980). *American kinship: A cultural account.* Chicago: The University of Chicago Press.

Schrodt, P., Baxter, L. A., McBride, M. C., Braithwaite, D. O., & Fine, M. A. (2006). The divorce decree, communication, and the structuration of coparenting relationships. *Journal of Social and Personal Relationships, 25,* 741–759.

Schwartz, S. H., & Bilsky, W. (1987). Toward a universal psychological structure of human values. *Journal of Personality and Social Psychology, 53,* 550–562.

Segrin, C., & Flora, J. (2005). *Family communication.* Mahwah, NJ: Lawrence Erlbaum.

Shore, B. (1991). Twice-born, once conceived: Meaning construction and cultural cognition. *American Anthropologist, 93,* 9–27.

Shotter, J. (1993a). *Conversational realities.* London: Sage.

Shotter, J. (1993b). *Cultural politics of everyday life.* Toronto, Canada: University of Toronto Press.

Shotter, J. (2000). Inside dialogical realities. *Southern Journal of Communication, 65,* 119–132.

Sias, P. M., Heath, R. G., Perry, T., Silva, D., & Fix, B. (2004). Narratives of workplace friendship deterioration. *Journal of Social and Personal Relationships, 21,* 321–340.

Sobchak, T. (1996). Bakhtin's "carnivalesque" in 1950s British comedy. *Journal of Popular Film & Television, 23,* 179–186.

Spanier, G. B. (1972). Romanticism and marital adjustment. *Journal of Marriage and the Family, 34,* 481–487.

Spano, S. (2001). *Public dialogue and participatory democracy: The Cupertino community project.* Cresskill, NJ: Hampton Press.

Stafford, L., & Kline, S. L. (1996). Women's surnames and titles: Men's and women's views. *Communication Research Reports, 13,* 214–224.

Stafford, L., & Merolla, A. (2007). Idealization, reunions, and stability in long-distance dating relationships. *Journal of Social and Personal Relationships, 24,* 37–54.

Stafford, L., Merolla, A. J., & Castle, J. D. (2006). When long-distance dating partners become geographically close. *Journal of Social and Personal Relationships, 23,* 901–919.

Stamp, G. H. (1994). The appropriation of the parental role through communication during the transition to parenthood. *Communication Monographs, 61,* 89–112.

Stamp, G. H. (2004). Theories of family relationships and a family relationships theoretical model. In A. Vangelisti (Ed.), *Handbook of family communication* (pp. 1–30). Mahwah, NJ: Lawrence Erlbaum.

Stamp, G. H., & Banski, M. A. (1992). The communicative management of constrained autonomy during the transition to parenthood. *Western Journal of Communication, 56,* 281–300.

Sternberg, M. (1982). Proteus in quotation-land: Mimesis and the forms of reported discourse. *Poetics Today, 3,* 107–156.

Stewart, J., & Zediker, K. (2000). Dialogue as tensional, ethical practice. *Southern Communication Journal, 65,* 224–242.

Strauss, A., & Corbin, J. (1998). *Basics of qualitative research: Techniques and procedures for developing grounded theory.* Thousand Oaks, CA: Sage.

Strine, M. S. (2004). When is communication intercultural? Bakhtin, staged performance, and civic dialogue. In R. Anderson, L. A. Baxter, & K. N. Cissna (Eds.), *Dialogue: Theorizing difference in communication studies* (pp. 225–242). Thousand Oaks, CA: Sage.

Suter, E. A., Bergen, K. M., Daas, K. L., & Durham, W. T. (2006). Lesbian couples' management of public-private dialectical contradictions. *Journal of Social and Personal Relationships, 23,* 349–366.

Suter, E. A., & Daas, K. L. (2007). Negotiating heteronormativity dialectically: Lesbian couples' display of symbols in culture. *Western Journal of Communication, 71,* 177–195.

Swidler, A. (2001). *Talk of love: How culture matters.* Chicago: The University of Chicago Press.

Tannen, D. (1984). *Conversational style: Analyzing talk among friends.* Norwood, NJ: Ablex.

Tannen, D. (1989). *Talking voices: Repetition, dialogue, and imagery in conversational discourse.* New York: Cambridge University Press.

Tannen, D. (2004). Talking the dog: Framing pets as interactional resources in family discourse. *Research on Language and Social Interaction, 37,* 399–420.

Tannen, D. (2006). Intertextuality in interaction: Reframing family arguments in public and private. *Text & Talk, 26,* 597–617.

Taylor, C. (1991). The dialogical self. In D. R. Hiley, J. F. Bohman, & R. Shusterman (Eds.), *The interpretive turn: Philosophy, science, culture* (pp. 304–314). Ithaca, NY: Cornell University Press.

Taylor, C. (1995). "You think it was a *fight?*": Co-constructing (the struggle for) meaning, face, and family in everyday narrative activity. *Research on Language and Social Interaction, 28,* 283–317.

Taylor, S. (2001). Locating and conducting discourse analytic research. In M. Wetherell, S. Taylor, & S. J. Yates (Eds.), *Discourse as data: A guide for analysis* (pp. 5–48). Thousand Oaks, CA: Sage.

Thatcher, M. (2006). Bakhtin applied: Employing dialogism to analyze the interplay of ideologies of individualism and community within the discourse of Alcoholics Anonymous. *Journal of Applied Communication Research, 34,* 349–367.

Therborn, G. (1980). *The ideology of power and the power of ideology.* London: Verso.

Todorov, T. (1984). *Mikhail Bakhtin: The dialogical principle* (W. Godzich, Trans.). Minneapolis, MN: University of Minnesota Press.

Toller, P. W. (2005). Negotiations of dialectical contradictions by parents who have experienced the death of a child. *Journal of Applied Communication Research, 33,* 46–66.

Triandus, H. C. (1995). *Individualism and collectivism.* Boulder, CO: Westview.

Trost, J. (1990). Do we mean the same by the concept of family? *Communication Research, 17,* 431–443.

Turner, J. H. (1986). *The structure of sociological theory* (4th ed.). Chicago, IL: The Dorsey Press.

Van Dijk, T. A. (Ed.). (1985). *Handbook of discourse analysis.* London: Academic Press.

Vangelisti, A. L. (1993). Communication in the family: The influence of time, relational prototypes, and irrationality. *Communication Monographs, 60,* 42–54.

Veroff, J., Sutherland, L., Chadiha, L., & Ortega, R. M. (1993). Newlyweds tell their stories: Predicting marital quality from narrative assessments. *Journal of Marriage and the Family, 55,* 317–329.

Voloshinov, V. N. (1986). *Marxism and the philosophy of language* (L. Matejka & I. R. Titunik, Trans.). Cambridge, MA: Harvard University Press. (Original work published in 1929)

Voloshinov, V. N. (1987). *Freudianism: A critical sketch* (I. R. Titunik, Trans.). Bloomington, IN: Indiana University Press. (Original work published in 1927)

Watzlawick, P., Beavin, J., & Jackson, D. (1967). *Pragmatics of human communication.* New York: Norton.

Wegar, K. (2000). Adoption, family ideology, and social stigma: Bias in community attitudes, adoption research, and practice. *Family Relations, 49,* 363–370.

White, P. R. R. (2003). Beyond modality and hedging: A dialogic view of the language of intersubjective stance. *Text, 23,* 259–284.

Williams, A., & Guendouzi, J. (2000). Adjusting to "the Home": Dialectical dilemmas and personal relationships in a retirement community. *Journal of Communication, 50,* 65–82.

Williams, R. (1983). *Keywords: A vocabulary of culture and society.* New York: Oxford University Press.

Wood, J. (1982). Communication and relational culture: Bases for the study of human relationships. *Communication Quarterly, 30,* 75–83.

Wood, J. T., Dendy, L. L., Dordek, E., Germany, M., & Varallo, S. M. (1994). Dialectic of difference: A thematic analysis of intimates' meanings for differences. In K. Carter & M. Prisnell (Eds.), *Interpretive approaches to interpersonal communication* (pp. 115–136). New York: SUNY Press.

Wood, L. A., & Kroeger, R. O. (2000). *Doing discourse analysis: Methods for studying action in talk and text.* Thousand Oaks, CA: Sage.

Wundt, W. (1904). *Volkerpsychologie.* Leipzig, Germany: Kroner.

Yael, M. (2002). The role of discourse markers in the construction of multivocality in Israeli Hebrew talk in interaction. *Research on Language and Social Interaction, 35,* 1–38.

Index

About the Author

Leslie A. Baxter is F. Wendell Miller Distinguished Professor of Communication Studies at the University of Iowa, where she has taught for 15 years. She has published over 130 books, book chapters, and articles on interpersonal and family communication. She is the recipient of many awards, including, from the National Communication Association, the Distinguished Scholar Award, the Bernard Brommel Family Communication Award, the Charles Woolbert Research Award, the Franklin Knower Article Award, and the Gerald Miller Book Award; the Berscheid-Hatfield Award from the International Association for Relationship Research (formerly INPR); and the inaugural WSCA Scholar Award from the Western States Communication Association.

Supporting researchers for more than 40 years

Research methods have always been at the core of SAGE's publishing program. Founder Sara Miller McCune published SAGE's first methods book, *Public Policy Evaluation*, in 1970. Soon after, she launched the *Quantitative Applications in the Social Sciences* series—affectionately known as the "little green books."

Always at the forefront of developing and supporting new approaches in methods, SAGE published early groundbreaking texts and journals in the fields of qualitative methods and evaluation.

Today, more than 40 years and two million little green books later, SAGE continues to push the boundaries with a growing list of more than 1,200 research methods books, journals, and reference works across the social, behavioral, and health sciences. Its imprints—Pine Forge Press, home of innovative textbooks in sociology, and Corwin, publisher of PreK–12 resources for teachers and administrators—broaden SAGE's range of offerings in methods. SAGE further extended its impact in 2008 when it acquired CQ Press and its best-selling and highly respected political science research methods list.

From qualitative, quantitative, and mixed methods to evaluation, SAGE is the essential resource for academics and practitioners looking for the latest methods by leading scholars.

For more information, visit **www.sagepub.com**.